Palgrave Philoso

Series Editor
Vittorio Bufacchi
Department of Philosophy
University College Cork
Cork, Ireland

The Palgrave Philosophy Today will help all philosophers, established and aspiring, to understand, appreciate and engage with the intricacies which characterize all the many faces of philosophy. They are ideal teaching tools as textbooks for more advanced students. These books may not be meant primarily for those who have yet to read their first book of philosophy, but all students with a basic knowledge of philosophy will benefit greatly from reading these exciting and original works, which will enable anyone to engage with all the defining issues in contemporary philosophy. There are three main aspects that make the Palgrave Philosophy Today series distinctive and attractive. First, each book is relatively concise. Second, the books are commissioned from some of the best-known, established and upcoming international scholars in each area of philosophy. Third, while the primary purpose is to offer an informed assessment of opinion on a key area of philosophical study, each title presents a distinct interpretation from someone who is closely involved with current work in the field.

More information about this series at
http://www.palgrave.com/gp/series/14672

Naomi Zack

Philosophy of Race

An Introduction

Naomi Zack
Department of Philosophy
University of Oregon
Eugene, OR, USA

Palgrave Philosophy Today
ISBN 978-3-319-78728-2   ISBN 978-3-319-78729-9   (eBook)
https://doi.org/10.1007/978-3-319-78729-9

Library of Congress Control Number: 2018937870

This Palgrave Macmillan imprint is published by the registered company Springer International Publishing AG part of Springer Nature
The registered company address is: Gewerbestrasse 11, 6330 Cham, Switzerland

Praise for *Philosophy of Race*

"Naomi Zack's book presents a panoramic view of race sweeping across centuries of philosophical thought, histories of immigration and assimilation, Brazilian, indigenous, and Hindu challenges to prevailing racial categories, and concluding with clarifying reflections on hot-button issues around identity politics and intersectionality. Epic in scope, Zack's highly informative survey offers an indispensable map for understanding the rise of race in US politics."

—Cynthia Willett, *Emory University, USA, and author of Irony in the Age of Empire: Comic Perspectives on Freedom and Democracy*

"Naomi Zack never disappoints. Unlike other philosophical engagements with race that prioritize the historical views of whites, Zack synthesizes sociological data and history to show how power creates the economic and political realities confronting racialized people. Zack accounts for practically every philosophical theorization of race, feminism, colonialism, and poverty present in the literature. This book needs to be in the hands of every philosopher teaching race, and on the shelf of every theorist claiming to write in the philosophy of race."

—Tommy J. Curry, *Texas A&M University, USA*

To Alex, Bradford, Jessica, Coco, and Winnie, Love, Gram.

Introduction to This Book

Many academic philosophers who are generally interested in social justice issues pertaining to racial and ethnic minority groups still do not clearly distinguish between Philosophy of Race and African American philosophy. And in American public discourse, African Americans are the primary racial subject. But the existence of other nonwhite groups in the United States and throughout the world calls for a shared discourse about the plurality of racial and ethnic injustices endured and resisted. It is therefore now useful to consider Philosophy of Race as a distinct academic subfield. Philosophy of Race has primarily emerged from African American philosophy, which not only carries an awareness of injustices suffered by other groups but has since the 1970s raised issues that redound to traditional ethics and political and social philosophy.

The main aim of this book is to introduce the reader to historical and contemporary issues in Philosophy of Race, with due regard for its debt to African American philosophy. African American philosophy has always had the burden of grappling with the legacy of US black chattel slavery, a burden that is exceptional because of the contrast between the ideals of a great democratic nation and its harsh realities for black Americans. Part of that contrast has been evident in a history of white dominance in higher education, perhaps especially among philosophers. The first line of defense against African American Philosophy was that it was not philosophy, because it focused too concretely on the experience of one human group. The greater generality of Philosophy of Race might thereby make it more acceptable to traditional philosophers. But might scholars of African American philosophy thereby suspect the progressiveness of Philosophy of Race, because it is more similar to the universal nature of philosophy as a discipline that has historically excluded African Americans and other nonwhite thinkers? Such suspicion can be allayed if Philosophy of Race turns out to be as progressive as African American philosophy.

It may seem strange for a more general form of thought to originate in a more particular one, that is, the origination of Philosophy of Race in African American Philosophy. But there is precedent for this kind of development in the history of philosophy: Bentham and Mill invented utilitarianism with a basic tenet that pleasure or happiness should be maximized, whereas contemporary consequentialism is more abstract in not specifying what should be maximized. Consequentialism *subsumes* utilitarianism. In this case, as with Philosophy of Race and African American philosophy, what occurs later is philosophically more general or abstract. And what occurs later here has a longer history than its origins. Philosophy of Race can be identified in the writings of Plato and Aristotle, when there was no version of African American Philosophy.

However, greater generality and abstraction need not entail erasure. It would be a mistake for Philosophy of Race to become so abstract as to reify "race," apart from the concerns of African Americans, Native Americans, Asian Americans, Middle Eastern Americans, Latin/x-Americans, and so forth. While it is important to be able to talk about shared experiences of injustice and reach for general, unifying moral and political principles, it is more important that everyone be able to claim this discourse, regardless of racial identity.

Philosophers have a long history of accepting or ignoring general and abstract, "race talk" that encompasses pluralities. In the nineteenth and early twentieth centuries, racial *ethnologists* sought to explain social and psychological differences between members of different racial groups on the assumption that human races had different "ranks." The white race was upheld as the most civilized, both morally and intellectually superior, while blacks were relegated to the bottom in culture, character, and intellect. This racist perspective was not a simple division of whites from blacks, because in-between whites and blacks, indigenes or AmerIndians, and "Orientals" or Asians, were also ranked. And even within what today would be consid-ered the white race, there was hierarchy, as in Madison Grant's valorization of Northern Europeans compared to Southern and Eastern Europeans, in his widely read 1916 *The Passing of the Great Race*. In its heyday, such race thinking was closely allied to a perspective of biological determinism and inevitable Darwinian conflict. This idea of the "survival of the fittest race" posited races as warring competitors for resources and honor and it meant that racial difference determined social and political destiny. Grant emphasized the connection between violence and race in referring to World War I, in his book's Introduction:

> The laws of nature operate with the same relentless and unchanging force in human affairs as in the phenomena of inanimate nature, and the basis of the government of man is now and always has been, and always will be, force and not sentiment, a truth demonstrated anew by the present world conflagration. (Grant 1916, p. 3)

The deeply racist Nazi ideology about Jews during World War II was in keeping with Grant's Northern European chauvinism, because Jews were considered Semites, a distinct nonwhite race, and Nazi propaganda portrayed Jews as both degenerate and dangerous. On a broader historical scale, moral worth was an integral part of official justifications for colonialism that included the enslavement, genocide, and material exploitation of Africans, Asians, and indigenous Americans and Australians.

While it is indisputable that ideas of human racial difference have historically been matters of life and death and there certainly have been physical and cultural differences among races, it is crucial to stay on a "meta" level in considering such differences as causes or justification for racial hierarchies. Ideas of biological racial difference and moral hierarchy were invented and posited to justify persecution and oppression by other names, undertaken by white Europeans for their own benefits, throughout the modern period (American Anthropological Association 1998; Eze 1997). Quite apart from explicit awareness of the injustice of such persecutions and oppressions, when interests of dominant groups were not believed to require genocide, slavery, or brutality, anti-nonwhite racism was not as violent. Also, intra-European racial ideologies calmed down following World War II, after Western European groups became more cooperative among themselves, partly as a result of Cold War anti-Soviet alignments and partly for gain in expanding, interdependent economies.

Despite ongoing discourse about justice and human equality (e.g., the 1948 UN Declaration of Universal Human Rights) and a certain amount of formal legal progress (e.g., the US Civil Rights Movement legislation of 1964–1965), the treatment of nonwhites by whites, both internationally and within rich Western nations such as the United States, has continued to be a flashpoint in society for experiences of injustice and oppression, or in a word, *racism*. While white-centered ethnology and racial differences as mere varieties may be subjects for social scientists, scholars in the humanities tend to focus on anti-nonwhite racism. This assumption that racial discourse is discourse about racism is shared throughout society. It is generally understood that the subject of race is too controversial to be casually broached among people of different races or ethnicities, without "trigger warnings," because when most people use the word "race," they are usually talking about racism. Those who can show that they suffer from racism may occupy positions of righteous blame and freely express their entitlements to redress (e.g., affirmative action), while those who are known to inflict racism on others are generally viewed as blameworthy and obligated to reform. Such assessments that some persons have been wronged by others who are thereby morally and socially guilty, add psychic and material weight to the discourse of race. Assessments of justice, injustice, and human worth are at stake and all of these are philosophical subjects, although they are seldom directly connected with racism in academic philosophy. That is, ethics and social and political philosophy may include racism as a separate or special topic, without making racism a core part of its scope. The result is that racism is treated under the subfield of African American Philosophy or Philosophy of Race. As a subject, racism is not viewed as belonging to ethics or social and political philosophy.

Over the twentieth century, the same biological sciences—anthropology, genetics, physiology, evolutionary biology, medicine—that had supported ideas of ranked racial difference underwent radical revisions of the scientific reality accorded to race. First, inherited physical race was separated from inherited culture that came to be understood as the result of historical events in human societies. French anthropologist Claude Lévi-Strauss and American anthropologist Franz Boas and his students pioneered much of the early twentieth century research that provided cross-cultural data for this separation of biological race from social culture (Lévi-Strauss 2014; Baker 1994). This separation of biological race from culture and psychic traits, by itself undermined biological racial determinism—that doctrine died in science—and ethnology as the study of inherited cultural aspects of race lost its credibility.

Second, and more striking, human racial divisions or *taxonomies* were abandoned by biological anthropologists and population geneticists. The sequence of the scientific divestment of race deserves emphasis. First, cultural, psychological, and moral traits associated with different races lost scientific support for those connections. And second, skepticism developed about distinct physical racial traits or group boundaries that could, independently of social custom and tradition, support human racial divisions or biological "race," in the biological sciences. When there was no longer good reason to posit distinct biological human races, there was no longer any scientific physical racial foundation for moral and intellectual differences between whites and nonwhites. Of course, race remains a subject in social anthropology and sociology, as well as throughout the humanities.

After the demise of credible biological racial determinism, violence in reaction to racial difference could no longer be either morally or intellectually justified. Violence against nonwhites who were innocent of wrongdoing, such as lynching, therefore came to be addressed as issues of illegitimate political power, violations of moral principles and human rights, or hate crimes. But, nevertheless, episodes such as unprovoked police homicide against unarmed African Americans (Zack 2015) and xenophobic expressions against nonwhite immigrants have persisted. It is on these grounds that progressive, racially egalitarian thinkers continue to conduct analyses and criticism related to race.

Philosophy of Race itself is now distinctive in ways that be traced through the history of Western philosophy. But the topical nature of the subjects or content of Philosophy of Race has also been strongly connected to progressive or liberatory aspirations, so that it might at times seem to be more normative than other philosophical subfields. This normativity is rarely simple sets of "oughts." Similar to other *critical theories*, such as Marxism, Freudianism, and feminism, Philosophy of Race provides analyses of social beliefs and practices, within new conceptual frameworks, or theories, which many (the public) would not accept without specialized education about institutional racism, intergenerational poverty, white privilege, and unconscious racism. The topicality of Philosophy of Race is not only normative, but it proceeds at a faster pace than more traditional philosophy, because its subject matter is in flux. Philosophy of Race moves at the speed of living history or current events. Philosophy of Race is also straightforwardly normative in attending to social injustice. Both critical theory normativity and injustice studies entail that philosophers of race are unlikely to have chosen this specialization after dispassionate casting about for something to do. Rather, doing Philosophy of Race is often the result of being invited, called, exhorted, obligated, or otherwise moved, *to do something* in reaction to observed and experienced injustice.

If its normative aspects sound as though Philosophy of Race is a somewhat ephemeral pursuit that is too specific or journalistic, too opinionated or "applied," to merit the attention of real or serious philosophers, we should consider the methodology of this subfield. Contemporary Philosophy of Race requires the same kind of patient analysis for understanding, and reasoning toward conclusions, which all subfields in philosophy require. The normative dimension is not a matter of personal opinion, but a methodological approach—humanistic scholars of race now believe that they are expected and obligated to tell their readers what should or could be done, after they have described certain problems. This is usually less exhortation, much less activism, and more explanation, theorizing, and hypothesizing—like the rest of philosophy.

The purpose of this book is to help construct an overview that will serve as a resource for students in thinking, talking, and writing about Philosophy of Race. It provides a concise description of the subfield, ideal for use in courses that need to cover extensive terrain within the limits of a fast-moving term or semester. Used on its own, this book serves as an introduction for students first encountering the Philosophy of Race. Additionally, the aim is to enable insight about how the claims of contemporary authors fit into bigger pictures in intellectual history, as well as "unpacking" likely assumptions and providing basic exposition of dense texts. At the same time, students will have an opportunity to construct their own perspectives and form opinions, through classroom lectures, facilitated discussions, and writing assignments.

There are three parts to this approach. The main part is the content of the major themes of the chapters. Two supporting parts within each chapter are a glossary of specialized terms (flagged by bold print) and questions for oral discussion and written assignments. Not assuming any background knowledge of Philosophy of Race on the part of the reader—who may be a student, a philosopher well versed in other areas of philosophy, an inquirer from a different discipline, or a general reader—this book takes a "bird's eye view" of the subfield of Philosophy of Race and strives to explain opposing perspectives.

The likely audience is philosophers and scholars in related fields seeking an introduction to Philosophy of Race, but primarily, undergraduate and graduate students of race, cultural diversity, morals and society, social philosophy, social-political philosophy, and related subjects in philosophy, the humanities, and social sciences. The overriding idea is to be comprehensive of this subfield, as developed by philosophers, from canonical to contemporary writers. We can see now, in considering the history of philosophy, that Philosophy of Race has always been relevant to its time and place and that tendency will be reflected in this work, in reference to historical and contemporary events. Finally, while any academic book of this nature, at this time, has underlying progressive commitments, this book seeks to avoid ideology or specific advocacy. The method is to untangle disputes and controversies through philosophical conceptual analyses that include both analytic and continental philosophy. Gender, class, ethnicity, and political events are brought in for real-world relevance.

I have striven to write clearly in presenting a short and hopefully useful book about a subject long important in life and more recently important in US academic fields. Obviously and inevitably, subjects dear to some will have been left out and not all relevant scholarship is included. The Part I and Part II Introductions provide brief chapter overviews of what follow. Comments are welcome from scholars, instructors, and students. Please email me at nzack@uoregon.edu.

References

American Anthropological Association. "AAA Statement on Race," 1998, http://www.americananthro.org/ConnectWithAAA/Content.aspx?ItemNumber=2583

Baker, Lee D., "The Location of Franz Boas Within the African American Struggle." Critique of Anthropology, 1994. Vol 14(2): 199–217.

Eze, Emmanuel Chukwudi, ed. *Race and the Enlightenment: A Reader*. Cambridge, MA: Blackwell, 1997.

Lévi-Strauss, Claude, Race and History, Charleston, SC: Nabu Press, 2014.

Madison, Grant. *The Passing of the Great Race or The Racial Basis of European History*. New York, NY: Scribner and Sons, 1916. http://www.jrbooksonline.com/pdf_books/passingofgreatrace.pdf

Naomi, Zack. *White Privilege and Black Rights: The Injustice of US Police Racial Profiling and Homicide*. Lanham, MD: Rowman and Littlefield, 2015.

Contents

List of Tables

Part I

Ideas and Realities of Human Race

Introduction

Evaluative ideas about human races in the history of Euro-American societies have not been neatly separated from beliefs that there are human races and that humankind is naturally or biologically divided into them. Beliefs that racial divisions naturally exist have usually been in the background of discussions about relations and interactions between racial groups. From a contemporary vantage point, the modern idea of biological race developed in the eighteenth and nineteeth centuries, has always been racist.

In Part I of this book, ideas of race in the canonical history of philosophy are considered first (Chapter 1). Insofar as those ideas now appear to be biased toward Eurocentrism or what some today would call ongoing white supremacy, it is important to also consider alternative ideas of race that were more egalitarian and inspired an historical tradition of resistance against racism and hope for a better future. The egalitarian tradition began in the ancient world, spanned Christianity, was taken up by abolitionists in England and the United States, and motivated the US Civil Rights Movement. Thinkers in fields outside of philosophy, as well as philosophers, contributed to that tradition and their work merits philosophical consideration in retrospect (Chapter 2). The subject of race in the modern period originated in the new sciences of biology and anthropology. For the first time, there was a universal scheme for dividing humankind. Biological race developed through monogenism, polygenism, evolutionary theory, and population genetics. Science of any kind is inherently self-revising and this has been especially true in the former science of race (Chapter 3).

Distinctively American pragmatist philosophy has lately directed positive attention to race, which is relevant insofar as the United States is the primary context for contemporary scholarship on race. Continental Philosophy has reflected liberatory intellectual phenomenology. Both of these philosophical traditions merit distinct and comparative consideration as alternatives to analytic philosophical approaches to race (Chapter 4). The idea and historical reality of ethnicity has been closely related to race, especially as affected by the movements of peoples. Ethnicity and race have overlapping meanings in different countries, as well as within indigenous societies (Chapter 5).

1

Ideas of Race in the Canonical History of Philosophy

To speak of human race is to speak of human races—if there were only one human race, that "race" would be the whole of humanity. To understand the history of ideas of race in Western philosophy, it is important to avoid anachronism and not interpret earlier forms of human **hierarchy** or status, as racial systems, where and when there were not yet fully developed ideas of human races as hereditary physical systems. Because we now know that many of the past beliefs concerning human racial taxonomy were not scientifically accurate in terms that scientists would accept today, we cannot rely on the existence of human racial **taxonomies** as a system of division timelessly given in nature. We also know that ideas of human race have changed over centuries and even decades, particularly in the USA (the main focus of this book), so it is useful to begin a discussion of race in the history of philosophy by stating five main meanings of the word "race" in contemporary intellectual discourse.

1. Race is biologically inherited and it causes both physical and cultural and moral traits that can be objectively compared in terms of human worth;
2. Race is biologically inherited but it causes only physical traits;
3. Race is a matter of superficial physical appearance, mainly skin color;
4. Race is a cultural artifact based on biology, even though the biological differences between societal or cultural races are arbitrary and unscientific;
5. Race is a social construction that reflects history, politics, and shared social traditions among dominant and subordinate human groups, each of which shares interlocking, intergenerational lines of family descent.

© The Author(s) 2018
N. Zack, *Philosophy of Race*, Palgrave Philosophy Today,
https://doi.org/10.1007/978-3-319-78729-9_1

Race as biologically inherited, with or without cultural and moral traits ((1) or (2)) was the dominant model and meaning of the word from the eighteenth to twentieth century, which is to say, over the modern period. Of course, biology as studies of living things predated modernity and has overflowed Western science. But biological distinctions with a basis in classification or taxonomy are distinctive to the modern period in the West, because modern biology began with **systematics** (Mayr 1942). The equation of racial difference with differences in appearance (3) also relies on a biological or hereditary physical foundation. And the contemporary conception of race as unscientific (4) refers to the science of biology. Race as a contemporary social construction (5) mirrors the experience of race as lived realities.

If we accept the starring role of biology in modern ideas of race, it needs to be shown why ideas of human difference that resembled race before modern biology should not be considered full-blown ideas of race, even though they may have had oppressive effects comparable to those of modern racism. Within the philosophical canon (containing ten to fifteen of the major historical figures), it makes sense to begin with Plato (427 BC–348 BC) and Aristotle (384 BC–323 BC) and then move on to Thomas Aquinas (1225–1274) and John Locke (1632–1704), followed by David Hume (1711–1776) and Immanuel Kant (1724–1804). G.W.F. Hegel (1770–1831), John Stuart Mill (1806–1873), and Friedrich Nietzsche (1844–1900) were influential philosophers of race over the nineteenth century. Altogether, canonical philosophers created a model of race with normative anti-nonwhite bias. Constructing a chronological account of their thought is disciplinarily appropriate, because philosophers typically begin inquiries with what past philosophers thought about a topic. And coincidentally or not, a consideration of race within or through the history of philosophy lines up with real-life historical events and narratives. For instance, all of the philosophers mentioned were aware of slavery as a legal institution in their own times. (The practice of slavery preceded ideas of race until it became coincident with race during the centuries of USA black chattel slavery.)

Race-Like Ideas in the Ancient World

Plato believed that the structure of the individual and of society were analogous—the state or society was the individual "writ large." The person has parts with distinct functions and so does society. The mind ideally rules the body and the passions, and the most intelligent and rational members of society should rule soldiers and workers. In the *Republic*, a "noble lie" about human hierarchy is suggested. Those setting up the Republic who were in charge of education, will have observed the characters of the young, testing them for memory, critical capacity (their ability not to be deceived), courage, composure, and discipline. Performance on these tests would determine the person's appropriate place in society—guardian-king, soldier (including military, police, and local administrators), or worker (laborers and mechanics).

The noble lie was to begin with a story of origins, when rulers and educators told the young that they had all had been born to the state through a process of "molding" underground, so that what they believed had been their education was in reality a dream. As creations of the state, all of the young were brothers, expected to love one another and the city as God that had fashioned them. But they were not equal, so they would be also be told:

> God in fashioning those of you who are fitted to hold rule mingled gold in their generation, for which reason they are the most precious—but in the helpers silver, and iron and brass in the farmers and other craftsmen. And as you are all akin, though for the most part you will breed after your kinds, it may sometimes happen that a golden father would beget a silver son and that a golden offspring would come from a silver sire and that the rest would in like manner be born of one another. (Plato 1964, 415, a–b, p. 659)

Some scholars have found a theory of race in these distinctions that included innate capacities (Kamtakar 2002). Moreover, Plato envisioned the Republic as a society that would function based on these differences and the noble lie would presumably sustain that structure by being retold to each new generation. However, Plato was not primarily interested in the different **identities** that resulted from his proposed race-like classifications—which he was quite open in labeling as what we would call "propaganda"—but in assigning societal roles based on individual capacities. The metallic categorizations were thus a heuristic device, because different individual capacities were to be determined before the metallic categorizations were applied as labels for the person. Also, the metallic categories were not hereditary as biological racial categories came to be, because gold parents could have silver offspring or silver parents.

Ironically, the closest resemblance to a theory of race in Plato's *Republic* is his introduction of the theory as a fabrication that Socrates is ashamed to propose: "You will think I have right good reason for shrinking when I have told [you about this noble lie]" (Plato 1964, 414c, p. 659). There is also great honesty in Plato's stated need to manipulate people into accepting a hierarchical, nondemocratic system. Both before and after modernity, subsequent political theorists who proposed race-like distinctions took pains to be convincing about the nature of the human differences supporting their categories.

Plato was the only race theorist who admitted that the differences were fictional, proxies for real differences that had nothing to do with their proxies.

After Plato, those who proposed race-like theories of human inequality were no longer ashamed to do so. Aristotle simply took historical and contemporary Greek status and role differences for granted. Rather than describing an ideal state as Plato did, Aristotle is famous for his historical beginning to political theory in Book I of *Politica* or *The Politics* (Aristotle 1941). According to Aristotle, the basic union is that of male and female, for the sake of reproduction. Barbarians may not distinguish between women and slaves, because they have no "natural ruler," but society is hierarchical for the Greeks. Where there are relationships between man and woman, and master and slave, the family arises. The family supplies "everyday wants" and when several families are united, a village appears, often ruled by an elder or king. Several villages united form a community and if it is self-sufficient, the state originates as a natural end or purpose of human life in its best form (Aristotle, *Politics*, I, 1252a–b).

However, for Aristotle, the basic unit of the state remains the household and a "complete" household consists of slaves and freemen. Aristotle notes that some believe the rule of a master over slaves is unnatural and the result of law, but he defends the naturalness of slavery as part of the management of a household, which requires "instruments." The slave is a kind of instrument, a "living possession" of the master: "The master is only master of the slave; he does not belong to him, whereas the slave is not only the slave of his master, but wholly belongs to him." Aristotle's division between master and slave is not merely a matter of social roles, arising by law or accident, or as for Plato, justified by a myth. Rather, the person who is a slave is *by nature* a slave—there is something inherent in such a person which makes him or her suitable for slavery. In addition to being the possession of another, a slave lacks the universal human capacity for **deliberation** or the ability to develop virtues, and **phronesis** or practical reasoning. Thus, in lacking deliberation, the slave is not a moral being, and in lacking phronesis, the slave cannot be a political agent. But the slave can perceive deliberation and phronesis in others and benefit from not having **autonomy** or being in charge of her own life. Given these differences between slaves and their masters, the main activity of the slave is physical labor (Aristotle, *Politics*, I. 5, 1252a–b, 1254a–b, quotes pp. 1128 and 1131).

Aristotle's description of the qualities of slaves does not convincingly stem from human traits that exist independently of the condition of slavery. That is, anyone who was enslaved might not be allowed to develop virtues or decide what action to take, and she might be forced to physically labor.

The inherent traits Aristotle ascribes to slaves are more plausibly the result of their enslavement. Moreover, Erick Raphael Jiménez identifies a proto-racist aspect to Aristotle's analysis of slavery in his description of Asians compared to Greeks, in terms of the influence of geography and climate on character traits. Jiménez argues that insofar as the majority of slaves during Aristotle's time were Asian, his analysis of slavery can be read as a justification for an existing practice that otherwise defied the principle that deliberation and phronesis were universal human traits. Jiménez quotes Aristotle:

> Those people who live in cold climates, as in Europe, are full of **thumos** or spiritedness, but lacking in intelligence and art. Hence they are generally free, but being without a constitution they cannot rule their neighbors. And Asians have intelligent and technical souls, but they lack thumos; hence they are always being ruled over and enslaved. But Greeks, being in the middle of these places, partake of both of them; for they have thumos and are intelligent. Hence they are always free and governed in the best way, and would be capable of ruling the world if they happened to form one city. (Jiménez 2014, quote p. 71, from Aristotle, *Politics*, VII.7, 1327b19–35, p. 1286)

Aristotle's use of geography and climate to compare traits of the members of human groups was taken up in full-blown biological theories of race during the modern period, as we will soon see. But to continue this history of slavery as an institution that would only later meld with theories of race, we should note that in both ancient Greece and Rome, slaves had a status close to animals. In Greece, slaves were referred to as "andropoda" or "man-footed beings," analogous to "tetrapoda," meaning "four-footed beings" or animals. In Rome, the differences in status were formal and official and slaves in tort law were treated the same as domestic animals (Finley 1983, p. 99). By 529–534 AD, Roman law in the *Code of Justinian* proclaimed, "Now the main division of the law on persons is this, that all human beings are either free or slaves" (Justinian 2014, p. 24).

The stigma of slavery was hereditary during the modern period, when inherited physical traits such as the dark skin of Africans, could serve as a proxy or symbol for slave status. By comparison, slaves in the ancient world were more easily freed and their heirs blended in with the rest of the population over several generations. Despite Aristotle's designation of slave work as physical labor, slaves in both ancient Greece and Rome practiced a variety of occupations, from crafts to policing in Athens, to teaching and medicine in Rome (Finley 1983). Thus, along with the practice of slavery in the ancient world, a certain rough human equality seems to have been widely acknowledged and taken for granted. Except for Aristotle's views, slavery was mainly a matter of social status, not a matter of the identity of persons who were slaves or anything they were intrinsically believed to be.

Ideas of Race by Christian Theological Philosophers

Christian theological philosophers displayed a need to justify slavery as a practice of inequality, but their arguments were weak. St. Augustine simply said, "Christ did not make men free from being slaves," which gave slavery the legitimacy of not having been prohibited in scripture or by the Catholic Church of his day (Noonan 1995, p. 191). Saint Thomas Aquinas, relying on a general principle of human equality, endeavored to show how slavery could be just by relegating it to merely external physical matters. Aquinas' primary authority was not the Christian bible or the Church, but another philosopher, the Roman stoic, Seneca (4 BC–65 AD) (Seneca was pagan advisor to the Emperor, Nero, who forced him to commit suicide (Kamp 1934). Seneca claimed that the whole person is not enslaved, but only his or her body, so that the slave's soul belongs only to the slave.

Aquinas claimed that pertaining to "the internal movement of the will," only God had to be obeyed. This meant that decisions and choices concerning nutrition, reproduction, marriage, and sexual activity were up to the slave. That is, according to Aquinas, the owner of a slave controlled only the slave's physical actions (Aquinas 1988, pp. 242–4). It is difficult to believe that Aquinas was so naïve as to imagine that slaves did have the kind of autonomy he posited. During Aquinas' period, slave owners could feed, breed, punish, and kill their slaves, as they wished (Melzer 1993, pp. 209–27). More likely, Aquinas was talking about what he thought should be the case, that slavery should be like the employment of free people who had private lives when they were not working.

Locke's Racism in Practice but Not in Theory

The core of John Locke's political philosophy was his posit of fundamental, God-given rights to "life, liberty, and estate (property)," which could not be violated by legitimate government. Locke assumed that these rights were restricted to European male property owners of some wealth and status, but he did not go out of his way to identify the groups who were excluded: the poor, women, indigenous peoples, or African slaves. While occupying the post of Secretary to the Council of Trade and Plantations, Locke owned stock in the slave-trading Royal African Company. By the time that Locke, as Secretary of the Lords Proprietors of the Carolinas, helped revise the fundamental constitution of that colony, black chattel slavery was established in the American colonies and the revised Carolina constitution allowed for the practice, including the power of life and death over slaves by their owners (Armitage 2004, p. 207). However, in his primary work in political philosophy, *The Second Treatise of Government* (Locke [1689] 1991), published in the same decade he worked on the Carolina constitution, Locke generally treated slavery as a great evil.

Locke argued for the legitimacy of enslavement of the captives of a just war, as a condition of labor that those enslaved tacitly consented to, instead of being put to death (Locke, *Second Treatise*, IV, 23–24, 1689, pp. 284–5). But otherwise, freedom was an absolute right for Locke. He wrote:

> This *freedom* from absolute, arbitrary power, is so necessary to, and closely joined with a man's preservation, that he cannot part with it, but by what forfeits his preservation and life altogether. For a man, not having the power of his own life, *cannot*, by compact, or his own consent, *enslave himself* to anyone, nor put himself under the absolute, arbitrary power of another to take away his life, when he pleases. (Locke, *Second Treatise*, IV, 23, 1689, p. 284)

Locke insisted that those who had the fundamental rights of life, liberty, and estate would not be expected to approve of a form of government that violated those rights, which would be the same as enslaving them. Insofar as government exists under the consent and for the convenience of those governed, when God-given freedom is taken away by government, the people have a right to rebel:

> And thus the community perpetually retains a supreme power of saving themselves from the attempts and designs of any body, even of their legislators, whenever they shall be so foolish, or so wicked, as to lay and carry on designs against the liberties and properties of the subject. For no man, or society of men, having a power to deliver up their preservation, or consequently the means of it, to the Absolute Will and arbitrary dominion of another; whenever anyone shall go about to bring them into such a slavish condition, they will always have a right to preserve what they have not a power to part with; and to rid themselves of those who invade this fundamental, sacred, and unalterable law of self-preservation, for which they entered into society. (Locke, *Second Treatise*, XIII, Sec. 149, Locke 1689, pp. 366–7)

William Uzgalis argues that Locke was innocent of racism, because just-war enslavement was not the same as colonial slavery, and as a principle of liberty, Locke objected to government violation of the rights of those who had consented to be governed. Uzgalis claims that Locke easily could have, but did not, use then-contemporary arguments by influential and highly regarded political theorists to justify either colonial slavery or the seizure of American Indian lands. Uzgalis therefore concludes that despite Locke's investments and participation in the Carolina constitution, his political philosophy was not racist (Uzgalis 2017). Leaving aside Locke's investment in the Royal African Company and his tacit approval of slavery in Carolina, and focusing only on Locke's political philosophy, it could be objected that the property-ownership of Locke's male British political subject had the effect of a racist exclusion of both black slaves and American Indians (among others). But it would be anachronistic to accuse Locke of racism in anything like the meaning of the word in subsequent centuries, because it is not clear that his acceptance of slavery was a bias against nonwhites, per se.

Nowhere in his writings does Locke discuss human races or suggest that there is a natural racial hierarchy. It does not seem to have occurred to him to think critically about the oppressive practices toward non-Europeans in his day, even though he does think in accord with general principles of fairness, which could be applied to what came to be considered racial difference. For instance, in his *Letter Concerning Toleration*, Locke argues against religious discrimination by comparing it to the injustice of discrimination based on physical appearance. Thus:

> Suppose this business of religion were let alone, and that there were some other distinction made between men and men, upon account of their different complexions, shapes, and features, so that those who have black hair (for example) or gray eyes, should not enjoy the same privileges as other citizens; that they should not be permitted either to buy or sell, or live by their callings, that parents should not have the government and education of their own children; that all should either be excluded from the benefit of the laws, or meet with partial judges; can it be doubted but these persons, thus distinguished from others by the colour of their hair and eyes, united together by one common persecution, would be as dangerous to the magistrate, as any other that had associated themselves merely upon the account of religion? (Locke 1963 *Letter Concerning Toleration*, p. 52)

This is a curious passage because Locke does not say that it would be wrong to deprive people of the privileges of citizenship based on their appearance, but rather that it should not be done because "common persecution" would unite "these persons" to pose a danger to the government. Locke here provides a purely pragmatic or instrumental argument against what we would call racial bias, today.

There is little if any scholarly evidence that the idea of human races was in circulation during Locke's time. Samuel Johnson defined "race" as family lines or animal breeds. And in the 1694 edition of the *Dictionnaire de l'Académie Française*, "race" was a line or lineage for both humans and animals (Hudson 1996). However, even if "race" as it came to be understood was a term in circulation when Locke wrote, there is a strong metaphysical basis for the absence of discourse about human races in Locke's thought. Locke's **nominalism**, inclined him to skepticism about the reality of many **natural kinds**. For Locke, the **essences** of things, or their qualities that make them what they are and from which their other qualities flow, are **nominal essences**, created by the mind, existing in the mind, and projected onto reality. Locke even went so far as to claim that whether a creature is a human being or an animal was a matter of decision. His example for this was "monsters," babies born with severe deformities, who he thought could be designated as either sheep or humans. That Locke did not simply assert the humanity of such individuals suggests that he did not hold the biological principle that animals can reproduce only their own kind (Locke 1975). Racial taxonomies that were developed later depended on exactly the idea of real racial essences, even though knowledge and acceptance of the biological principle that humans had to give birth to other humans did not preclude various kinds of "dehumanization" based on nonwhite racial categorization.

Ideas of Human Races After Biology

By 1700, the British slave trade was well underway and recognized as an important part of the colonialist economic system. Slaves were typically taken from the West Coast of Africa to the Caribbean or American colonies, from which the agricultural products of slave labor would be shipped back to England. Profits from the slave trade created a favorable export balance for England in competition with Spain (MacInnes 1934; Davies 1957). The existence of African slavery before there were ideas of human races underscores the primacy of economic and political motivations for slavery, compared to prejudice or discrimination based on racial differences.

The development of systematics in the science of biology was used to justify slavery in the age of Enlightenment, when principles of human dignity and equality were otherwise espoused. The taxonomies of biology that later influenced anthropology afforded sophisticated frameworks in which moral, political, aesthetic, and intellectual distinctions among human races could be drawn. Hume, Kant, Hegel, Mill and Nietzsche had well-developed ideas of human racial difference that in some cases not only reflected general views in circulation when they wrote, but made perspectives that would now be considered racist, more emphatic, as well as more influential because written by famous philosophers.

Pre-modern theories of slavery proved to be place-holders for fully developed theories of race, and black chattel slavery became the paradigm case in the New World. When David Hume considered human history and civilization in the mid-eighteenth century, he could insultingly refer to racial differences in an almost offhand way. Aaron Garrett and Silvia Sebastiani emphasize Hume's ongoing assumption that blacks were naturally inferior to whites, as evident in multiple versions of a footnote in his chapter "Of National Characters" in *Essays, Moral, Political and Literary*. The version of this note in the 1777 posthumous edition of Hume's *Essays* began, "I am apt to suspect the negroes to be naturally inferior to the whites. There scarcely ever was a civilized nation of that complexion, nor even any individual eminent either in action or speculation" (Garrett and Sebastiani 2017; Hume 1875a, b, p. 249).

Hume's Explicit Racism

Hume first referred to racial differences in the 1754 edition of his *Essays* during a public intellectual debate about whether the human species had one origin—***monogenism***—or several corresponding to each race—***polygenism***. Eighteenth-century monogenists believed that differences in climate, geography, and food caused racial differences, which they did not think were permanent but could change over a few generations, when people changed environments. The polygenists believed that Africans, Asians, and Indians were permanently inferior to whites, because their inferiority was part of their original, unchanging racial identities. As a doctrine, polygenism posited strong racial differences and in keeping with this, in the first version of Hume's infamous footnote, he referred not to different human races, but ***species***, a more general taxonomic division than race, which does not allow for interbreeding:

I am apt to suspect the negroes and in general all the other species of men (for there are four or five different kinds) to be naturally inferior to the whites. There never was a civilized nation of any other complexion than white, nor even any individual eminent either in action or speculation. (Hume 1964, 252, n.1)

Hume developed a general thesis that differences in human groups or "national characters" were *moral*, the result of history, custom, and psychology, rather than physical factors. According to Hume, cultural differences had cultural causes, because of the strong human tendency toward imitation of those nearby and a near-universal sentiment of sympathy. However, this moral/cultural nature of causes of human difference apparently did not apply to groups living under extremes of temperature—particularly the inhabitants of Africa—and it is when Hume is discussing exceptions to moral causes of difference in temperate climates that his footnote appears. It is puzzling that Hume draws such strong differences based on race, because in his essay "Of the Populousness of Ancient Peoples, written before 1754, when the harshest version of the infamous footnote first appeared, Hume also refers to the uniformity of the human species:

> Stature and force of body, length of life, even courage and extent of genius, seem hitherto to have been naturally, in all ages, pretty much the same. The arts and sciences, indeed, have flourished in one period, and have decayed in another... . As far, therefore, as observation reaches, there is no universal difference discernible in the human species. (Hume 1875b, p. 382)

Garrett and Sebastiani relate Hume's defense of extreme polygenism to his desire to develop a theory of human nature and culture in terms of human history. Richard Popkin has discussed the infamous footnote as "Hume's Racial Law," noting that it cannot be explained in terms of conformity to a prevailing consensus, because Hume had plenty of objections and criticisms from both monogenists and those such as James Beattie who were more open-minded about the achievements and abilities of non-Europeans (Popkin 1977–1978). Beattie noted that Europeans had only been civilized for about 2000 years and that Hume did not know enough about Negro civilizations to draw the generalization he did (Beattie 1997). Hume could have preserved both tolerance and consistency in his moral theory, by at least suggesting that as members of the human species, "n"egroes (the word had a small 'n' until about 1930) also developed distinct cultures from moral causes, even if those moral causes were influenced by extremes of climate. But despite numerous opportunities to do that, he did not change his assessment. I think we can say without anachronism that Hume's views of human races were deeply prejudiced, because of the radical change in the methods he used to describe the histories of blacks and whites. Also, as Garrett and Sebastiani point out, his prejudice or racism was not limited to blacks, because he wrote that the difference between European whites and Amerindians was as great as the difference between European whites and animals (Garrett and Sebastiani 2017)!

Kant's White Supremacist Raciology and Dignitarianism

Immanuel Kant is best known by philosophers for his work in metaphysics, epistemology, and ethics. In 1755, he received a license to teach Philosophy in Königsberg, his home town, and his most popular courses from which he made a living for the next 40 years, were anthropology and geography. According to Kant, anthropology comprised the histories and studies of human culture, morality, and psychology; geography was made up of the studies of biological racial taxonomy. The effect of this division was that studies of nonwhites were relegated to geography. Kant's cultural analyses in *Anthropology from a Pragmatic Point of View* remain philosophically valid, because of its focus: "what man makes, can, or should make of himself as a freely acting being" (Kant 1996, p. 3). But Kant's 'geographical' views of human races made him the leading raciologist of the eighteenth century and were highly influential for what became the social science of anthropology, over the nineteenth century (Count 1950, pp. xx–xxi; 704–5, n.2, 1946).

Kant did not argue for the existence of human races but simply accepted received opinion in the same way Hume did: "The reason for assuming the Negroes and Whites to be fundamental races is self-evident" (Kant 1950, p. 19). Overall, Kant put forth and advanced **ethnological** Eurocentric theses about differences in human reason, morality, and taste, e.g., his often quoted, "The white race possesses all motivating forces and talents in itself" (Kant 1994, p. 117). In his more detailed analysis of human history, Kant posited a somewhat transcendental or at least nonempirical taxonomy of human races, arguing from the existence of mixed-race individuals to pure-raced parents, all of whom were descended from the same human "stem." That is, unlike Hume, Kant was a monogenist and his definition of races, besides hybridity resulting from interbreeding, included physical traits that are constant over generations in different environments. However, Kant also recognized *sports*, who do not generate hybrids in interbreeding, and *varieties*, or those that maintain resemblances but are not races; there were also special *strains*, or deviations that generate hybrids, but disappear after environmental change (Kant 1950, p. 17).

These rather elaborate and now-antiquated distinctions show that Kant struggled for clarity in reconciling the idea of race with known facts about human physical differences at the time, but they did not preclude his unfounded and bigoted assumptions about nonwhite inferiority. Kant was very outspoken about his characterization of blacks as intellectually inferior, as in another often-quoted remark, "This fellow was quite black from head to foot, a clear proof that what he said was stupid" (Kant 1965, pp. 110–1). Kant wrote about differences among the anthropological "national characters" of the French, Spanish, English, and German "distinctive feeling of the beautiful and the sublime," and he chauvinistically exalted the Germans. In considering Africans, however, his discourse changed from anthropology to race in a geographical sense, with acknowledgment of Hume:

> The Negroes of Africa have by nature no feeling that rises above the trifling. Mr. Hume challenges anyone to cite a single example in which a Negro has shown talents, and asserts that among the hundreds of thousands of blacks who are transported elsewhere from their countries, although many of whom have even been set free, still not a single one was ever found who presented anything great in art or science or any other praise-worthy quality, even though among the whites some continually rise aloft from the lowest rabble, and through superior gifts earn respect in the world. So fundamental is the difference between these two races of man, and it appears to be as great in regard to mental capacities as in color. (Kant 1994, pp. 55–6)

Finally, while Kant did not explicitly exclude Africans and other nonwhites from the moral domain of autonomous agents and subjects, his rule-based formulation of the *categorical imperative*, his most general moral principle, implied their exclusion. Kant's moral agent and subject were obligated to act under a general principle that he could will everyone else would follow (Kant 1994, pp. v–xi). He believed that women did not have sufficient rationality to act morally, or to appreciate the sublime and, of course, he thought that blacks lacked both reason and taste.

Nevertheless, Kant had at least one other formulation of the categorical imperative that yields a simpler emphasis on human dignity: Act so that you treat everyone, including yourself, as an end and never a means. The rationale for this formula of "the end in itself" is that a rational being regards his own existence as intrinsically valuable (Kant 1994, 36, n.21, Sec. 2). Kant's distinction between goods of exchange that have prices and human beings who have dignities also supports an egalitarian interpretation of his moral system (Kant 1994, pp. 73 and 77).

The **dignitarian** (intrinsic worth) aspect of Kant's moral system inspired twentieth century human rights doctrines, from the 1948 United Nations Universal Declaration of Human Rights, to a number of post-World War II constitutions for newly formed governments. Nevertheless, the aspirational influence of Kant's moral thought is somewhat irrelevant to understanding just how serious Kant was about his bigoted, chauvinistic remarks and whether they should be considered an integral part of his moral and political philosophy, as well as his theory of race. Toward answering these questions, Bernard Boxill has shown how Kant's teleology was related to his moral philosophy, of which his views on race were an integral part, and Robert Bernasconi has analyzed Kant's dehumanizing attention to the Khoikhoi.

On a political level, Boxill examines how Kant's racist views are compatible with other aspects of his thought insofar as he was concerned with the progress toward perfection of humanity as whole. This **teleological** development would, according to Kant, require that weaker groups perish. Boxill argues that even though Kant may have condemned colonialism and slavery in his later years, he displayed no real concern for their victims, as human beings (Boxill 2017).

Bernasconi observes that Kant was the first to define "race" as a term for large groups of people with heritable difference, in his 1775 essay, "On the Different Races of Human Beings" (Kant 1950). Bernasconi compares Kant's discussions of the Khoikhoi, also known as the Hottentots, with that of Jean-Jacques Rousseau. Rousseau discussed the culture and perspectives of the Hottentots, whereas Kant simply treated them as objects without subjectivity (Bernasconi 2014). This was damaging to any attempt to include nonwhites in the moral universe, because Kant was the preeminent theorist of moral dignity who based intrinsic human worth on the fact that a person's life was subjectively valuable to that person. Kant's **racialism**, or belief in the existence of human races, was thus indistinguishable from his **racism** or weighted comparison of races in terms of superior and inferior human worth (Appiah 1990).

Hegel's Geographical Racism

In contrast to Kant, Hegel's reliance on geography was directly tied to Western history insofar as nonwhite racial categories were imposed on people in Africa, Asia, and the Americas during the so-called "Age of Discovery." By the time Hegel addressed race in the early nineteenth century, the effects of colonialism had concretely changed ways of life in many non-European parts of the world: lands were taken, cultures disrupted, inhabitants brutalized, tortured, killed, enslaved, or subjected to hostile foreign rule. But more than that, geography for Hegel was an expression of abstract *spirit* and he wrote African people out of human history, on that basis:

> *Africa Proper* is the characteristic part of the whole continent as such. We have chosen to examine this continent first, because it can well be taken as antecedent to our main enquiry. It has no historical interest of its own, for we find its inhabitants living in barbarism and slavery in a land which has not furnished them with any integral ingredient of culture. From the earliest historical times, Africa has remained cut off from all contacts with the rest of the world; it is the land of gold, forever pressing in upon itself, and the land of childhood, removed from the light of self-conscious history and wrapped in the dark mantle of night. Its isolation is not just a result of its tropical nature, but an essential consequence of its geographical character (Hegel, 1997).

If Africans and their descendants have suffered the most severe and enduring racism in modernity, Hegel was undoubtedly a major architect of the fictional subhuman characteristics that were ascribed to them in justification of such treatment.

J.S. Mill's Racial Exclusions

John Stuart Mill's classic proclamation of freedom of speech, *On Liberty*, survives today as a defense of the need to allow even the most heinous views free expression, so that those with rational and benevolent opinions are continually required to remember and restate why they hold them. Mill's advocacy of freedom of speech was not based on the intrinsic value of freedom of expression but on the utilitarian benefits to society when the most enlightened are prepared to give reasons for their beliefs. However, as Thomas McCarthy points out, Mill qualified his principles of liberty with paternalism, so that they would not apply to everyone. Mill began *On Liberty* with the qualification that the principles therein were "meant to apply only to human beings in the maturity of their faculties," and not to "those backward states of society in which the race itself may be considered in its nonage…. Despotism is a legitimate mode of government in dealing with barbarians, provided the end be their improvement and the means justified by actually effecting that end." John Stuart Mill, like his father James, was a career administrator in the East India Company that administered the affairs of the British government in India (McCarthy 2009, p. 168). We can see that public and personal history constricted and biased his humanism.

Nietzsche's Racial Eugenicism

Mill's views on the maturity of human races can be viewed as a legacy from the metaphor of childhood that Hegel used to describe Africans. Nietzsche, however, was not so much concerned with the conventions of European white supremacy in his discussions of race, as he was with a vision of reactionary overthrow of democratic and egalitarian principles. Bernasconi notes that although Nietzsche was positive about Jews, who were considered a nonwhite race in the late nineteenth century, he defended both slavery and colonialism and was very pejorative about blacks. Bernasconi points out that Nietzsche advocated the creation of a pure, blonde, European race, through breeding—he was a racial **eugenicist**. Furthermore, Nietzsche's view of race, which some of his apologists have seen as a matter of spirit only, was belied by his claim that "it is not in the least possible that a human being might *not* have the qualities and preferences of his parents and ancestors in his body" (Bernasconi 2017).

Conclusion

Plato inadvertently introduced the idea of race by proposing to tell some groups of people that they were inferior to other groups, by birth. Aristotle did not have an idea of race but accepted slavery as a natural institution and believed that Asians, the majority of those enslaved in his time, had character traits that made them suitable for that status. The Romans, like the Greeks, viewed slaves as household property, along with domestic animals, but they did not identify slaves by race. Slavery was accepted by the Church founders and Saint Aquinas, and although there was a sense that it required moral justification, their qualifying arguments were weak. John Locke justified the type of slavery that could be imposed on the losing side in a just war, but for normal government, he rejected slavery as a violation of fundamental human rights.

Hume was the first canonical philosopher to mention human races and explicitly assert nonwhite inferiority. Kant cited Hume as an authority for black inferiority, but also developed his own complex system of race and a white supremacist perspective of racial differences in reason, morality, and aesthetic taste. Although Kant was a monogenist and thought that all races derived from the same stem, he posited different racial essences as determining degrees of intellectual capacity and moral worth. Hegel was as derogatory about nonwhites, especially Africans, as Hume and Kant, but he believed that geography or environment was the main determining factor of racial differences. Despite his overall liberalism and endorsement of representative government, John Stuart Mill restricted freedom of expression to European individuals and groups who were advanced or "mature". Nietzsche took evaluative racial hierarchies for granted. He attributed an historical decline in European vitality to race-mixing and advocated the creation of a new, fierce, blond race.

The history of ideas of race in the canon of Western philosophy was not emancipatory to those non-European groups who were enslaved, oppressed, and exploited over the centuries of colonialism. However, the point of exploring this history is not to blame or castigate revered philosophers. Rather, the task is to determine the extent to which their ideas about race were integral parts of their thought and philosophical systems that traditionally have been more central to philosophical scholarship than the subjects of racialism or racism. It is also important to recognize their influence on subsequent scientific and popular ideas about race. Even if the racism(s) of these thinkers is an integral part of their philosophical systems, some believe it remains conceptually possible to expand their domains to include non-whites and non-Europeans in erstwhile unfairly advantaged communities that contained the privileged subjects in the history of moral and political philosophy. For instance, contemporary universalist **dignitarian** thought is deeply connected to Kant's ideas about the intrinsic value of human individuals (Rosen 2012).

Glossary

autonomy—self-rule, being in charge of one's own life.

biological racial determinism—idea that inherited human racial traits determine social, psychological, physical, and cultural traits.

deliberation—for Aristotle, the intellectual activity of practical wisdom that allows one to practice or develop virtues.

dignitarian—pertaining to the intrinsic value of human individuals.

essences—qualities of things that make them what they are and cause their other qualities.

ethnology—nineteenth-century studies of the history of human cultures that related cultural differences to inherited racial traits.

eugenics—practice and ideology of improving the quality of humanity by regulating who can have children, and with whom.

identity—what a person is, naturally or in society.

intrinsic worth (dignity)—valuable in itself (to itself).

monogenist(ism)—belief that all human groups, including races, had the same origins.

moral—adjective connoting human culture, ethics, psychology, and studies thereof.

nominalism—philosophical doctrine that the distinguishing marks of a certain type of thing or of all types of things are matters of language and human decision and convention, rather than what actually exists in nature or in the external world.

natural kind—a type of thing that exists on its own in nature, without human invention.

Philosophy of Race—descriptive and normative philosophical inquiry into racial differences and injustice related to them.

polygenist(ism)—belief that human groups, especially races, had different origins.

phronesis—for Aristotle, practical reasoning about how to act.

racialism—belief that there are human races or that humankind is divided into races.

racism—negative assessment of some human races and their members, compared to others.

species—most common division in biological taxonomy; members of a species share its defining traits and can breed amongst themselves but not with members of other species.

systematics—biological naming and classifying living things as individuals and groups, in relation to one another.

teleology—determination or causation by an end goal.

thumos—(Greek) spiritedness.

Essay and Discussion Questions

1. Why do you think it's important to avoid anachronism in discussing ideas resembling race before the modern period?
2. What are the main differences between Plato and Aristotle's views of who should be enslaved?
3. Do you think Locke's failure to extend fundamental rights to women, the poor, and non-Europeans means that his political philosophy was not based on his avowed principles of liberty and freedom?
4. What are the implications of the fact that Africans were enslaved before a biological concept of human races were developed?

5. Hume was a polygenist and Kant was a monogenist. Explain how their assessments of racial differences were or were not related to their different beliefs about human origins.

6. Explain and critically evaluate the difference between Kant's claim that Africans lacked intelligence and reason and that they lacked taste.

7. How did Kant's reliance on racial essences and Hegel's on geography influence their views of human races?

8. What are the implications of John Stuart Mill's restrictions of liberty to Europeans?

9. In what ways was Nietzsche a racialist? Was he also a racist?

10. How might a philosopher's views on race be relevant to other aspects of that thinker's work? How are nonracial views held by a philosopher related to that thinkers' views on race?

References

Aquinas, Saint Thomas. *On Law, Morality, and Politics*, edited by William P. Baumgarth and Richard J. Regan. S.J. Indianapolis, IN: Hackett, 1988.

Appiah, K. Anthony. "Racisms." *Anatomy of Racism*, edited by David Theo Goldberg. Minneapolis, MN: University of Minnesota, 1990, pp. 3–17.

Armitage, David. "John Locke, Carolina, and the Two Treatises of Government." *Political Theory*, vol. 32, no. 5, Oct. 2004, pp. 602–27.

Aristotle. "Politica." *The Basic Works of Aristotle*, edited by Richard McKeon. New York, NY: Random House, 1941, pp. 1127–33.

Beattie, James. "'A Response to Hume' from *An Essay on the Nature and Immutability of Truth, in Opposition to Sophistry and Skepticism*." *Race and the Enlightenment: A Reader*, edited by Emmanuel Chukwudi Eze. Cambridge, MA: Blackwell, 1997, pp. 34–7.

Bernasconi, Robert. "Kolb's Pre-racial Encounter with the Hottentots and Its Impact on Buffon, Kant, and Rousseau." *Graduate Faculty Philosophy Journal*, Special Issue on Race in the History of Philosophy, New School University, 2014, pp. 101–24.

Bernasconi, Robert. "Nietzsche as a Philosopher of Racialized Breeding." *Oxford Handbook of Philosophy and Race*, edited by Naomi Zack. New York, NY: Oxford University Press, 2017.

Boxill, Bernard. "Kantian Racism and Kantian Teleology." *Oxford Handbook of Philosophy and Race*, edited by Naomi Zack. New York, NY: Oxford University Press, 2017.

Count, Earl W. "The Evolution of the Race Idea in Modern Western Culture During the Period of the Pre-Darwinian Nineteenth Century." *Transactions of the New York Academy of Sciences*, vol. 8, 1946, pp. 139–65.

Count, Earl W., ed. *This is Race: An Anthology Selected from the International Literature on the Races of Man*. New York, NY: Henry Schuman, 1950.

Davies, K.G. *The Royal African Company*. London: Longmans Green, 1957, pp. 1–37.

Eze, Emmanuel Chukwudi. "The Color of Reason: The Idea of 'Race' in Kant's Anthropology." *Anthropology and the German Enlightenment*, edited by Katherine Faull. London: Bucknell and Associates Press, 1994, Chap. IV, vol. 8, reprinted in *Race and the Enlightenment*, edited by Eze, pp. 103–31.

Finley, M.I. *Ancient Slavery and Modern Ideology*. New York, NY: Penguin, 1983.

Garrett, Aaron, and Silvia Sebastiani. "David Hume on Race." *Oxford Handbook of Philosophy and Race*, edited by Naomi Zack. New York, NY: Oxford University Press, 2017.

Hegel, Georg Wilhelm Fredrich. "'Geographical Bases of World History,' from *Lectures on the Philosophy of World History*." *Race and the Enlightenment: A Reader*, edited by Emmanuel Chukwudi Eze. Cambridge, MA: Blackwell, 1997, p. 124.

Hudson, Nicholas. "From 'Nation' to 'Race': The Origin of Racial Classification in Eighteenth-Century Thought." *Eighteenth-Century Studies*, vol. 29, no. 3, Spring 1996, pp. 247–64.

Hume, David. "Of National Characters." *Essays Moral, Political and Literary*, edited by T.H. Green and T.H. Grose. London: Longmans, Green and Co., 1875a, Essay XXI.

Hume, David. "Of the Populousness of Ancient Nations." *Essays Moral, Political and Literary*, edited by T.H. Green and T.H. Grose. London: Longmans, Green and Co., 1875b, Essay XI.

Hume, David. "Of National Characters." *The Philosophical Works*, edited by Thomas Hill Green and Thomas Hodge Grose. Darmstadt, West Germany: Scientia Verlag Aalen, 1964, 4 vols., 3: 252, n.1.

Jiménez, Erick Raphael. "Aristotle on Natural Slavery: The Race Question." *Graduate Faculty Philosophy Journal*, Special Issue on Race in the History of Philosophy, New School University, 2014, pp. 53–80.

Justinian. *Digest of Justinian*. Translated by Charles Henry Monro. Cambridge, MA: Cambridge University Press, 2014, Book I, vol. 3, p. 24.

Kamp, H. W. "Concerning Seneca's Exile." *The Classical Journal*, vol. 30, no. 2, 1934, pp. 101–8.

Kamtakar, Rashama. "Distinction Without a Difference: Race and Genos in Plato." *Philosophers on Race: Critical Essays*, edited by Julie K. Ward and Tommie L. Lott. Oxford, UK: Blackwell, 2002, pp. 1–13.

Kant, Immanuel. "On the Different Races of Man or On the Different Races of Human Beings." *This Is Race: An Anthology Selected from the International*

Literature on the Races of Man, edited by Earl W. Count. New York, NY: Schuman, 1950, pp. 16–24.

Kant, Immanuel. *Observations on the Feeling of the Beautiful and the Sublime.* Translated by John T. Goldthwait. Berkeley, CA: University of California Press, 1965.

Kant, Immanuel. "Grounding for the Metaphysics of Morals." *Kant's Ethical Philosophy*. Translated by James W. Ellington. Indianapolis, IN: Hackett, 1994, Warner A. Wick, Introduction.

Kant, Immanuel, *Anthropology from a Pragmatic Point of View.* Translated by Hans H. Rudnick and edited by Victor Lyle Dowdell. Carbondale: Southern Illinois University Press, 1996.

Kant, Immanuel. "Of National Characteristics, from Physical Geography." Race and the Enlightenment, edited by Eze, Chap. 4.

Locke, John. *A Letter Concerning Toleration.* Latin and English Texts Revised and edited by Mario Montuori. The Hague: Martinus Nijhoff, 1963.

Locke, John. *An Essay Concerning Human Understanding*, edited by Peter H. Niddich. Oxford: Oxford University Press, 1975, Book IV, Chap. iii, Sec. 5, pp. 338–40; iii, 27, pp. 414–5; iv, 27, p. 454.

Locke, John. *Two Treatises of Government*, edited by Peter Laslett. Cambridge: Cambridge University Press, (1689) 1991.

MacInnes, C. M. *England and Slavery.* Bristol: Arrowsmith, 1934, pp. 13–21.

Mayr, Ernst. *Systematics and the Origin of Species.* Cambridge: Harvard University Press, 1942.

McCarthy, Thomas. *Race, Empire, and the Idea of Human Development.* Cambridge, MA: Cambridge University Press, 2009.

Melzer, Milton. *Slavery: A World History.* 2 vols. New York, NY: Da Capo Press, 1993.

Noonan, John T., Jr. "Development in Moral Doctrine." *The Context of Casuistry*, edited by James F. Keenan and Thomas A. Shannon. Washington, DC: Georgetown University Press, 1995, pp. 188–204.

Plato. "Republic." *The Collected Dialogues of Plato*, edited by Edith Hamilton and Huntington Cairns and translated by Paul Shorey. New York: Bollingen Foundation, Pantheon Books, Random House, 1964, pp. 575–844.

Popkin, Richard H. "Hume's Racism." *Philosophical Forum*, vol. 9/2, no. 2–3, 1977–1978, pp. 211–26.

Rosen, Michael. *Dignity: Its History and Meaning.* Cambridge, MA: Harvard University Press, 2012.

Uzgalis, William. "John Locke, Racism, Slavery, and Indian Lands." *Oxford Handbook of Philosophy and Race*, edited by Naomi Zack. New York, NY: Oxford University Press, 2017.

2

Egalitarian Spiritual and Legal Traditions

Ideas tend to drift toward **consensus** led by those with the strongest influence and highest status in their fields. The ideas about race developed by famous philosophers, as discussed in Chapter 1, became the consensus and common sense about race throughout society from about the late 1700s until about 1960. Whether these philosophers independently came up with their views or produced them to comply with and support economic and political forces such as colonialism and slavery, is a question for psychology, **intellectual history**, and the **sociology of knowledge**, which has not yet been fully addressed. But, regardless of how that question comes to be answered, more than the ideas about race in the history of philosophy are needed to approach a full historical account of the idea of race. Some ideas that did not prevail in their times, or influence public policy, are closer in egalitarian spirit to contemporary educated ideas about race than canonical philosophical thought. And those submerged egalitarian ideas regarding race were rooted in older spiritual and religious traditions in the West.

From the ancient world through modernity, there were **egalitarian** perspectives and voices about what we would now consider human racial difference—"now consider," because the ideas of human difference before the modern period were not based on the fully developed, modern concept of biological race. In addition, many of these perspectives shaped egalitarian law in the United States, not fully in the Constitution, but specifically in legislation enacted right after the Civil War and following the Civil Rights Movement of the 1950s and 60s. Even brief consideration of several spiritual/religious and formal legal ideas of race provide an historically

© The Author(s) 2018
N. Zack, *Philosophy of Race*, Palgrave Philosophy Today,
https://doi.org/10.1007/978-3-319-78729-9_2

grounded egalitarian account of human racial difference that is a powerful antidote to ideas of race in the canonical history of philosophy.

One could give a revised historical account of ideas about race from religious and spiritual egalitarian views, right up to prevailing egalitarian views of the present. But to view such a constructed or even made up counter-narrative as a real historical record would be misleading. Many of the egalitarian views that were submerged in the past, especially views of those who were victims of racism and oppression would not have been necessary without those circumstances. Also, egalitarian actions by the most powerful were sometimes undertaken with aims other than the defeat of racism. For example, the federal legislation passed during **Reconstruction** was widely perceived to be a means for punishing white Southerners, after the Civil War. And some parts of the Civil Rights legislation were motivated by concern for United States moral standing during the Cold War, rather than sincere desire to defeat racism within the United States.

This chapter proceeds historically through highlights of the spiritual/religious and legal egalitarian traditions. We have seen that both Plato and Aristotle ranked human beings according to basic worth: Plato advocated that rulers use a metaphor of precious and base metals to create propaganda that would justify human rankings based on talent and merit. Aristotle thought that there were natural slaves. He also thought that Asians lacked the spirit for self-rule and, coincidentally or not, Asians were a large proportion of the slave population of ancient Greece. However, there were thinkers in both the ancient world and early and medieval Christianity, who thought that human beings were equal in important ways. During the modern period, egalitarian ideas were also expressed at the same times as the most privileged racist ideas, for example, in philosopher George Berkeley's project for a seminary that would include American Indians, and within philosophy, James Beattie's challenge to David Hume's easy assumptions about the existence of a hierarchy of human races. Moreover, the subjects or victims of racist ideas about human difference have often worked within the Christian tradition, particularly nineteenth-century free black writers and activists.

Even though all citizens do not obey their laws and laws are not always applied, Western democratic countries, especially the United States, do have egalitarian principles in their foundational documents and amendments to them. These principles have often been drawn upon by those resisting societal racist practice. It is also important to add to egalitarian laws within nations, consideration of how the United Nations, in the 1948 Universal Declaration of Human Rights, provided the aspirational foundation for contemporary global egalitarianism.

One important difference between the philosophical racist tradition and the egalitarian religious-legal tradition is the relation between theory and practice. The philosophers who constructed racist theories were not the same people who directly benefitted from them—slave owners and traders and those who exploited free black labor. But after the US institution of slavery was established and later under **Jim Crow**, the theorists of egalitarianism were often also activists, especially during the Civil Rights Movement. As a result of this difference, the egalitarian tradition can be viewed as a part of real history and not only the history of ideas or the history of philosophy. This egalitarian tradition includes: ancient egalitarians and early Christians, Hume's critics, modern Christians, and nineteenth-century black egalitarians, American formal equality, and the Universal Declaration of Human Rights.

Ancient Egalitarians and Early Christians

Cosmopolitans, Stoics, and early Christians established a tradition of **discourse** about human commonality and equality that was to endure as motivation for subsequent religious and secular egalitarians. While racial differences were not their direct subjects, the early spiritual humanitarian tradition has continued to motivate much antiracist thought, to this day.

Cosmopolitanism is a perspective on other individuals and groups that are tolerant of personal and cultural differences and is not restricted by political borders, language, morals, beliefs, or customs. The origins of cosmopolitanism derive from Diogenes of Sinope (412–404—323 BCE), who replied when asked where he came from, "I am a citizen of the world." Diogenes lived in a barrel on the streets of Athens and defied most of the conventions of his day. He was said to have "raised his leg" at a banquet, on those who threw him bones as though he were a dog. When Alexander the Great introduced himself to him, saying "I am Alexander, the great king," Diogenes replied, "And I am Diogenes the dog." In later life, Diogenes's poverty resulted in his living as a slave and working as a tutor for his owner's children. But in his sale as a slave, he listed rule over others as one of his skills, further demonstrating a lack of deference for the existing social order (Laëtius 1853).

Several contemporary philosophers have taken up cosmopolitanism as an inclusive social doctrine with relevance to attitudes toward racial difference. Kwame Anthony Appiah indicates the scope of this influence with reference to his own background:

These three ideas then, I, a twenty-first century American citizen of Anglo-Ghanian ancestry, want to borrow from a citizen of Sinope who dreamed of global citizenship twenty-four centuries ago: (1) We do not need a single world government; but (2) we must care for the fate of all human beings inside and outside our own societies; and (3) we have much to gain from conversation with one another across our differences. (Appiah 2007, p. 2377)

We saw in Chapter 1 that the great theologian philosopher, Saint Thomas Aquinas (1225–1274) unsuccessfully tried to show how slavery could be just by associating its conditions with the control and regulation of only external physical matters. Aquinas' primary authority was the Roman stoic, Seneca (4 BC–65 AD) Indeed, Cosmopolitanism influenced **Stoicism**, the school of philosophy founded by Zeno of Citium (234–362 BCE) in Athens and enduring through the third century AD, in Rome, as well as Greece. Stoics advocated an inner removal from the ups and downs of fortune, including personal pain, based on the principle that we should care only about what is under our control.

Stoics also emphasized human commonality and love. The Roman statesman, Marcus Tullius Cicero (106–43 BCE) was perhaps the most famous stoic in this regard. Although a slave owner, he emphasized generosity and kindness to strangers, as in these often-quoted lines:

> The friendly soul who shows one lost the way,
> Lights, as it were, another's lamp from his.
> Though he has lit another's, his own still shines. (Cicero 2000, 1:51)

Cosmopolitan sentiments were also expressed by early and medieval Christian theologians. Jesus told his disciples not to be more concerned about convention than their own actions. He defended his disciples for breaking with the tradition of their elders by not washing their hands before eating: "Not that which goeth into the mouth defileth a man; but that which cometh out of the mouth, this defileth a man" (Mathew 15:11). Saint Paul posited the unity of mankind by building upon such cosmopolitanism, in a new dimension. Paul did not flout tradition within the same realm it operated, but posited human unity in a new spiritual realm:

> For you are all children of God through faith in Christ Jesus. For as many of you who were baptized into Christ have put on Christ there is neither Jew nor Greek; there is neither slave nor freeman; there is no male and female: for you are all one in Jesus Christ. And if you belong to Christ, then you are Abraham's offspring, heirs according to the promise. (Galatians 3: 26–9)

Paul's unity was nonmaterial insofar as Christians held that the mind-soul was separate from the physical body. Thus, Paul's Epistle to the Romans, Chapters 7, 14: "For we know that the law is spiritual: but I am carnal, sold under sin."

James Beattie's Challenges to David Hume and George Berkeley's Activism

The **idealist** philosopher George Berkeley, Bishop of Cloyne in the Church of Ireland (1685–1753) is not well known for his thoughts about race. As a clergyman, he believed there was a common human nature and he had a degree of missionary zeal to increase the number of Christians. Berkeley was actively involved in charitable works to help the poor in England but he thought that Christianity could best be revitalized through missionary programs in the New World. In the 1720s he began efforts to found a seminary in Bermuda, which would turn out pastors from "the English youth of our plantations" and "a number of young American Savages." Berkeley thought that training American Indians in morality, religion, and civic responsibility would enable them to spread Christianity among their people. He also advocated "gospel liberty" for black slaves, although not emancipation.

The British Parliament pledged a grant of £20,000 or about 80 million dollars, today (Reddit 2017), for Berkeley's seminary. He received a charter from the Crown and collected private contributions. In 1728, he traveled to Rhode Island with his wife (he had married for the first time that same year). The couple settled on a farm outside of Newport, where they hoped that food for the seminary would eventually be produced. The parliamentary grant did not materialize and when the Berkeleys returned to England in 1931, he donated the farm to Yale University (Gaustad 1979, pp. 24–50).

Berkeley presupposed that nonwhite people could be educated, which did not occur to many of his contemporaries, especially David Hume. His emphasis on religion and commitment to the furtherance of Christianity was undoubtedly conservative or at best ameliorative, regarding race. But although he did not advocate changes in political policy toward nonwhites in the British colonies, the effort and expectations he poured into the Bermuda project was a unique undertaking, compared to the activism of other philosophers.

David Hume's remarks about race were offhand, as noted in Chapter 1. His disparagement of nonwhites as deficient in achievements was taken up by Kant who produced a white supremacist theory of human racial hierarchy that influenced the new science of anthropology, well through the nineteenth century. Kant dismissed the ideas of Hume's "Scottish critics," who included James Beattie. Beattie (1735–1803), a Presbyterian clergyman, mainly objected to Hume's atheism and he was active in blocking Hume from securing university employment in Scotland (Schmidt 2003, pp. 410–20). Beattie also offered incisive challenges to Hume's remarks about race (as well as other aspects of his philosophy) in his *An Essay on The Nature and Immutability of Truth in Opposition to Sophistry and Skepticism* (1770).

A number of scholars have noted that Beattie's criticism of Hume was in reality an application of Hume's own principle that cultural differences among human groups are the result of cultural practices over time. Beattie noted that Europeans had taken many generations to develop more advanced cultures and he brought forth the examples of cultural achievements in Africa, Mexico, and Peru, to refute Hume. He remarked that Hume himself did not know any Africans. He argued that assumptions of the inferiority of slaves in Europe would also apply to Europeans who were backward in culture because they were not educated (Popkin 1977; Palter 1995).

Overall, the force of Beattie's criticism of Hume was based on his Christian commitment to a common human nature and his adherence to the Scottish historical school, which held that human actions needed to be understood in their own cultural circumstances. Beattie also advocated seeking out such understanding of the behavior of people in cultural circumstances that were radically different from one's own (Schmidt 2003, pp. 410–11); Beattie's views of non-European races were remarkably progressive and **empirical**. Although he may have been motivated by religious conviction (particularly in his general antagonism toward Hume), his approach to equality was based on empirical studies, rather than the faith in an egalitarian afterlife held by Saints Paul and Aquinas.

Christianity and Nineteenth-Century Black Egalitarians

The **abolitionist movement** against American slavery before the Civil War is often associated with Mennonites, Quakers, New England intellectuals and white **suffragists**. However, there were substantial contributions from free black people, both in the United States and England. These thinkers often relied on religious argument and textual interpretations of the bible. For instance, Andrew Harris, 1938 graduate of the University of Vermont, was one of the first black antislavery advocates and he became a Presbyterian minister in 1841 (Thornton 2015). His 1839 address to the American Anti-Slavery Society included these words:

The Bible says the love of money is the root of all evil; and if the love of money is a predominant passion anywhere, it is in this land. Yet, without disputing the correctness of the declaration, it seems to me that slavery has developed a passion in the human heart that is stronger than the love of money; for they refuse to gratify this disposition which the bible says is the root of all evil, through the influence of that still deeper root of evil, prejudice. (*Emancipator* 1839)

Some nineteenth-century black writers also addressed science and politics, but their engagement with Christianity was important for encouraging wider multitudes toward racial justice and countering derogatory ideas about blacks. The majority of all Americans were religious in the nineteenth century and traditional emotions about race, as associated with religion, continue to have motivating force in the early twenty-first century. The prevailing nineteenth-century religious view among Christians was that Africans were the descendants of Ham, who had been cursed by Noah, unto his descendants through Canaan—"Cursed be Canaan; a servant of servants shall he be unto his brethren" (Genesis 9:23). Their black skin was believed to be evidence of the curse that condemned them to slavery, because of their ancestor's sin (Goldberg 2005).

Albert Mosley sums up this bible-focused religious strain in antislavery writings of free black men on both sides of the Atlantic:

They accepted Christianity as the source of revealed truth, and they accepted the Biblical account of the sons of Noah (Shem, Japheth, Ham) as the progenitors of the present races. But they make clear that Noah's curse on Canaan had invalidly been taken to be a curse on all the children of Ham. The curse was on Canaan and his descendants, and Africans were descendants of Cush, not of Canaan. (Mosley 2017, p. 89)

Mosley chronicles the bible-centered writings of a number of free black intellectuals. African slaves were emancipated in 1772 in England and they criticized proslavery thought and the slave trade. Ignatius Sancho (1729–1780), an educated and prominent musician, provided a meeting place for antislavery discussion in his place of business as a grocer. Olaudah Equiano (1745–1797), a former slave who became a trader and had been able to buy his freedom from the king, was his friend. Both Sancho and Equiano agreed with the views of their friend, Quobna Cugoano (1757–1791), who had been a slave in Granada and Virginia. Cugoano saw a value in slavery as a means to convert Africans to Christianity. But he interpreted Noah's curse on Ham, as applying to only Canaan and his descendants, so that Ham's other sons were unscathed; Canaanites, who were not Africans, deserved to be cursed because they were wicked, although they had no distinguishing physical features.

American free black antislavery writers included David Walker (1796–1830), Martin Delaney (1812–1885), Alexander Crummell (1819–1898), Edward Blyden (1832–1912), and of course, Frederick Douglass. Walker was born free in North Carolina and became a member of the African Methodist Episcopal (AME) church. He considered whites enemies of blacks according to a biblical interpretation: Whites descended from Noah's son Ham but have deceptively attributed that descent to blacks. Delaney was also born free in West Virginia and became a doctor by assisting white abolitionist doctors. He thought that before the flood, everyone was rouge in color but that Noah's sons developed different complexions, with Ham the darkest due to climate conditions after settling in Africa.

Alexander Crummell (1819–1898) was born in New York City. His mother was a free woman and his father a former African slave. He was the first black graduate of Queens College, Cambridge and became an Episcopal priest. He believed that Africans needed to unite and in 1853 he moved to Liberia to spread Christianity. But he returned to the United States in 1873, and in 1897 he founded the American Negro Academy. Crummell's biblical scholarship sought to prove that it was not Ham who was cursed by Noah, but his son Canaan. Ham was the first member of the Negro race, but Canaan went to Judea, Ethiopia, and then Europe and his descendants were not Negroes. The descendants of Noah's son Cush were Negroes, but they carried no curse.

Edward Blyden (1832–1912), born in the Virgin Islands, was encouraged by a Dutch Reformed minister to study in the United States and then immigrate to Liberia. Like Crumell, Blyden's interpretation of race after the flood was that the curse applied to Canaan and not all of the descendants of Ham; the other descendants of Ham who migrated to Africa, were blameless. Blyden also believed that Africans became slaves because of their sin of turning away from God.

Mosley notes that Frederick Douglass, although not a religiously motivated thinker himself, was well aware of the importance of religion in solving the problems related to slavery. Douglass thought that blacks would eventually assimilate into white society, claiming, "Drive out the Negro and you drive out Christ, the Bible, and American liberty with him" (Mosley 2017, Douglass quotation, p. 88).

Religious abolitionist activists included heroic women. Sojourner Truth (1797–1883) adopted her name and became an itinerant preacher as the result of a religious experience in 1843, when the Spirit called to her to speak the truth. In her dictated autobiography, *The Narrative of Sojourner Truth*, Truth remembered how she had responded to disrupters of a religious tent meeting:

> Shall I run away and hide from the Devil? Me, a servant of the living God? Have I not faith enough to go out and quell that mob, when I know it is written- "One shall chase a thousand, and two put ten thousand to flight"? I know there are not a thousand here; and I know I am a servant of the living God. I'll go to the rescue, and the Lord shall go with and protect me. (Painter 1996, p. 105)

Like Truth, Harriet Tubman (1820–1913) was born in slavery and became a dedicated abolitionist, known as "Moses" for her success on the Underground Railway. After escaping from slavery in Maryland, she returned to that state 19 times to escort others to freedom. During the Civil War, Tubman worked for the Union Army as a cook, nurse, and armed scout and spy. She led the raid freeing 700 at Combahee Ferry. Tubman is described by biographers as "deeply spiritual," and like Truth, her faith allowed for righteous indignation:

> I prayed all night long for my master. Till the first of March; and all the time he was bringing people to look at me, and trying to sell me. I changed my prayer. First of March I began to pray, 'Oh Lord, if you ain't never going to change that man's heart, kill him, Lord, and take him out of the way.' (Bradford 1971, pp. 14–5)

American Formal Equality

By about 1970, after the success of the **Civil Rights Movement**, formally, or according to written law, the United States appeared to be an egalitarian society in terms of race. A good part of the legal gains for African Americans and other racial minorities were based on interpretations of the Bill of Rights, the first ten amendments to the US Constitution. Rights originally stated as applying to everyone were now applied to those who had been deprived of them. The post-civil rights movement legal structure and its legal antecedents have often been viewed by the majority of Americans as proof that racism and discrimination are isolated aberrations in US society. Much academic scholarship from 1970 on has been dedicated to showing how the United States began and persists as an anti-nonwhite racist society. But the record of formal equality remains important as a well-**promulgated** commitment to egalitarianism. Indeed, in the context of civil rights education and public discourse, certain milestones of American egalitarianism are recognized and honored, so we should consider them here, beginning with constitutional rights before the Civil Rights Movement and followed by key events in the Civil Rights Movement and its aftermath.

Civil Rights in the US Constitution

The Bill of Rights to the US Constitution (1789) is recognized as divided into two parts: First Amendment liberties and rights pertaining to religion, speech, press, assembly, and petition; and liberties and rights pertaining to crime and due process. In both cases, liberties are protections against harms by government and rights are entitlements to equal protection by government. Although the language of the Bill of Rights appears to include all citizens, only male property owners could vote in most locales and for the purpose of US congressional representation, as well as taxation, slaves were to count as three-fifths of free persons (Blackpast.org 2017). Until the Emancipation Proclamation, local practice and courts upheld the rights of slave owners over slaves, including the return to their owners of escaped slaves residing in non-slave states, as in the infamous *Dred Scott v. Sanford* decision of 1857. But during the period of Reconstruction over the decade following the Civil War, African Americans were legally granted many rights for the first time. Some claimed that these Amendments were passed to punish the members of the former Confederacy, but for a while, the new rights, as delineated in Table 2.1, were real (Allard 2006).

After the Reconstruction era federal legislation, there followed a period of extreme antiblack racism composed of racist segregation, agricultural peonage, and both random and organized violence, including **lynching** by the Klu Klux Klan and other groups (Klarman 2004; Ayers 2007). By 1960, many African Americans were denied their right to vote and under "**Jim Crow**," schools and other public facilities, from swimming pools to churches, were racially segregated. For instance, despite the Civil Rights Act of 1875, in *Plessy v. Ferguson*, 163 US 537 (1896) the US Supreme Court upheld state racial segregation laws for public facilities under the doctrine of "separate but equal." That is, the Court held that racial segregation was legal

Table 2.1 US Civil Rights Legislation, from 1865–1875 (*Source From United States House of Representatives 2017*)

Amendment/Act	Public law/US code	Main provisions
Thirteenth Amendment	P.L. 38-11; 13 Stat. 567; P.L. 38–52; 13 Stat. 774–775	Abolished slavery and involuntary servitude, except as punishment for a crime. Approved by the 38th Congress (1863–1865) as S.J. Res. 16; ratified by the states on December 6, 1865
Civil Rights Act of 1866	14 Stat. 27–30	Guaranteed the rights of all citizens to make and enforce contracts and to purchase, sell, or lease property. Passed by the 39th Congress (1865–1867) as S.R. 61
Fourteenth Amendment	14 Stat. 358–359	Declared that all persons born or naturalized in the US were citizens and that any state that denied or abridged the voting rights of males over the age of 21 would be subject to proportional reductions in its representation in the US House of Representatives. Approved by the 39th Congress (1865–1867) as H.J. Res. 127; ratified by the states on July 9, 1868
Fifteenth Amendment	16 Stat. 346; 16 Stat. 40–41	Forbade any state to deprive a citizen of his vote because of race, color, or previous condition of servitude. Approved by the 40th Congress (1867–1869) as S.J. Res. 8; ratified by the states on February 3, 1870
First Ku Klux Klan Act (Civil Rights Act of 1870)	16 Stat. 140–146	Prohibited discrimination in voter registration on the basis of race, color, or previous condition of servitude. Established penalties for interfering with a person's right to vote. Gave federal courts the power to enforce the act and to employ the use of federal marshals and the army to uphold it. Passed by the 41st Congress (1869–1871) as H.R. 1293
Second Ku Klux Klan Act (Civil Rights Act of 1871)	16 Stat. 433–440	Placed all elections in both the North and South under federal control. Allowed for the appointment of election supervisors by federal circuit judges. Authorized US Marshals to employ deputies to maintain order at polling places. Passed by the 41st Congress (1869–1871) as H.R. 2634
Third Ku Klux Klan Act (1871)	17 Stat. 13–15	Enforced the 14th Amendment by guaranteeing all citizens of the United States the rights afforded by the Constitution and provided legal protection under the law. Passed by the 42nd Congress (1871–1873) as H.R. 320
Civil Rights Act of 1875	18 Stat. 335–337	Barred discrimination in public accommodations and on public conveyances on land and water. Prohibited exclusion of African Americans from jury duty. Passed by the 43rd Congress (1873–1875) as H.R. 796

provided that the different facilities were equal—even though they rarely, if ever, were equal. Racial violence by whites against blacks was more prevalent in the South, but not limited to the South, and perpetrators were neither arrested nor convicted. The National Association for the Advancement of Colored People (NAACP) reports that between 1882 and 1967, 4773 lynchings occurred, of which 3446 of the victims were black (NAACP 2017).

The Jim Crow system continued through World War I and World War II until its dismantlement began in the military in 1948 and the Civil Rights Movement began in the 1950s. Again, the historical record tells a compelling story, although in this case it is somewhat ambivalent, as delineated in Table 2.2.

Truman's desegregation of the military, the Supreme Court decision in *Brown*, and Johnson's civil rights legislation were all partly motivated by international pressure against American racism, during the Cold War with the Soviet Union (Zack 2016, pp. 108–14). The milestone events themselves were clearly not all positive and there were many evident defeats. However, even an uneven account supports an historical narrative of progressive struggle toward equality. The success of progressive struggle in turn supports the idea that equality is attainable, so that struggle itself is part of an egalitarian political tradition.

Table 2.2 Key events in the Civil Rights Movement

July 26, 1948—President Truman ended segregation in the military with Executive Order 9981: "It is hereby declared to be the policy of the President that there shall be equality of treatment and opportunity for all persons in the armed services without regard to race, color, religion, or national origin"

May 17, 1954—The US Supreme Court unanimously ruled in *Brown v. Board of Education of Topeka*, Kans. that segregation in public schools is unconstitutional, on the grounds that segregation itself is "inherently unequal" and psychologically damaging to children

August 1955—There was great public outcry after 14-year-old Chicagoan Emmett Till, was kidnapped while visiting family in Mississippi, brutally beaten, shot, and dumped in the Tallahatchie River, for speaking to a white woman. Protests continued after his murderers were acquitted by an all-white jury and the defendants later boasted about their actions in an interview published by Look magazine

December 1, 1955—In Montgomery, Alabama, Rosa Parks, a member of the NAACP refused to give up her seat at the front of the "colored" section of a bus, to a white passenger. After Parks's arrest, the Montgomery black community launched a bus boycott that lasted over a year, until the buses were desegregated on December 21, 1956. Reverend Martin Luther King, Jr., president of the Montgomery Improvement Association (MIA), led the boycott

(continued)

Table 2.2 (continued)

January and February 1957—Martin Luther King, Charles K. Steele, and Fred L. Shuttlesworth established the Southern Christian Leadership Conference with King as president. The SCLC organized the civil rights movement based on principles of nonviolence and civil disobedience

September 1957—In response to a school desegregation initiative, Arkansas Governor Orval Faubus ordered nine black students blocked from entering all-white Central High School in Little Rock. President Eisenhower sent federal troops and the National Guard to intervene on behalf of the students, who become known as the "Little Rock Nine"

February 1, 1960—In Greensboro, N.C., four black students from North Carolina Agricultural and Technical College began a sit-in at a segregated Woolworth's lunch counter, where they were refused service. Many similar nonviolent protests followed throughout the South. By August, the original four protesters were served lunch at the same Woolworth's counter. Student sit-ins continued to be effective throughout the South, integrating parks, swimming pools, theaters, libraries, and other public facilities

April 1960—In Raleigh, N.C., The Student Nonviolent Coordinating Committee (SNCC) was founded for black youth at Shaw University. SNCC later became more radical under the leadership of Stokely Carmichael (1966–1967)

May 4, 1961—Over the spring and summer, student volunteers begin taking bus trips through the South to test new laws prohibiting segregation in interstate travel facilities, including bus and railway stations. Several of the freedom rider groups were attacked by angry white mobs. The freedom rider program was sponsored by The Congress of Racial Equality (CORE) and the Student Nonviolent Coordinating Committee (SNCC), with over 1000 black and white volunteers

October 1, 1962—James Meredith became the first black student to enroll at the University of Mississippi. Violence and riots led President Kennedy to send in 5000 federal troops

April 16, 1963—Martin Luther King, Jr. was arrested and jailed during antisegregation protests in Birmingham, Alabama, where he wrote "Letter from Birmingham Jail," arguing that individuals have the moral duty to disobey unjust laws

May 1967—Commissioner of Public Safety Eugene "Bull" Connor ordered fire hoses and police dogs turned on black demonstrators. The televised and published images gained international support for the American civil rights movement

June 12, 1967—Mississippi's NAACP field secretary, 37-year-old Medgar Evers was murdered outside his home in Jackson. Byron De La Beckwith was tried twice in 1964 with hung juries, but convicted in 1997

August 28, 1967—Martin Luther King, Jr. led 200,000 people in the March on Washington, DC. At the Lincoln Memorial, King delivered his "I Have a Dream" speech

September 15, 1967—Four young girls (Denise McNair, Cynthia Wesley, Carole Robertson, and Addie Mae Collins) attending Sunday school in Birmingham, Alabama, were killed when a bomb exploded at the Sixteenth Street Baptist Church. Riots followed, with deaths of two more black youth

January 23, 1964—The 24th Amendment abolished the poll tax, instituted in 11 southern states after Reconstruction to make it difficult for poor blacks to vote

(continued)

Table 2.2 (continued)

Summer 1964—The Council of Federated Organizations (COFO), a civil rights group network including CORE and SNCC, launched a massive effort to register black voters during the Freedom Summer. Delegates were sent to the Democratic National Convention to attempt to unseat the official all-white Mississippi contingent

July 2, 1964—President Johnson signed the Civil Rights Act of 1964, the most sweeping civil rights legislation since Reconstruction, prohibiting discrimination of all kinds based on race, color, religion, or national origin, and providing the federal government with powers to enforce desegregation

August 4, 1967—After a six-week federal investigation backed by President Johnson, the FBI reported that in Neshoba Country, Mississippi, the bodies of three civil-rights workers (two white and one black) who had been working to register black voters (Andrew Goodman, James Earl Chaney, and Michael Schwerner) were found in an earthen dam. After investigating the burning of a black church, they had been arrested by the police on speeding charges, incarcerated for several hours, and then released after dark into the hands of the Ku Klux Klan members who murdered them

February 21, 1965—In Harlem, New York, Malcolm X, black nationalist and founder of the Organization of Afro-American Unity, was shot to death, likely by members of the Black Muslim faith, which Malcolm had recently abandoned in favor of orthodox Islam

March 7, 1965—In Selma, Alabama, Blacks began a march to Montgomery in support of voting rights but were stopped at the Pettus Bridge by a police blockade. Fifty marchers were hospitalized after police use tear gas, whips, and clubs against them. The incident, known as "Bloody Sunday," was considered the catalyst for pushing through the voting rights act five months later

August 10, 1965—Congress passed the Voting Rights Act of 1965, making it easier for Southern blacks to register to vote. Literacy tests, poll taxes, and other requirements that were used to restrict black voting, were made illegal

August 11–17, 1965—In Watts, California, race riots erupted

September 24, 1965—Asserting that civil rights laws alone are not enough to remedy discrimination, President Johnson issued Executive Order 11,246, which enforced Affirmative Action for the first time. It required government contractors to "take affirmative action" toward prospective minority employees, in all aspects of hiring and employment

October 1967—In Oakland, California, the Black Panthers were founded by Huey Newton and Bobby Seale

April 19, 1967—Stokely Carmichael, a leader of the Student Nonviolent Coordinating Committee (SNCC), coined the phrase "Black Power" in a speech in Seattle, defining it as an assertion of black pride and "the coming together of black people to fight for their liberation by any means necessary." This resolution alarmed those who believed the civil rights movement's effectiveness and moral authority required nonviolent civil disobedience

June 12, 1967—In *Loving v. Virginia,* the Supreme Court ruled that prohibiting interracial marriage is unconstitutional. Sixteen states that still banned interracial marriage were forced to revise their laws

July 1967—Major race riots occurred in Newark (July 12–16) and Detroit (July 23–30)

April 4, 1968—Martin Luther King, age 39, was shot to death on the balcony outside his hotel room, in Memphis, Tennessee. Escaped convict and avowed racist James Earl Ray was convicted of the murder

(continued)

Table 2.2 (continued)

April 11, 1968—President Johnson signed the Civil Rights Act of 1968, prohibiting discrimination in the sale, rental, and financing of housing

April 20, 1971—The Supreme Court, in *Swann v. Charlotte-Mecklenburg Board of Education,* upheld busing to achieve integration of public schools. Although largely unwelcome (and sometimes violently opposed) in local school districts, court-ordered busing plans in cities such as Charlotte, Boston, and Denver continued until the late 1990s

March 22, 1988—Overriding President Reagan's veto, Congress passed the Civil Rights Restoration Act, expanding the reach of nondiscrimination laws within private institutions receiving federal funds

November 22, 1991—After two years of debates, vetoes, and threatened vetoes, President Bush signed the Civil Rights Act of 1991, strengthening existing civil rights laws and providing for damages in cases of intentional employment discrimination

April 29, 1992—In Los Angeles, California, the first race riots in decades erupted in south-central Los Angeles after a jury acquitted four white police officers for the videotaped beating of African-American Rodney King

June 23, 2003—In the most important Affirmative Action decision since the 1978 *Bakke case* that limited affirmative action, the Supreme Court (5–4) upheld the University of Michigan Law School's policy. The Court ruled that race can be one of many factors considered by colleges when selecting students, because it furthers "a compelling interest in obtaining the educational benefits that flow from a diverse student body"

June 21, 2005—The ringleader of the Mississippi civil rights murders in August 1964), Edgar Ray Killen, was convicted of manslaughter

February 2007—Emmett Till's 1955 murder case, reopened by the Department of Justice in 2004, was officially closed. The two confessed murderers, J. W. Milam and Roy Bryant, were dead of cancer by 1994, and prosecutors lacked sufficient evidence to pursue further convictions

May 10, 2007—James Bonard Fowler, a former state trooper, was indicted for the murder of Jimmie Lee Jackson 40 years after Jackson's death. The 1965 killing had led to historic civil rights protests in Selma

January 2008—Senator Edward Kennedy (D-MA) introduced the Civil Rights Act of 2008 that ensured federal funds are not used to subsidize discrimination, holding employers accountable for age discrimination, and improving accountability for other violations of civil rights and workers' rights

January 2009—In *Ricci v. DeStefano,* a lawsuit brought against the city of New Haven, 18 plaintiffs—17 white people and one Hispanic—argued that results of the 2003 lieutenant and captain exams were thrown out when it was determined that few minority firefighters qualified for advancement. The City claimed they threw out the results because they feared liability under a disparate-impact statute for issuing tests that discriminated against minority firefighters. The plaintiffs claimed that they were victims of reverse discrimination under the Title VII of the Civil Rights Act of 1964. The Supreme Court ruled (5–4) in favor of the firefighters, writing that New Haven's "action in discarding the tests was a violation of Title VII"

(continued)

Table 2.2   (continued)

June 2013—In *Shelby County v. Holder,* the Supreme Court struck down Section 4 of the Voting Rights Act, which established a formula for Congress to use when determining if a state or voting jurisdiction requires prior approval before chang- ing its voting laws. Currently under Section 5 of the act, nine states with a history of discrimination must get clearance from Congress before changing voting rules, to ensure that racial minorities are not adversely affected. The 5–4 decision did not invalidate Section 5, but made it toothless. Chief Justice John Roberts said the formula Congress now uses, which was written in 1965, had become outdated. "While any racial discrimination in voting is too much, Congress must ensure that the legislation it passes to remedy that problem speaks to current conditions," he said in the majority opinion. In dissent, Judge Ruth Bader Ginsburg said, "Hubris is a fit word for today's demolition of the V.R.A." (Voting Rights Act)

June 2014—The new museum, the National Center for Civil and Human Rights, opened in Atlanta

September 2014—In addition to an FBI civil rights inquiry, the Justice Department opened a civil rights investigation into police practices in Ferguson, Missouri where Michael Brown, an unarmed black teenager, was shot and killed by a white police officer on August 9

December 2015—After a Justice Department report in March documenting civil rights violations by the Ferguson Police Department, Ferguson officials reached an agreement with the Justice Department, avoiding a civil rights lawsuit, and involving new taxes to pay for planned improvements but requiring a local vote.
(Infoplease 2000–2017; Borgna and Haney 2018; The Leadership Conference 2017)

The Universal Declaration of Human Rights

In the aftermath of World War II, in 1945, the United Nations was formed in a mission to keep and preserve peace. In 1948, the UN General Assembly issued the Universal Declaration of Human Rights (UDHR), an assertion of aspirational spiritual and legal humanism that asserted universal human equality, for the first time in the West (UN General Assembly 1948).

UDHR is remarkable for its egalitarian assertion of human rights, as both **liberties** and **entitlements**. And the ground put forth for universal rights is equality, even though the reasons for it are vague in the Preamble: "Whereas recognition of the inherent dignity and of the equal and inalienable rights of all members of the human family is the foundation of freedom, justice and peace in the world." Most readers could not say what is meant by "the human family" or by "rights" outside of a national context, but the spirit of this beginning is intuitively well understood. Article 1 emphasizes inclu- siveness: "All human beings are born free and equal in dignity and rights. They are endowed with reason and conscience and should act towards one another in a spirit of brotherhood." And Article 2 makes clear that "all" is taken seriously: "Everyone is entitled to all the rights and freedoms set forth in this Declaration, without distinction of any kind, such as race, colour, sex, language, religion, political or other opinion, national or social origin, property, birth or other status."

UDHR draws on rights recognized in democratic countries in articles 3–13: individual liberties, rights to life and security. Articles 14–21 that address civil liberties draw on the same kinds of established sources. But articles 21–28 go further, beyond established democratic consensus, proclaiming rights to individual development and security for the ill, unemployed, old, and disabled, with special attention to mothers and children (United Nations, General Assembly 1948). Such aspirational and inspirational entitlements marked an important new development in the egalitarian counter-tradition.

Conclusion

It is not surprising that there is agreement toward egalitarianism, between the Western spiritual and religious tradition and both founding documents and civil rights legislation in the United States and the UDHR. Despite a constitutional separation between church and state (no state religion and no religious qualifications for liberties and rights), American political leaders have been avowedly religious, if not specifically Christian. Thus, formal American law pertaining to rights and liberties shares an aspirational quality with the religious egalitarian tradition. UDHR makes no reference to religion but it is in the same egalitarian tradition as religious humanism. Both religion in this sense and law appeal to elevated moral principles.

Two **tensions** are evident in the consideration of the history of egalitarian ideas about race that were submerged in their times. The first is tension between egalitarian ideas, as in the thought of Cosmopolitans, Stoics, and Christians, with the acceptance and legality of practices of human chattel slavery during the same time periods. The second tension is between just egalitarian laws and the racial injustice resulting from their lack of application or outright lawlessness. Both of these tensions have and continue to consist of sets of ideas accompanying or influencing opposed practices and actions. Tensions, like contradictions, call for deeper understanding of how events pull in different directions from ideas.

The tension associated with Cosmopolitanism, Christian thought, and Stoicism on the one hand, and the practice of slavery on the other, can be

Owners violence not acceptable

understood in terms of the nonmaterial spirituality of the egalitarian ideas in question. Thus, Cosmopolitans, Stoics, and Christians have all emphasized the interior life of individuals—their thoughts, hopes, dreams, and self-protective attitudes; we have also seen that Christians posited equality in an afterlife, which did not require equality in the here and now.

The tension between just and egalitarian laws and unjust or lawless practice can be understood through a broad understanding of how law works. There is nothing magical about any law that automatically makes its content lived reality. For laws to affect society, they must be promulgated, applied to new areas of life, broadly understood by the population, and enforced with penalties for lawbreakers. Laws also need to be interpreted by courts if there is disagreement about application or punishment. Without promulgation, application, understanding, and enforcement, practices that contradict just laws can easily coexist with them. For instance, there are just laws involving racially egalitarian voting in the United States, according to the 1965 Federal Voting Rights Act, but there has been continuing evidence that many African Americans are denied legal opportunities to vote by local authorities. Also, voting rights and antidiscrimination federal legislation was in place, although often not implemented or applied, before the Civil Rights Movement. The coexistence of inequalities both before and after the Civil Rights Movement, with egalitarian law, underscore the importance of applying laws, with penalties for those who violate them.

The United Nations (1948) Universal Declaration of Human Rights was a supreme culmination of both the Western spiritual/religious egalitarian tradition and the rights and liberties set forth in the US Constitution. Insofar as there is no world government to enforce UDHR, it remains aspirational, at best furnishing ideals within and between the UN's member nations. In moral, humanitarian terms, UDHR presides over many struggles to achieve and protect human rights, throughout the world. On the one hand, UDHR and the UN might be criticized by progressives for lack of practical effectiveness. But on the other hand, UDHR is immensely important as a humanistic document that spans, without replacing, many spiritual and religious motivations and goals, without recourse to divinities.

The positive to neutral ideas of racial difference considered in this chapter will be further nuanced by accounts of a tradition of resistance to racial oppression in American philosophy in Chapter 4. First, while we are on a **descriptive**, rather than a normative plane of inquiry, it will be useful to turn to the history of science concerning race and the present consensus about the reality of race within the biological sciences, in Chapter 3.

Glossary

abolitionist movement—political and social movement to end American slavery.

Affirmative Action—controversial policy of giving nontraditional candidates better chances than white males for admission and hiring in social institutions, government entities, and large corporations.

Civil Rights Movement—period of peaceful protest and demonstration from 1954–1968, seeking to end segregation and secure equal rights for African Americans.

Cosmopolitanism—a perspective on other individuals and groups that is tolerant of personal and cultural differences and is not restricted by political borders, language, morals, beliefs, or customs.

descriptive—accounts of how things are.

discourse—forms of communication, including reading, writing, conversation, public speaking, and demonstration.

due process—treatment according to fair and just rules by legal authorities.

egalitarianism—view that human beings are equal in important ways.

empirical—a method of inquiry or body of knowledge that is based on known facts.

entitlements—benefits due to people, such as education or health care.

intellectual history—history of ideas, chronological accounts of the thoughts of major thinkers and their intellectual influences.

Jim Crow—racist system against American blacks, primarily in the US South from the late 1870s through the mid 1950s.

liberty—freedom from external constraint; what people have a right to do without interference from others, including government.

lynching—killing by a mob, without trial or due process for an alleged offense; in the late nineteenth and early twentieth centuries in the US South and Midwest, lynching was often carried out as festival, with children present and souvenirs of the victim's body parts taken away.

NAACP—NAACP (National Association for the Advancement of Colored People).

normative—accounts of how things should be or change, how people should act.

promulgation—broadcast of a law so that those it applies to know it.

Reconstruction—decade after the Civil War when African Americans were granted rights and protections to support their free status.

sociology of knowledge—study of the societal context of ideas and the influence of ideas in society.

Stoicism—school of philosophy founded by Zeno of Citium (234–362 BCE) in Athens and enduring through the third century AD, in Greece and Rome. Stoics emphasized fortitude and universal human brotherhood.

suffragists—advocates for securing women's right to vote.

Essay and Discussion Questions

1. What is the difference between egalitarian theory and egalitarian practice? Give examples.
2. Is cosmopolitanism relevant to contemporary race relations? Explain either way.
3. Does one have to believe in a religion as a person of faith, to accept the value of its teachings? Explain.
4. If Beattie criticized Hume for his ideas about race, from ulterior motives, does that weaken the validity of his criticism?
5. Why was Ham's curse important to nineteenth-century African American writers?
6. Why was it necessary to "re-do" the Reconstruction Amendments with Civil Rights legislation?
7. What do you think will be necessary to make formal equality a reality in the United States?
8. What purpose does the UN Universal Declaration of Human Rights serve?
9. Audre Lorde is famous for having said that you cannot dismantle the master's house with the master's tools. Is that true? How does it apply to the usefulness of the egalitarian tradition?
10. What would you add to the egalitarian tradition that has not been discussed in this chapter?

References

Allard, Phil. "Civil War: Reconstruction Moderate v. 'Radical' Plans for Reintegrating the South." *Issues and Controversies in American History*, Facts. Com, 2006. http://www.philwrites.com/H_reconstruction.htm.

Appiah, Kwame Anthony. "Global Citizenship." *Fordham Law Review*, vol. 75, 2007, pp. 2375–91. http://ir.lawnet.fordham.edu/flr/vol75/iss5/3.

Ayers, Edward L. *The Promise of the New South: Life After Reconstruction*. Oxford and New York, NY: Oxford University Press, 1992 and 2007.

Beattie, James. *An Essay on the Nature and Immutability of Truth in Opposition to Sophistry and Scepticism (1770)*. Canongate, GB: Denham and Dick, 1805. https://archive.org/details/essayonimmutabil00beatuoft.

Blackpast.org. "The Three-Fifths Clause of the United States Constitution (1787)." http://www.blackpast.org/aah/three-fifths-clause-united-states-constitution-1787#sthash.3SQ6CVN3.dpuf. Consulted May 28, 2017.

Bradford, Sarah Hopkins. *Scenes in the Life of Harriet Tubman*. Freeport: Books for Libraries Press, 1971.

Brunner, Borgna, and Elissa Haney. "Civil Rights Timeline: Milestones in the Modern Civil Rights Movement." *Infoplease*,. April, 2018. https://www.infoplease.com/spot/civil-rights-timeline.

Cicero. *On Obligation (De Officiis)*, edited and translated by P.G Walsh. Oxford, UK: Oxford University Press, 2000, pp. ix–x.

Dennis, Dermid. "James Beattie (1735—1803)." *Internet Encyclopedia of Philosophy*. http://www.iep.utm.edu/beattiej/#H3. Consulted May 27, 2017.

Emancipator. "Andrew Harris." Black Abolitionist Archive, University of Detroit Mercy, May 13, 1839. http://research.udmercy.edu/digital_collections/baa/Harris_03939spe.pdf. Consulted May 29, 2017.

Gaustad, Edwin S. *George Berkeley in America*. New Haven and London: Yale University Press, 1979.

Goldenberg, David M. *The Curse of Ham: Race and Slavery in Early Judaism, Christianity, and Islam* (Jews, Christians, and Muslims from the Ancient to the Modern World). Princeton, NJ: Princeton University Press, 2005.

History, Art, and Archives, United States House of Representatives, Constitutional Amendments and Major Civil Rights Acts of Congress Referenced in Black Americans in Congress, 2017. http://history.house.gov/Exhibitions-and-Publications/BAIC/Historical-Data/Constitutional-Amendments-and-Legislation/. Consulted May 28, 2017.

Infoplease. *Civil Rights Timeline*, Sandbox Networks, Inc., 2000–2017, https://www.infoplease.com/spot/civil-rights-timeline. Consulted May 28, 2017.

Klarman, Michael J. *From Jim Crow to Civil Rights: The Supreme Court and the Struggle for Racial Equality*. Oxford and New York, NY: Oxford University Press, 2004.

Laëtius, Diogenes. *Lives and Opinions of Eminent Philosophers*. Translated by C.D. Yong. London: Henry G. Bohn, 1853, "Diogenes," Book VI, pp. 224–48.

Leadership Conference. "Civil Rights Chronology," Civil Rights 101, 2017. http://www.civilrights.org/resources/civilrights101/chronology.html. Consulted May 28, 2017.

Mosley, Albert. "'Race' in Eighteenth and Nineteenth-Century Discourse by Africans in the Diaspora." *The Oxford Handbook of Philosophy and Race*, edited by Naomi Zack. New York, NY: Oxford University Press, 2017, pp. 80–89.

NAACP. "History of Lynching." April 2017. http://www.naacp.org/history-of-lynchings/.

Painter, Nell Irvin. *Sojourner Truth: A Life, a Symbol*. New York: W. W. Norton, 1996.

Palter, Robert. "Hume and Prejudice." *Hume Studies*, vol. XXI, no. 1, April 1995, pp. 3–24.

Popkin, Richard H. "Hume's Racism." *The Philosophical Forum*, vol. 9, no. 2–3, 1977, pp. 211–26, Boston, MA.

Reddit, Ask Historians. "How Do Pounds from the 1700s Translate into USD Today?" https://www.reddit.com/r/AskHistorians/comments/3wz8an/how_do_pounds_from_the_1700s_translate_into_usd/. Consulted May 28, 2017.

Schmidt, Claudia M. *David Hume: Reason in History*. College Park, PA: Pennsylvania State University Press, 2003.

Thornton, Kevin Pierce. "Andrew Harris, Vermont's Forgotten Abolitionist." *Vermont History*, vol. 83, no. 2, 2015, pp. 119–56.

United Nations, General Assembly. "Universal Declaration of Human Rights (UDHR)." 1948. http://www.un.org/en/universal-declaration-human-rights/.

Zack, Naomi. *Applicative Justice: A Pragmatic Empirical Approach to Racial Injustice*. Lanham, MD: Rowman & Littlefield, 2016.

3

Race According to Biological Science

Many scholars now consider race to be a **social construction**. This means that racial categories, such as "black," "white," or "Asian," are not based on natural or inevitable human differences but are the result of social ideas, values, and practices, which could be otherwise, with the same biology. There are two ways in which human races have been social constructions. The first way pertains to the biological foundations for race in science. Ideas of race, as first developed and then unraveled by scientists are the subject of this chapter. The second way that race is socially constructed pertains to attitudes, biases, stereotypes, generalizations, and real-life practices concerning members of different racial groups and that will be the subject of the chapters of Part II.

We should start by saying what we mean by the word "race." First, as noted at the beginning of Chapter 1, the plural "races" are the subject, because if there were only one race, it would be the whole of humanity and discourse about racial differences would be pointless. "Race" is an ordinary word in English that we use to categorize individuals as belonging to or having the traits of one or more of a specific number of groups. Most people belong to one race—that is how they view themselves and how others view them. In the United States, the major races are specified by the US Census. The Population Estimates Program (PEP) interprets the data from the US Census, which is in turn used by institutions throughout society. This is how that process begins:

Population estimates use the race categories mandated by the Office of Management and Budget's (OMB) 1997 standards: White; Black or African American; American Indian and Alaska Native; Asian; Native Hawaiian and Other Pacific Islander. These race categories differ from those used in Census

© The Author(s) 2018
N. Zack, *Philosophy of Race*, Palgrave Philosophy Today,
https://doi.org/10.1007/978-3-319-78729-9_3

2010 in one important respect. Census 2010 also allowed respondents to select the category referred to as Some Other Race. When Census 2010 data were edited to produce the estimates base, respondents who selected the Some Other Race category alone were assigned to one of the OMB mandated categories. For those respondents who selected the Some Other Race category and one or more of the other race categories, the edits ignored the Some Other Race selection. (U.S. Census Bureau, PEP 2017)

While the Census relies on respondents to identify themselves by race, it is expected that every respondent can be identified by one of the five major racial categories, even those who select "some other race."

We can see from the PEP account that US Census data about race is not inert information that is left in its original form of how respondents have categorized themselves. Instead, the responses become structured data by classifying people into one of five categories. On this level, and on many other levels throughout the US society, there is thus a system of race: White, Black, American Indian, and Alaskan Native; Asian; Native Hawaiian, and Other Pacific Islander.

The primary philosophical question concerning race in terms of science is whether human races exist. But the term "science" must be further specified. Since racial categories entered Western culture, with the beginning of the science of biology in the modern period, biology, including individual heredity, evolution, and population genetics has been the major science of race. Philosophers and others have claimed that the question of whether race is real according to biological science is important, if most people in society believe that race is real according to biological science and researchers in the social sciences and humanities accept that belief in their studies of race. If there is such widespread belief in the reality of race, the question is whether these beliefs about race and biology are true.

Biologists have found traits that can be associated with each of the five racial groups of the social racial **taxonomy** or system of classification. But that in itself does not mean that race is a *biological taxonomy*, according to biologists. In other words, it is possible that most people think that race is real in biology but have assumed this only because there are biological traits, which can be studied by biologists that are associated with race, such as skin color. For the human race to be biologically real, there would need to be a taxonomy of human race that was independently accepted and relied upon by biologists. The general term *race* has since Charles Darwin's research, referred to specific kinds of subdivisions within animal and plant species, which biologists have independently discovered (Darwin and Wallace 1858). Asking if the human race is real for biologists means asking if biologists have independently discovered that human beings are divided into races. The discovery of races within animal and plant species has not been based on the prior social ideas about such races. For human race to be a valid biological taxonomy, it should also not be based on prior social ideas about races.

But even independent biological discovery does not address fully address the scientific requirements for a taxonomy of human race. Consider the concept of pets, in this regard. There could be a taxonomy for the five most common pets: dogs, cats, fish, birds, and rabbits. Each of these kinds of animals has traits that can be, and are, studied in biology. But that does not mean that their social classification under pets corresponds to a biological system of classification used by biologists. The philosophical issue about race and biology is whether the social taxonomy of human race corresponds to a valid independent taxonomy in biology. The skepticism here is analogous to Jerry Fodor's critique of scientific reductionism, the idea that because all material things are ultimately made up of particles studied by physicists, all of the other sciences can be **reduced** to physics. Fodor's example is economics. Every economic transaction, be it on paper, verbal, electronic, or plastic, does have a physical correlate that can ultimately be explained by physics, in terms of atoms and electrons and whatever else physicists find relevant. But the main categories in the system of money do not line up with categories independently studied in physics. For instance, the branch of physics that would study the particles in the paper, or sound, are very different from the branch that would study electronics. This can be summarized as saying that the science of economics cannot be reduced to the science of physics (Fodor 1974). Similarly, the societal system or taxonomy of race may not be reduced to a system or taxonomy in biology.

If the idea of race commonly accepted in society—call it *the ordinary idea of race*—does not correspond to a scientific idea of race and the ordinary idea of race assumes or has embedded in it, belief that such correspondence exists, then there is something wrong with the ordinary idea—it is a false idea. To understand this issue more fully requires understanding the history of race in science leading up to contemporary biology. This history consists of: early ideas of race in biology, racist ideas of race in biology, transitional ideas of race in biology, races as populations, and further considerations of how populations are now studied. The history of science is important here, because it is in the nature of science to revise previous findings and theories as new information is acquired. That is, science, including biology and the human sciences therein, is **revisionist**—it is constantly revising itself as a valued methodology in light of new evidence (Radnitzky and Andersson 1978; Goodstein 2011).

Early Ideas of Race in Early Biology

The scientific study of race originated at the same time that the modern science of biology originated. Biology originated with methodologies of classification and taxonomies or *systematics*. We can see this coincidence between early race and early biology through the ideas of several influential early biologists. Before the study of race by biologists, there were of course systems of human classification and division, from the ancient world through medieval times. Groups of people were and continue to be distinguished and divided based on many factors, including: sex, wealth, royalty or commoner status, nationality, religion, class, language, occupation within society. Some of these divisions are hereditary and others can form in single life times. However, there was no one universal taxonomy of humankind that divided all human beings into a set number of inherited groups, before the idea of biological race. **Universal human racial taxonomy** has had two parts: (1) assignment of individuals to racial categories and (2) value assessments of different racial groups, and their members. As we shall see, both were combined to different extents in the early history of modern science. However, noteworthy in the early history, before full-blown assessment, were Francois Bernier, Carolus Linnaeus, Johann Friedrich Blumenbach, and George-Louis Leclerc.

Seventeen-century French physician and philosopher Francois Bernier (1625–1688) is credited with having created the modern biological idea of race. Bernier became famous for his travels, after spending twelve years as a physician in the Mughal Court in India. He was the first person to measure the speed of sound and a colleague and friend of John Locke's. In 1684, Bernier first published his "Nouvelle Division de la Terre" ("New Division of the Earth") anonymously and prestigiously in *Journal des Scavans* (the first academic journal in Europe). Bernier divided humankind into races or species (he used these terms interchangeably), based solely on physical traits. He presented skin color, hair type, and bodily shape as more fundamental criteria for human classification than geographical origin or location and he claimed that there were four or five species or races, according to those criteria: (1) The "first race," made up of people from Europe, North Africa, the Middle East, India, part of South-East Asia, and the native population of the Americas; (2) The African negroes; (3) The East and Northeast Asian race; and (4) The Lapps (Stuurman 2000, pp. 4–6).

Bernier posited the greatest differences between 1 and 2 and referred to 1. The "first race" as "we" throughout his text. Bernier's ideas of four or five races or species set the stage for subsequent biological thought about race, until well into the twentieth century. The influence was extensive, including philosophers who provided theoretical support, as we saw in Chapter 1.

By the mid-1700s, Carolus Linnaeus (1707–1788), a Swedish botanist, physician, and zoologist, was highly acclaimed for his classifications of plants and animals. He invented the early three-kingdom system for classifying natural beings (below kingdom was: phylum/division, class, order, family, genus and species). In Linnaeus's *Systema Naturae*, humans were first classified as primates and then given their own category, *Homo sapiens*. Homo sapiens had four *varieties* (types within species) according to skin color and geography: Europæus albus (white European), Americanus rubescens (red American), Asiaticus fuscus (brown/yellow Asian) and Africanus Niger (black African). Linnaeus later associated each variety with a *humor* or temperament: Europeans–Sanguine; Americans–Choleric; Asians–Melancholy; Black–Phlegmatic (Smedley and Smedley 2011, pp. 218–9).

Stephen Jay Gould (1941–2002), eminent twentieth-century paleontologist and evolutionary biologist explains how Johann Friedrich Blumenbach (1752–1840) a great admirer of Linnaeus, changed racial taxonomy from mere physical difference, to difference plus assessment or valuation. Gould begins by asking how white Europeans came to be called "Caucasian," after a mountain range over Russia and Georgia. Blumenbach invented this name in *De Generis Humani Varietate Nativa* (*On the Natural Variety of Mankind*) (1975–1995), because he thought that this area was populated by very beautiful people and was likely where humans originated. Blumenbach changed very little of Linnaeus's taxonomy, except to add the Malay variety within Asians, as a fifth racial group.

Gould suggests that Blumenbach's greater influence compared to Linnaeus was based on the geometry: the fifth race made it possible to present pictorially a model in which two pairs of races radiated out from the white race. Blumenbach also proposed that after a common origin, nonwhite racial groups formed as "degenerations" resulting from different climate conditions. He was not overtly racist against nonwhite groups and did not think that any particular mark of inferiority set Africans apart, writing of "the good disposition and faculties of these our black brethren" and maintaining a library of black authors in his home. Gould thinks that Blumenbach's commitments to moral equality were at odds with his appealing five-group model and that his use of an aesthetic ideal, rather than a moral one, for Caucasians, was a way to resolve that dilemma (Gould 1994).

French Naturalist and mathematician George-Louis Leclerc, Comte de Buffon (1707–1788) wrote the 36 volume, *Histoire Naturelle, générale et particulière, avec la description du Cabinet du Roi* (translated as *Natural History*) and his colleagues added eight posthumous volumes. Buffon took up Blumenbach's idea of degeneration and Charles Darwin (1809–1882), credited him for beginning an evolutionary approach to the study of humanity by introducing the idea of "unity of type" and through that, comparative anatomy. In a strong departure from Linnaeus (with whom he shared birth and death years), Buffon described racial differences as effects of differences in climate and emphasized gradations of difference between races, rather than abrupt species-type discontinuities. While such differences were inherited, Buffon also considered them changeable, even in single lifetime. Buffon's enthusiasm about breeding projects to improve races anticipated eugenics. Although, as we will soon see, eugenics did not aim to "improving" nonwhite races (Nelson 2010).

Racist Ideas of Race in Nineteenth-Century Biology

Racism is unjustified bias about people and groups because of their racial identities. **Racialism** is thought or action based on the belief that human races are real and the differences among races are important. The racism in nineteenth-century ideas of biological race is evident in the writings of George Cuvier, Louis Agassiz, and Joseph de Gobineau, as well as the research of Samuel Morton. This strain of nineteenth-century race science handily supported the eugenics movement.

Blumenbach may not have intended to express bias about nonwhite races, but his aesthetic **valorization** of whites as Caucasians, nevertheless legitimized, inspired, and justified subsequent explicitly racist accounts of human racial taxonomy. For instance, French naturalist and zoologist George Cuvier (1769–1832) departed from Blumenbach's five-race taxonomy, positing three distinct races—Caucasian, Mongoloid, and Ethiopian. Cuvier not only agreed with Blumenbach's ideas about Caucasian beauty but held the white race to be "superior to others by its genius, courage and activity." He described the black race in ways that set the stage for racial hierarchy:

> [M]arked by black complexion, crisped or woolly hair, compressed cranium and a flat nose. The projection of the lower parts of the face, and the thick lips, evidently approximate it to the monkey tribe: the hordes of which it consists have always remained in the most complete state of barbarism. (Cuvier 1831, p. 50)

Attempts made to reinforce popular ideas of racial hierarchy, especially in mid-nineteenth century America, built on work such as Cuvier's, moving into speculations about differences in mental endowment that were based on unreliable empirical data. Gould chronicles some of this work in *The Mismeasure of Man*, including the *craniometric* or skull measurement studies conducted by physician Samuel George Morton (1799–1851). Based on skull size, Morton, who believed that human races were different species, rather than varieties (greater differences were posited between species than between varieties) claimed in *Crania Americana* that whites had the biggest skulls and blacks the smallest. Gould casts doubt on the accuracy of Morton's measurements that included substituting bird seed for birdshot in measuring the volumes of black skulls, which resulted in less volume (Gould 1996, pp. 82–103). Gould does not impute overt racist motives to Morton but summarizes several inaccuracies in his data collection:

> All miscalculations and omissions that I have detected are in Morton's favor. He rounded the negroid Egyptian average down to 79, rather than up to 80. He cited averages of 90 for Germans and Anglo-Saxons, but the correct values are 88 and 89. He excluded a large Chinese skull and an Eskimo subsample from his final tabulation for mongoloids, thus depressing their average below the Caucasian value. (Gould 1996, p. 101)

It should also be emphasized that there is no evidence that brain size is positively correlated with intelligence. As Ashley Montagu put it in 1942: "What the racist never mentions is that the average volume of the brain of Neanderthal man was 1550 cubic centimeters—150 cubic centimeters greater than that of modern whites!" (Montagu, p. 71).

Gould also discusses the career of Swiss naturalist Louis Agassiz (1807–1873), who became a professor at Harvard in 1848 and in 1859 founded the University's Museum of Comparative Zoology, directing it for the rest of his life. Agassiz was highly revered (the Museum website continues to honor him (Museum of Comparative Zoology 2017)), but he was what we would today consider a virulent racist. Although he opposed slavery, he believed that African Americans were a distinct species. In the great nineteenth-century debate about **monogeny** (one human origin) versus **polygeny** (multiple human origins), Agassiz began as a monogenist in Europe but was persuaded to polygenism by American colleagues and his experiences with black Americans who waited on him in a hotel. Besides his polygenism, Agassiz believed that races should be ranked in human worth:

> There are upon earth different races of men, inhabiting different parts of its surface, which have different physical characters; and this fact presses upon us

the obligation to settle the relative rank among these races, the relative value of the characters peculiar to each, in a scientific point of view. As philosophers it is our duty to look it in the face.

Of Africa, he wrote:

There has never been a regulated society of black men developed on that continent. Does not this indicate in this race a peculiar apathy, a peculiar indifference to the advantages afforded by civilized society? (Gould 1996, pp. 78 and 79)

Agassiz believed that after the Civil War, blacks would remain in the South and that they should be educated only in manual labor; he was an adamant segregationist, as well as a great admirer of Morton, whom he visited in Philadelphia when Morton had collected 600 of his eventual total collection of over 1000 skulls (Gould 1996, pp. 80–82).

This discussion would be incomplete without mention of the French avowed elitist Joseph Arthur de Gobineau (1816–1882), who responded to the French Revolution by publishing *An Essay on the Inequality of the Human Races*, in 1848 (the same year Harvard hired Agassiz). Gobineau's ideas were well received by white supremacists and anti-Semites in the United States. Although, the extirpated form of his 1200 word tome that circulated left out his claims that most Americans were not racially pure (Gobineau believed that the downfall of all great civilizations was the result of race mixing.) (Richter 1958).

Racist science in the twentieth century also supported the **eugenics movement** restricting inclusion and reproduction of members of groups considered inferior to others. British scholar Francis Galton (1822–1911), a relative of Darwin, is considered the founder of the eugenics movement, although his efforts were not effective in England. In the United States, Charles Davenport (1866–1944), Director of the Eugenics Records Office, was highly influential, leading to congressional passage of the Johnson-Reed Immigration Act of 1927, which limited immigration to 2% of nationalities then residing in the US, and restricted entry from Southern and Eastern Europe (U.S. State Department 2017; The Immigration Act of 1924/The Johnson-Reed Act (Gillham 2001)).

Transitional Scientific Ideas of Race

Biological science became less speculative and more empirical over the late nineteenth and early twentieth centuries, a trend that continued after World War II. Also, egalitarian thought about racial differences developed in response to the Jim Crow regime in American life. However, many progressive thinkers were uncertain about the scientific reality of physical race and mainly addressed social racism. Nevertheless, there was a marked period of transition in expert and educated thought, following the broad popularity of racist science. Shared within this transitional thought was a background agreement that physical race was real, but that social, moral, and psychological issues associated with physical race were neither inherited nor determined by physical race, but were the results of history and persisting cultural traditions and practices.

The great scientist of evolution, Charles Darwin, related his ideas about race to contemporary hereditary theory in his time. When Darwin wrote, it was not yet known that hereditary material of genes, chromosomes, DNA, RNA, and so forth, functions separately from the traits resulting from it, and that this hereditary material is not part of the observable physiology and anatomy of animals. Darwin subscribed to **pangenesis**, a theory of heredity going back to the ancient world, which held that changes in somatic or bodily cells "drifted" to reproductive cells, with effects on subsequent heredity. He argued in favor of a common origin for all human races, based on his knowledge that racial traits are **clines**, occurring in gradations in nature, over different geographical and climactic differences. His attitude toward the intellectual aptitude of Africans was favorable and his impressions of indigenous people were positive; he opposed slavery (Darwin 1889).

Darwin was primarily focused on physical hereditary and the changes within species over time. His political and social views were incidental to his main work. But evolutionary theory and his principle of "survival of the fittest" were misapplied to society in support of **social Darwinism**, a doctrine used to justify slavery, Jim Crow, Native American genocide, and disregard for the suffering of poor people of all races (Rutledge 1995). Still, beyond oppressive appropriation of his ideas, Darwin is important to keep in mind in terms of scientific theories relevant to race, because he introduced scientifically disciplined empirical observation to his theories of evolution and emphasized the importance of heredity over time, both of which supported more modern theories of human difference.

Social Darwinism notwithstanding, ideas of racial hierarchy changed in the social sciences during the twentieth century. There was a paradigm shift in the separation of hereditary physical race from the social aspects of race. The research and theoretical work of three anthropologists were important in this regard: Franz Boas (1858–1942); Ashly Montague (1905–1999); and Claude Lévi-Strauss (1908–2009).

Boas is widely considered "the father of American Antropology" and his research, popular writing, and exhibitions about cultural difference influenced the next generation of cultural anthropologists. He presented his core ideas first in a 1911 pamphlet version of *The Mind of Primitive Man*, which was published as a book in many editions over subsequent decades (Boas 1911). The title was provocative, because Boas insisted that differences in racial intellectual achievement were fully the result of cultural and environmental differences, rather than determined and unchangeable at birth. He also consistently argued for cultural relativism throughout his career, against the idea that there were objectively more advanced races or cultures, which he denounced as biased and chauvinistic. Boas specified the task of anthropology to study aspects of cultures that made them distinct, such as migration, food, parenting, illness, and interactions with other cultures. Boas himself conducted such **ethnological studies**, with a focus on the Kwakiutl Indians on the coast of British Columbia (White 1963). He thus directly addressed realities of what we now consider cultural difference, but which in the nineteenth-century were considered racial difference. The acceptance of Boas's work meant that what was left in considering "race," apart from its cultural constituents, would have been biological or physical race, without a mental, moral, or psychic component.

Lévi-Strauss took a more theoretical approach to Boas's efforts to combat both ideas of social Darwinism and simplistic evolutionary views of race and culture (e.g., "survival of the fittest"). In his 1952 pamphlet, *Race and History*, he described race as a "social myth" and explained how race was both distinct from culture and part of it. Lévi-Strauss rejected the idea that different cultures were at different stages of progress in civilization and he postulated a universal human ability to cooperate in exchanges, within all "fully adult" human cultures. In a 1971 United Nations Educational, Scientific and Cultural Organization (UNESCO) lecture, "Race and Culture," Lévi-Strauss argued that cultures have a right to preserve their own cultural practices without interference from other cultures. He claimed that racial diversity was the result, and not the cause, of cultural diversity, by analyzing the social or cultural construction of physical race, in terms of both random and structured cultural practices. In "Réflexion," his last UNESCO talk at the age of 97 in 2005, he claimed that cultural diversity and biological diversity were analogous phenomena that should both be preserved (Müller-Wille 2010). But the focus of his thought was on the relation between race and culture and he retained the idea that biological races existed, albeit as products of culture.

Montague became famous for his 1942 *Race: Man's Most Dangerous Myth*. He noted that scientific attempts to divide humankind into races had been arbitrary and based on incomplete understanding of the traits considered important. He drew a very clear line between race as studied by biology and common ideas of race in society:

> In biology race is defined as a subdivision of species which inherits physical characteristics distinguishing it from other populations of the species. In this sense there are many human 'races.' But this is not the sense in which many anthropologists, race-classifiers, and racists have used the term. (Montague 1942, p. 9)

Montague was also active in UNESCO efforts to address "the question of race" through a series of statements.

Despite progressive tendencies in anthropology, eugenics became one of the core programs of Nazi Germany during World War II. The Nazis were directly aware of and opposed to egalitarian advances in thought about race in American Anthropology, for instance, they burned Boas's *The Mind of Primitive Man* in the 1930s and revoked Boas's German PhD (Tax 2017). Soon after the revelations of German extermination of over 12 million Jews, Roma, and other ethnic groups, related to the ideology of Aryan racial superiority, the United Nations addressed international anxiety that the same thing could happen again, with "Four Statements on the Race Question," written in 1950, 1951, 1964, and 1967 and published altogether by UNESCO in 1969 (UNESCO 1969).

Claude Lévi-Strauss was one of the authors of the first statement and Ashley Montague recorded and revised it after criticism. L.C. Dunn recorded the early results in 1951, which supported a minimal concept of biological race after stating that Homo sapiens were a single species and that systems of racial classification or the concept of race could not be universally applied. Thus, Part 1 of this first UNESCO statement asserted:

> Scientists are generally agreed that all men living today belong to a single species, Homo sapiens, and are derived from a common stock, even though there is some dispute as to when and how different human groups diverged from this common stock. The concept of race is unanimously regarded by anthropologists as a classificatory device providing a zoological frame within which the various groups of mankind may be arranged and by means of which studies of evolutionary processes can be facilitated. In its anthropological sense, the word "race" should be reserved for groups of mankind possessing well-developed and primarily heritable physical differences from other groups.

Many populations can be so classified but, because of the complexity of human history, there are also many populations which cannot easily be fitted into a racial classification. (UNESCO 1951, Part 1)

In Part 5, this first UNESCO Statement on Race also distinguished between physical racial traits that could be studied, and mental characteristics as more dependent on the social environment than heredity:

> Most anthropologists do not include mental characteristics in their classification of human races. Studies within a single race have shown that both innate capacity and environmental opportunity determine the results of tests of intelligence and temperament, though their relative importance is disputed. When intelligence tests, even nonverbal, are made on a group of nonliterate people, their scores are usually lower than those of more civilized people. It has been recorded that different groups of the same race occupying similarly high levels of civilization may yield considerable differences in intelligence tests. When, however, the two groups have been brought up from childhood in similar environments, the differences are usually very slight. Moreover, there is good evidence that, given similar opportunities, the average performance (that is to say, the performance of the individual who is representative because he is surpassed by as many as he surpasses), and the variation round it, do not differ appreciably from one race to another. (UNESCO 1951, Part 5)

We can see that this statement strikes a compromise between Boas's notion of intellectual equality among human groups and Montague's claim that race is not a scientific term, on the one hand, and ideas that intellectual differences between races can be studied scientifically, on the other.

In an Introduction to the complete UNESCO 1969 publication of all four statements, Belgian biologist, and anthropologist Jean Heirneaux summarized the biological arguments against physical hierarchical analyses of ideas of racial hierarchy in a retrospective essay, "Biological Aspects of the Race Question" (Heirneaux 1969). Heirneaux argued that human endowments are the result of interactions between hereditary and culture, leaving little reason to conclude that inherited factors dominate either individual or group capacities and achievements. Moreover, when environmental or cultural factors are changed, mental inequalities between racial groups either decrease or are reversed. He summed up:

> No genetic difference between peoples, however, has ever been proved in this sphere. Admittedly, research on this point is very difficult. There is no psychological test by which the innate factor in mental capacities or affective

tendencies can be measured alone. But whenever the conditions for the mental development of two populations begin to resemble each other, the differences in the average of the test results are reduced or eliminated; they tend to become reversed when the inequalities of the environment are reversed. (Heirnaux 1969, p. 15)

Heirnaux also suggested that then-contemporary methods in biology used the term "race" in two senses—to refer to distinct groups that mostly bred within themselves and to refer to more broad classificatory schemes such as three or five major races. However, he went on to say that the use of the term "race" as a classificatory scheme leaves out the details of evolution on a population level and is therefore not true to underlying science:

> The evolutionary unit is the **population**; those which are grouped together, in the classifications, as major stocks may have very different evolutionary histories…. The contemporary anthropologist does not regard the human race as naturally divided into white people, yellow people, black people, or any other sub-division, but as composed of a vast number of populations, each with its own history of development. Taken together, they form a continuum such that any attempt at classification according to selected combinations of characters leads to the conclusion that many populations are unclassifiable. (Heirnaux 1969, pp. 11 and 12)

Heirnaux's 1969 UNESCO Four Statements overview represented loss of confidence in the biological aspects of human races for geneticists and anthropologists. His summary of the complex relation between heredity and environment makes problematic any claims that important human abilities, particularly intelligence, are inherited based on the race. And even if such traits are correlated with specific racial membership, it would be false to claim that their presence or absence is caused or determined by the racial membership. However, Heirnaux's methodological approach to scientific studies of race leaves open the question of whether human races exist. It rests with the idea of a population as the main human evolutionary unit but does not explicitly say whether populations are scientific versions of races or not.

Races as Populations in Science

Over the second half of the twentieth century, the biological human sciences, including medicine, population genetics, individual genetics, and biological anthropology moved toward a consensus that there is no independent scientific foundation for human racial taxonomies, apart from societal views of such differences. However, along the way, the idea of populations appealed to many as a plausible scientific construct that could be a foundation or substitute for ideas of race as understood in society. Heirnaux's UNESCO overview can be interpreted as suggesting that reference to either races or populations is simply a matter of how classification is done—either by "lumping" or "splitting." This view of races as collections of populations implies that there is nothing misleading in using the larger categories of races instead of the more detailed categories of populations, so that it's just a question of how much detail a researcher prefers, almost as a matter of taste.

It seems banal to say that human populations exist. Skeptics about race can agree that populations, or groups geographically bounded that breed within themselves, are the units in which human beings evolve. Members of a population share hereditary similarities that distinguish them from members of other populations. But the question is whether populations are races, as racial taxonomy has been understood. In the late 1960s, Alice Brues's definition of a race as a population was widely quoted: "a division of the species that differs from other divisions by the frequency with which certain hereditary traits appear among its members" (Brues 1977, p. 1). However, to simply assert that races are populations, while it may harmonize controversy, skirts the same problems attending posits of biological race. Criteria for a population are neither self-evident nor widely agreed upon and the number of human populations has ranged from less than fifty to hundreds of thousands (Garn 1965; Relethford 1997, chap. 14). So if races are viewed as populations, the result will not resemble a simple or obvious taxonomy of four or five races.

However, a more serious problem than the arbitrary nature of their number follows the methodological use of populations to replace races—the idea of a population may be incoherent as a scientific concept, independent of prior social standards. In 1972, geneticist Richard Lewontin published a study reporting data on the diversity *within* seven human populations that were considered races in society: Caucasian, African, Mongoloid, South Asian Aborigines, Amerinds, Oceans, and Australian aborigines. Lewontin found that 85.4% of the human genetic variation, including variation associated with blood groups as associated with races, was within these populations, not between them. Variation between the populations was 8.5%, with geographical variation accounting for 6.3%. Lewontin wrote: "Since… racial classification [as based on populations] is now seen to be of virtually no genetic or taxonomic significance either, no justification can be offered for its continuance" (Lewontin 1972; Sapp 2012).

Lewontin's findings, which used molecular-genetic techniques and statistical analysis of 17 polymorphic sites (locations of multiple forms of a single gene) means that there is greater genetic variation between any two individuals in the same social race than between averages of the races as groups. If the genetic or hereditary material is the primary physical mechanism for race as a taxonomy of human groups, then there is no support for such a taxonomy in modern science.

Subsequent genetic research has supported Lewontin's findings and conclusion. After the human genome was mapped, both Craig Venter of the Institute of Genetic Research and Francis Collins of the National Institutes of Health reported that their research yielded no distinct genes for race or human races (Sapp 2012). Traits such as skin color, facial features, and hair texture may reliably be used to determine racial identity in society, and different types of these traits are more frequent in some populations than others, but these traits do not vary consistently between races and are superficial in genetic terms.

The mapping of the human genome, like Lewontin's research, is directly relevant to contemporary racial taxonomy or classification. However, human populations have also been studied historically in terms of genetic traits associated with different geographical regions. Luigi Cavalli-Sforza, who pioneered much of the twentieth-century research on population lineage, has explained that the genetic markers used to trace populations are not related to physical traits associated with race in society (Cavalli-Sforza 2000, pp. 61–6). Also, population studies are a weak form of taxonomy because there is nothing objective to determine how much of human history needs to be considered. Geographically isolated populations branch off and that is reflected in genetic difference. But the system of branching and the detail of branching are considered arbitrary (Cavalli-Sforza et al. 1996, p. 19). Genetic research and evolutionary biology following Cavalli-Sforza's research in the 1990s have confirmed and even strengthened the conclusion of his findings that common sense ideas of race are not supported in the biological sciences. Nevertheless, racial categories continue to be used in increasing detail in medicine, law, and popular searches for ancestry (Krimsky and Sloan 2011).

Further Considerations About Population Studies

It is important to note that the scientific consensus about the nonexistence of race in biological science and the failure of social racial taxonomy to be independently supported in population studies has not been smoothly received by all philosophers, or by all scientists, for that matter, much less understood by the public. Two related projects from philosophy of science merit consideration: races as clades and races as geographical groups that are currently accepted in science. A third usage related to public policy also merits consideration in terms of the US Census.

With reference to Cavalli-Sforza's work, Robin Andreasen has proposed that the ordinary idea of race could be given a scientific foundation as a system of clades. Most animals above the species level of classification are **clades**—multigenerational groups with distinctive traits who have a common ancestor and split within a larger group. Andreasen proposes that all human groups can be viewed as clades of an original population that originated in Africa (Andreasen 1998). The current scientific consensus is that modern humans originated in Africa about 150,000 years ago and migrated to Australia and Eurasia about 50,000 years ago (University of Cambridge 2007). However, the population-tracking genes used by Cavalli-Sforza are not linked to what we think of as racial traits, so the idea of races-as-clades would not be an independent scientific foundation for ordinary *racial* classification. Also, clades are not usually applied to groups below the species level, such as races, so either races-as-clades would get reconfigured as species, or if treated as groups more specific than species, there would have to be a scientific way to identify them, which is the primary problem.

Contemporary population studies that avoid classification in terms of geographical continental ancestry have been used to support social ideas of race. Rosenberg et al. report on their 2002 study in this regard:

> We studied human population structure using genotypes at 377 autosomal microsatellite loci in 1056 individuals from 52 populations. Within-population differences among individuals account for 93 to 95% of genetic variation; differences among major groups constitute only 3 to 5%. Nevertheless, without using prior information about the origins of individuals, we identified six main genetic clusters, five of which correspond to major geographic regions, and subclusters that often correspond to individual populations. General agreement of genetic and predefined populations suggests that self-reported ancestry can facilitate assessments of epidemiological risks but does not obviate the need to use genetic information in genetic association studies. (Rosenberg et al. 2002, p. 2381)

Philosopher Michael Hardimon proposes that Rosenberg's research can provide a foundation for a "minimalist concept of race," that he specifies as: a group of human beings distinguished from other groups by visible physical features, whose members share a common ancestry and that originates from a distinctive geographical location. By a "minimalist concept of race," Hardimon seeks to avoid racist connotations of race, while preserving a biological basis for race (Hardimon 2017). His proposal seems to relate to common sense insofar as ordinary people do assume that racial identity means exactly that one's ancestors were from Europe, Africa, Asian, and so forth. However, Hardimon's minimalist specifications would also coincide with all Homo sapiens who have visible physical features distinct from other animals, and a common ancestry that resided in Africa, according to the out-of-Africa thesis, or else a common ancestry that resided on planet earth. Also, continental ancestry does not always coincide with appearance, because even apparently random genetic testing sometimes reveals ancestry at odds with a person's racial appearance. For instance, students at West Chester University in Pennsylvania who participated in DNA ancestral tests were surprised to find out that they have genetic material associated with continents different from their racial self-identification and appearance (Foeman 2017).

Some social scientists and social-political philosophers, for instance, Quayshawn Spencer, have claimed that the meaning of the term "race" is exactly the meaning assigned to it in society, as reflected in US Census categories. The reasoning is that a vast majority of respondents select entries from those categories and the categories line up with human biological traits (Spencer 2014). However, the philosophical question is whether that coincidence is sufficient to establish the scientific reality of race. The coincidence is one aspect of the meaning of race in society, but the census makes no mention of the validity of its categories, so this approach simply by-passes the questions of the reality of race according to the biological sciences, in favor of a social science approach.

Returning now to the biological sciences themselves, it is important to note an explanation for the nonexistence of human races in terms of requirements for racial formation within species. In their 2011 *Race? Debunking A Scientific Myth*, physical anthropologist Ian Tattersall and geneticist Rob DeSalle explain that as *Homo sapiens*, the only surviving human species, evolved, there was interbreeding between different geographical groups through migrations, war, colonization, trade, and so forth. This genetic *rearticulation* prevented the formation of races—human "populations" were never sufficiently isolated from other populations to acquire the distinct characteristics of races. Moreover, the differences identified as racial differences are recent in Homo sapiens evolution, only about 50,000 years (Tattersall and De Salle 2011). This means that differences considered racial differences may not have always existed in our species.

Evolutionary studies of human group formation reflect a shift in biological studies of race from systems of classification to genetic history. John Relethford well sums up this current situation in a recent article, "Biological Anthropology, Population Genetics, and Race":

> We now have a much better view of human variation that has emerged from an ever increasing body of evidence from molecular genetics and genomics and the application of the models and methods of population genetics. To assess the utility (or lack thereof) of biological definitions of race and studies of racial classification, global patterns of human genetic variation must be examined within the context of the basic principles of population genetics and the genetic history of the human species. (Relethford 2017, p. 160)

Conclusion

A story has been told in this chapter about race in science over the modern period. Race was a new universal system of human classification that was invented along with modern biology. Ideas about race began as neutral human varieties based on the geographical divisions. Racist assessments and valuations of different races, which justified colonization, resource appropriation, black chattel slavery, indigenous genocide, and later forms of oppression, were added by Europeans and Americans to racial taxonomy, favoring whites. Based on both empirical evidence and egalitarian ideals, these hierarchical assessments were removed from scientific ideas of race, substituting ideas of populations, instead. However, the population idea failed as a substitute for race, because there are greater genetic variations within populations than between them. The only way to winnow down existing human populations numbering between fifty and hundreds of thousands, to match social ideas of race with smaller numbers of races, is to start with social ideas of race, thereby undermining the scientific independence of biological race. Besides these issues of classification, evolutionary studies of populations identify human groups that overlap but do not coincide with, common sense ideas of race. Moreover, these groups indicate ancestry or lines of descent within populations that still reside where their ancestors did and ongoing migrations and genetic mixtures in highly mobile global society have not preserved those divisions.

On a purely physical biological level, the story could end here, but the public is generally unaware of the current state of science regarding the nonexistence of races as they are known in society and some philosophers have tried to save the connection between social and scientific ideas. Their success would depend on philosophy being able to tell science what it does, or should, consider real. So, we are left in an impasse between biological science, in which ideas of race originated and society and its spokespersons who seek to retain race.

However that impasse is resolved, many thinkers, especially in Pragmatic and Continental philosophical traditions, have avoided a scientific starting point for inquiries about race, by addressing race in terms of human existence within societies with racialist and racist systems or addressing race by beginning with the social facts of racism. Several of those projects will be discussed in Chapter 4.

Glossary

clades—multigenerational groups with distinctive traits forming after a split with a larger group, who have a common ancestor.

clines—traits that gradually change into other traits over geographical and climactic differences.

ethnological studies—anthropological studies of specific practices within different cultures.

eugenics movement—thought and policies based on the idea that only people judged superior relative to others should be permitted to have offspring.

monogeny—doctrine that all human varieties have a common evolutionary origin.

pangenesis—out of date theory that changes in bodily cells "drift" to genetic material, changing what can be inherited.

polygenism—doctrine that different human races have different evolutionary origins.

population—term for a group used by evolutionary biologists and anthropologists for a group of people in the same geographical area who breed mainly among themselves.

racialism—thought or action based on the belief that human races are real and the differences among races are important.

reduction—translating the terms for entities and principles studied in one science to entities and principles studied in another more basic or more rigorous science.

revisionism—changing knowledge as a valued practice.

social construction—an idea, thing, or practice that is created in society and not the result of anything natural or self-evident.

social Darwinism—late nineteenth and early twentieth-century misapplications of Darwinian evolution to support oppression and/or neglect of circumstances of nonwhites and poor in society.

valorization—positive value assessment.

Essay and Discussion Questions

1. How were modern ideas of race different from older ideas of division within society?
2. Explain how description and assessment figured into racialist and racist ideas of race.
3. How was the idea of biological race retained by transitional thinkers such as Franz Boas and Claude Lévi-Strauss?
4. Explain the difference between classificatory and evolutionary-historical genetic descriptions of human groups.
5. How is the genetic difference within and between groups relevant to whether or not races exist in science?
6. What are some problems with the idea of populations? If races were defined as populations, what problems would follow?
7. Critically engage Andreasen's suggestion that races are clades.
8. Critically engage Hardimon's idea of "minimal race."
9. What can be concluded from the fact that some people have genetic material related to ancestral origins that are different from how those people identify racially?
10. Explain why the status of race as a real system in science is important for how we think about race.

References

Andreasen, Robin O. A New Perspective on the Race Debate. *The British Journal for the Philosophy of Science*, vol. 49, no. 2, 1998, pp. 199–225.

Boas, Franz. "The Mind of Primitive Man." *Science*, New Series, vol. 13, no. 321, Feb. 22, 1911, pp. 281–89.

Brues, Alice Mossie. *People and Races*. New York, NY: Macmillan, 1977.

Cavalli-Sforza, Luigi, Paolo Menozzi, and Alberto Piazza. *The History and Geography of Human Genes*. Princeton, NJ: Princeton University Press, 1996.

Cavalli-Sforza, Luigi. *Genes, People, and Languages*. Translated by Mark Seielstad. New York: Northpoint Press, 2000.

Cuvier, George. *The Animal Kingdom: Arranged in Conformity with Its Organization*, edited by H. Murtrie. New York: G&C&H. Carvill, 1831. https://archive.org/details/animalkingdomar03graygoog.

Darwin, Charles, and Alfred Wallace. "On the Tendency of Species to Form Varieties; and on the Perpetuation of Varieties and Species by Natural Means of Selection." *Journal of the Proceedings of the Linnean Society of London*, vol. 3, no. 9, 1858, pp. 45–62. Version of Record Online: Apr. 13, 2011. https://doi.org/10.1111/j.1096-3642.1858.tb02500.x, http://onlinelibrary.wiley.com/doi/10.1111/j.1096-3642.1858.tb02500.x/abstract.

Darwin, Charles. "On the Races of Man." *The Descent of Man, and Selection in Relation to Sex*. New York: D. Appleton & Co., 1889, Chap. 7. https://genius.com/Charles-darwin-the-descent-of-man-chapter-7-on-the-races-of-man-annotated.

Fodor, J. A. "Special Sciences (Or: The Disunity of Science as a Working Hypothesis)." *Synthese*, vol. 28, no. 2, Oct. 1974, pp. 97–115.

Foeman, Anita. "DNA Tests, and Sometimes Surprising Results." *The New York Times*, Apr. 20, 2017. https://www.nytimes.com/2017/04/23/us/dna-ancestry-race-identity.html?_r=0.

Garn, S. M. *Human Races*. Springfield, IL: Charles Thomas, 1965.

Gillham, Nicholas W. "Sir Francis Galton and the Birth of Eugenics." *Annual Review of Genetics*, vol. 35, no. 1, 2001, pp. 83–101.

Goodstein, David. "How Science Works." *Reference Manual on Scientific Evidence*. Washington, DC: National Academies Press, 2011, 3rd ed., Chap. 4, pp. 37–54.

Gould, Stephen Jay. "The Geometer of Race." *Discover*, vol. 15, no. 11, 1994, pp. 65–9.

Gould, Stephen Jay. *The Mismeasure of Man*. London and New York: Norton, 1996.

Hardimon, Michael O. "Minimalist Biological Race." *Oxford Handbook of Philosophy and Race*, edited by Naomi Zack. New York, NY: Oxford University Press, 2017, pp. 150–59.

Heirneaux, Jean. In UNESCO, "Four Statements on the Race Question," 1969, pp. 8–16. http://unesdoc.unesco.org/images/0012/001229/122962eo.pdf.

Krimsky, Sheldon, and Kathleen Sloan, editors. *Race and the Genetic Revolution: Science, Myth, and Culture*. New York, NY: Columbia University Press, 2011.

Lewontin, Richard. "The Apportionment of Human Diversity." *Evolutionary Biology*, vol. 6, 1972, pp. 381–98. Marine Library/Stacks. http://www.philbio.org/wp-content/uploads/2010/11/Lewontin-The-Apportionment-of-Human-Diversity.pdf.

Montague, Ashley. *Race: Man's Most Dangerous Myth*. New York, NY: Columbia University Press, 1942. https://archive.org/stream/mansmostdangerou032948mbp/mansmostdangerou032948mbp_djvu.txt. Consulted June 6, 2017.

Montague, Ashley. *The Idea of Race*. Lincoln: University of Nebraska Press, 1965.

Müller-Wille, Staffan. "Claude Lévi-Strauss on Race, History, and Genetics." *BioSocieties*, vol. 5, 2010, pp. 330–47.

Museum of Comparative Zoology, Harvard University. 2017. http://www.mcz.harvard.edu/about/history.html.

Nelson, William Max. "Making Men: Enlightenment Ideas of Racial Engineering." *American Historical Review*, vol. 115, no. 5, 2010, pp. 1364–94.

Population Estimates Bureau. "Race." United States Census, 2017. https://www.census.gov/quickfacts/meta/long_RHI225215.htm.

Radnitzky, Gerard, and Gunnar Andersson, editors. *Progress and Rationality in Science*. Dordrecht: D. Reidel, 1978.

Relethford, John H., *The Human Species: An Introduction to Biological Anthropology*. Mountain View, CA: Mayfield, 1997.

Relethford, John H. "Biological Anthropology, Population Genetics, and Race." *The Oxford Handbook of Philosophy and Race*, edited by Naomi Zack. New York, NY: Oxford University Press, 2017, pp. 160–69.

Richter, Melvin. "The Study of Man: A Debate on Race." *Commentary*, Feb. 1, 1958. https://www.commentarymagazine.com/articles/the-study-of-man-a-debate-on-race/.

Rosenberg, Noah A., Jonathan K. Pritchard, James L. Weber, Howard M. Cann, Kenneth K. Kidd, Lev A. Zhivotovsky, and Marcus W. Feldman. "Genetic Structure of Human Populations." *Science*, vol. 298, no. 5602, Dec. 20, 2002, pp. 2381–85. http://science.sciencemag.org/content/298/5602/2381/tab-pdf.

Rutledge, M. Dennis. "Myths and Realities: African Americans and the Measurement of Human Abilities." *The Journal of Negro Education*, vol. 64, no. 3, 1995, pp. 243–52.

Sapp, Jan. "Race Finished," Jan Bookshelf. *American Scientist*. Mar./Apr., 2012. http://www.americanscientist.org/bookshelf/pub/race-finished.

Smedley, Audrey, and Brian D. Smedley. *Race in North America: Origin and Evolution of a Worldview*. Boulder, CO: Westview Press, 2011, 4th ed.

Spencer, Quayshawn. "A Radical Solution to the Race Problem." *Philosophy of Science*, vol. 81, no. 5, Dec. 2014, pp. 1025–38.

Stuurman, Siep. "François Bernier and the Invention of Racial Classification." *History Workshop Journal*, no. 50, Autumn, 2000, pp. 1–21. JSTOR, www.jstor.org/stable/4289688.

Tattersall, Ian, and Rob DeSalle. *RACE? Debunking a Scientific Myth*. College Station, TX: Texas A&M University Press, 2011.

Tax, Sol. "Franz Boas, German-American Anthropologist." *Encyclopedia Britannica*, May 2, 2017. https://www.britannica.com/biography/Franz-Boas#ref210125.

UNESCO, United Nations. "Four Statements on the Race Question," 1950, 1951, 1967, 1970, published in 1969. http://unesdoc.unesco.org/images/0012/001229/122962eo.pdf.

University of Cambridge. "New Research Confirms 'Out of Africa' Theory of Human Evolution." *ScienceDaily.* http://www.sciencedaily.com/releases/2007/05/070509161829.htm. Accessed June 9, 2017.

U.S. State Department. "The Immigration Act of 1924 (The Johnson-Reed Act)." Office of the Historian. https://history.state.gov/milestones/1921-1936/immigration-act. Consulted June 3, 2017.

White, Leslie A. "The Ethnography and Ethnology of Franz Boas." *Bulletin of the Texas Memorial Museum*, no. 6, Apr. 1963.

4

Ideas of Race in Twentieth Century American and Continental Philosophy

American or pragmatist philosophy and continental philosophy begin and end with human life and subjectivity in society. In both philosophical traditions, the starting point is not the physical sciences, because both American and continental philosophy use methods of describing and analyzing actual human experience. Scholars of race in each of these philosophical traditions have the goal of understanding practical, political, social, emotional, and moral aspects of racial experience, rather than the intellectual and empirical justification for ideas about race, taken cognitively, or as strains of abstract thought or objective knowledge. Such thinkers have emphasized the importance of the human subject, as prior to the practice of science. The underlying insight is that human beings invent science, shape it, practice it, and change it.

W.E.B. Du Bois (1868–1963) provided clear examples of the subject matter and methods of American philosophy in terms of race and Edmond Husserl (1859–1938), developed a strain of phenomenology in continental philosophy that has proved relevant to race. We will begin with them and then, with their primary methodological insights in mind, consider subsequent American and continental philosophers who provide perspectives different from both the canonical thought of Chapter 1 and the scientific aspects of race of Chapter 3. In many senses American and continental philosophers have furthered the progressive and inspirational thought and action discussed in Chapter 2.

© The Author(s) 2018
N. Zack, *Philosophy of Race*, Palgrave Philosophy Today,
https://doi.org/10.1007/978-3-319-78729-9_4

W.E.B. Du Bois and Edmond Husserl

In his 1923 essay, "The Superior Race," Du Bois relates his conversation with a white supremacist. After discussing difficulties of identifying the black group, Du Bois is asked, "But what is this group; and how do you differentiate it; and how can you call it 'black' when you admit that it is not black?" Du Bois answers, "I recognize it quite easily and with full legal sanction; the black man is a person who must ride Jim Crow in Georgia" (Du Bois 1923, p. 60). Du Bois's trenchant response serves to define blackness in terms of the social status and circumstances of members of a group of people in late nineteenth-century America. This is an historically contextualized definition of blackness, based on the experience of black people. Du Bois here presents experience as a reality more compelling than abstract criteria for being black or whether the black race could be independently identified in science as a group with inherited physical and/or cultural traits. In defining race this way, Du Bois was practicing philosophical **pragmatism**. Pragmatism is a tradition in American philosophy that turns toward the real-life consequences of ideas, principles, and hypotheses in order to understand and analyze them.

We can also see that Du Bois practiced sociology as a pragmatist, in his first research project. In *The Philadelphia Negro*, first published in 1899, Du Bois designed and carried out an empirical study of the circumstances of African Americans in Philadelphia. Aldon Morris explains how the late nineteenth- and early-twentieth century practice of professional sociology that Du Bois first encountered, was not an empirical science, testable by data, with documented sources. Rather, sociology at that time was a form of speculative theory that Du Bois called "car-window sociology," as in musings from a Pullman car while traveling through the South on holiday (Du Bois 1967, p. 51). Soon after the publication of *The Philadelphia Negro*, Du Bois wrote in *Souls of Black Folk*:

> To the car-window sociologist, to the man who seeks to understand and know the South by devoting the few leisure hours of a holiday trip to unravelling the snarl of centuries,—to such men very often the whole trouble with the black field-hand may be summed up by Aunt Ophelia's word, "Shiftless!" They have noted repeatedly scenes like one I saw last summer. We were riding along the highroad to town at the close of a long hot day. A couple of young black fellows passed us in a mule team, with several bushels of loose corn in the ear. One was driving, listlessly bent forward, his elbows on his knees,—a happy-go-lucky, careless picture of irresponsibility. The other was fast asleep in the bottom of the wagon. As we passed we noticed an ear of corn fall from the wagon. They never saw it,—not they. A rod farther on we noted another ear on

the ground; and between that creeping mule and town we counted twenty-six ears of corn. Shiftless? Yes, the personification of shiftlessness. And yet follow those boys: they are not lazy; to-morrow morning they'll be up with the sun; they work hard when they do work, and they work willingly. They have no sordid, selfish, money-getting ways, but rather a fine disdain for mere cash. They'll loaf before your face and work behind your back with good-natured honesty. They'll steal a watermelon, and hand you back your lost purse intact. Their great defect as laborers lies in their lack of incentive beyond the mere pleasure of physical exertion. They are careless because they have not found that it pays to be careful; they are improvident because the improvident ones of their acquaintance get on about as well as the provident. (Du Bois 1904, p. 154)

The early sociology that Du Bois sought to revise was steeped with racist normative assumptions, in keeping with Jim Crow white supremacy, speculative and biased biological science, and racist political ideology. Unlike Du Bois's approach, such sociologists did not take up the perspectives of their human subjects.

The intellectual inferiority of Negroes was a basic assumption throughout science and society. But Du Bois was confident about his own intellectual abilities and he rejected doctrines of general Negro inferiority. From a Howard BA, he earned a Harvard MA and PhD and would have been granted a PhD at the University of Berlin, but for lack of a one-term residency requirement. He knew that the unchallenged racist sociology of his day lacked empirical foundations. And he aimed to make sociology a real science through study of African Americans and thereby also demonstrate that racial inequality was the result of racism and not inherited inferiority. Through interviews, statistical research, and analyses, all informed by history, Du Bois developed social science methodology, assisted by student and community researchers and informants. Among other findings, Du Bois showed how the following worked in black communities: the relation of crime to unemployment; class divisions among African Americans; American black agency through community organization, primarily the black church; activism as a way to correct injustice (Morris 2015).

Du Bois's methodology reflected nascent grass roots work in his time. In Edward Baltzell's 1967 introduction to Du Bois's *Philadelphia Negro*, he notes that when this book, which was to fall out of print for almost 50 years, was published in 1899, the leaders of the Settlement House movement had already begun to call for fact-based studies of contemporary society. Beatrice Webb (Potter) and Charles Booth in Great Britain and Jane Addams in the United States abandoned a priori theorizing to study social facts, living and working among the very groups who were their subjects (Du Bois 1967, xvi–xii).

Du Bois influenced subsequent social scientists and his work may also have coincided with or anticipated Arthur Bentley's thought. Bentley, in *The Process of Government* (discussed in Chapter 2), called for attention to political activities and interests as a way to understand how what he called "government" and we would today call "political power" operates in society. Bentley's contribution, like Du Bois's, was neglected. Bentley was a white outsider to mainstream academia, a journalist and an independent scholar and Du Bois was a scholar who was excluded because of his race. Bentley's book was published in 1908, without any mention of Du Bois, although they shared the same rejection of car window or arm chair theorizing. But, Du Bois knew the leading pragmatists of his day and Bentley was in touch with John Dewey, so they may have interacted indirectly. The grounds on which they both rejected speculative arm-chair theory are very comparable. In *Dusk of Dawn*, published in 1940, Du Bois contrasted his method with Herbert Spencer in providing his own intellectual history for *The Philadelphia Negro*:

> Herbert Spencer finished his ten volumes of Synthetic Philosophy in 1896. The biological analogy, the vast generalizations, were striking, but actual scientific accomplishment lagged. For me an opportunity seemed to present itself … I determined to put science into sociology through a study of the condition and problems of my own group. I was going to study the facts, any and all facts, concerning the American Negro and his plight, and by measurement and comparison and research, work up to any valid generalization which I could. (Du Bois 1967, p. 51, cited by Digby in Du Bois 1967, p. xviii)

And in his *Process of Government*, Bentley suggested how his call for empiricism might be applied to racial difference within society:

> I am not denying that there may be actual differences in nervous complexity (and so capacity) between physical races of men just as there may be between individuals. I am not denying the significance of the skulls of Pithecanthropus and of the Neanderthal man. The whole point concerns the interpretation of social activity and organization in terms of such differences. Against the exaggerated emphasis that is placed on slight shadings of capacity stated in anatomical or physiological terms, I am appealing to a whole world of social facts, and asking their analysis on their own merits. (Bentley, p. 249)

But there is a difference in how Bentley and Du Bois analyzed race. Bentley's attack on racialist analyses of group differences within society was not motivated by progressive ideals, that is, his attack was not normative, but purely methodological. By contrast, Du Bois attack on the same sources was motivated by his desire to show how racism was unjust.

Du Bois also knew Franz Boas quite well and approved of his work in distinguishing between biological race and culture (as discussed in Chapter 3) (Shenk 2015). However, Du Bois's definition of "the black man" as "a person who must ride Jim Crow in Georgia" is something different from an empirical sociological or anthropological analysis, or even a psychological one and it goes beyond pragmatic description. Du Bois's definition differs from criteria for membership in a racial group or distinctions between heredity and environment, or the social causes of disadvantaged racial traits. It signals a concern with the experience of individuals, as definitive of race. And in that vein, Du Bois was not focused on oppression only, because he had his eye on what could be possible in the future—he was interested in the aspirations of American black people. He called what he presented as a primary aspiration, **destiny**. In his 1897 address to the American Negro Academy, he said:

> But while race differences have followed mainly physical race lines, yet no mere physical distinctions would really define or explain the deeper differences–the cohesiveness and continuity of these groups. The deeper differences are spiritual, psychical, differences. …Manifestly some of the great races of today–particularly the Negro race–have not as yet given to civilization the full spiritual message which they are capable of giving. For the development of Negro genius, of Negro literature and art, of Negro spirit, only Negroes bound and welded together, Negroes inspired by one vast ideal, can work out in its fullness that great message we have for humanity. Negroes are … a nation stored with wonderful possibilities of culture, their destiny is not a servile imitation of Anglo-Saxon culture, but a stalwart originality which shall unswervingly follow Negro ideals. (Du Bois 1897)

This kind of faith in the future of a race as a striving and deserving cultural group is a moral prediction, not a scientific one. It is a vision of something better to come, which should come. In that sense, Du Bois's proclamation of that faith in a shared, glorious Negro racial destiny was clearly intended to inspire others to share his faith. This practice of **rhetoric**, or as we shall see later with Cornel West, **prophecy**, has become an integral part of American Philosophy of Race, specifically African American philosophy.

The criticism of science in continental philosophy has been even more forceful than in American philosophy, because the question has not been how to improve science by making it more realistically informed, but how to relate science to human subjectivity and values. Edmund Husserl (1859–1938) first raised this foundational question in terms of the assumption that objective knowledge is possible in the natural sciences, including geometry. Husserl argued that perception and observation, the factual foundation for objectivity, occurs on an individual level, to individual consciousness. But subjective experience does not have a vocabulary in the natural sciences and instead, perception and observation are translated into objective language that does not refer to anything which has been experienced by individual consciousness. The result is that, rather than being based on fact, so-called objective science is based on fiction, on experiences that are only imagined. Another way of describing this problem is that we describe our observations with terms that refer to universal abstract qualities that we never directly experience. We then assume that we are thereby describing a shared world but others who "share" that world are in the same position as we are. They, like us, have to proceed from their own unique conscious experience, to an imagined experience described in language that may not exactly refer to what they have experienced. Husserl described the result of this disconnection as a crisis, because human beings have become alienated from knowledge that is presented as an ultimate value, although it fails to describe or address their spiritual needs.

Husserl's solution to fictional ideas of objectivity in science was that the individual knower engage in an *epoché* or bracketing of the existence or objective property of any object of consciousness and then proceed with description of the object, as an object of consciousness. He proposed that this would lead to knowledge about the structures of consciousness and ultimately a philosophical system of genuine knowledge, which could be a foundation for the natural sciences. That process and its resulting general principles are modern **phenomenology**, of which Husserl is considered the founder (Husserl 1970, pp. 3–18).

Husserl's criticism of the natural sciences would apply to the social sciences insofar as they have developed by accepting the methods and factual knowledge of the natural sciences as their own model and ideal. However, there are difficulties in building a theory of social science knowledge based on phenomenological *epoché*, because social experience varies more than physical perception (Gorman 1975, pp. 396–403). And there is further variation, based on racial difference. Such racial experience of the social world can and has been phenomenologically described by continental philosophers. Continental philosophy has been more existential than abstractly phenomenological, concerning race, yielding **existentialist** phenomenology, a departure from Husserlian phenomenology that is nonetheless deeply indebted to it.

American Philosophy and Race

American philosophy is the work of philosophers in the United States who also tend to be pragmatists. Classic Pragmatism consists of the philosophical work of Charles Sanders Peirce (1839–1914), William James (1842–1910), Josiah Royce (1855–1916), John Dewey (1859–1952), and George Herbert Mead (1863–1931). Pragmatism declined after Dewey but in the 1970s, it began a renaissance and revision through the work of Richard Rorty (1931–2007), Hilary Putnam (1926–2016), and Robert Brandom (1950–). At different stages of pragmatism's heyday, decline, and revival, the work of African American pragmatist philosophers have engaged the classical and renascent sources, as well as Du Bois's foundational contributions to American Philosophy of Race. Alain LeRoy Locke (1885–1954), James Baldwin (1924–1987), and Cornel West (1953) are major figures in both the American and pragmatist traditions and they in turn engage the work of other African American writers and activists. The secondary literature about Locke, Baldwin, and West also contains reclaimed and new contributions. African American philosophers have also worked directly in the pragmatist tradition as it was first developed by white pragmatist philosophers. For instance, William T. Fontaine (1909–1968), who was the first African American employed in the ivy league, at the University of Pennsylvania, developed ideas in social philosophy influenced by the work of Mead (Fontaine 1942). More recent philosophers of race, such as V. Denise James, have taken up classical pragmatism in terms of African American feminist philosophy (see Chapter 10) (James 2009, 2013). Altogether, the overlap of American Philosophy of Race with classical and contemporary pragmatism has yielded a new comprehensive body of work.

Alain Locke was the first African American Rhodes scholar and he received his PhD in Philosophy from Harvard University. But because he was black, he was able to secure academic employment only in historically black colleges. He chaired the philosophy department of Howard University for 32 years, until 1953. Locke was famous as a founder of the Harlem Renaissance, supporting and helping to publicize the work of black novelists, poets, historians, and artists. The Harlem Renaissance began in the 1920s and flourished for about 12 years, becoming better known after it was over. Locke's 1925 anthology, *The New Negro*, was a focal point for the new identities and racial pride of the era. However, Locke disagreed with Du Bois about the purpose of creative projects: Du Bois insisted that black art have a political and moral message, but Locke emphasized the importance of individual self-expression, with universal human themes (Du Bois 1897; Locke 1928). According to Locke, such self-expression was neither narcissistic nor frivolous, but could be a means for individual reflection and group development in racist society. Locke wrote:

> Up to the present one may adequately describe the Negro's 'inner objectives' as an attempt to repair a damaged group psychology and reshape a warped social perspective. Their realization has acquired a new mentality for the American Negro. And as it matures we begin to see its effects; at first, negative, iconoclastic, and then positive and constructive. In this new group psychology we note the lapse of sentimental appeal, then the development of a more positive self-respect and self-reliance; the repudiation of social dependence, and then the gradual recovery from hyper-sensitiveness and 'touchy' nerves, the repudiation of the double standard of judgment with its special philanthropic allowances and in the sturdier desire for objective and scientific appraisal; and finally the rise from social disillusionment to race pride, from the sense of social debt to the responsibilities of social contribution, and offsetting the necessary working commonsense acceptance of restricted conditions, the belief in ultimate esteem and recognition. Therefore, the Negro today wishes to be known for what he is, even in his faults and shortcomings, and scorns a craven and precarious survival at the price of seeming to be what he is not. (Locke 1925, p. 11)

In this passage, Locke describes and calls for internal psychological change through creative work. While this might have the same effect as what he called Du Bois's call for "propaganda," there is a strong implication that it would be more effective toward progress in race relations than propaganda, as well as positively changing how blacks viewed themselves.

Locke's philosophical career reflected broad social struggles of African Americans for intellectual recognition. Leonard Harris, who has researched both Locke's philosophy and his life, relates his distressing and moving experiences in retrieving Locke's legacy, in an essay aptly entitled, "Looking for Alain Locke." In 1983, Harris began his quest for Locke's philosophical work at the Alain Locke Archives at Howard University, the Beinecke Library, Yale University, and the Community Art Center in Chicago. Harris's search for Locke's work and his attempts to find a publisher for a biography about Locke was shadowed by his search for Locke's physical remains. It turned out that Locke's ashes had been kept in a can, in a paper bag, in an archive vault at Howard University, from his 1954 cremation until 2007—they were finally interred in the Congressional Cemetery in 2014 (Harris 2017). Harris finally succeeded in publishing both a biography of Locke and an anthology of philosophical commentary on Locke's work (Harris 2008, 1989/1999).

Jacoby Adeshi Carter, Harris's student and colleague, wrote a definitive exposition of Locke's work for the *Stanford Encyclopedia of Philosophy*, in 2012, an entry that informs, interprets, and analyses, as well as it vindicates. Through his graduate studies at Harvard, Locke was directly influenced by the classical pragmatists, Dewey, James, and Royce. Carter notes that although Locke was directly educated in pragmatism, Du Bois has been claimed as the primary pragmatist by philosophers of race. One reason for this is that Locke's work has been unavailable for so long, while Du Bois's writings were constantly in print over the twentieth century. Another reason is that Du Bois wrote as much for general readers as academics, whereas Locke's philosophical prose is not as accessible.

Locke's 1917 doctoral dissertation, *The Problem of Classification in Theory of Value*, was written under the advisement of Ralph Barton Perry (1876–1957), a student of William James, who specialized in pragmatic theories of value and perception. Locke argued that values are rooted in human attitudes as "emotionally mediated experience," so that emotions determine values. Value-norms function as stereotypes for emotions and they determine habits of action. Value-modes are culturally, historically, and geographically relative. Based on experience, reason and judgment may enter into the assessment of a value-norm, but its mode, for instance, as aesthetic, logical, religious, or moral, cannot be changed by experience. The result of the functionality of value for Locke was that the same things could be valued in different ways. Also, the value-norm could be changed if its determining emotional attitude changed. Locke believed in pluralities of values and thought that obstacles to such plurality were based on *absolutism*, or an insistence of value uniformity, as well as dogmatic and arbitrary.

Carter further explains that Locke developed the concept of *ethnic race* as inherited identity that is primarily cultural and social, rather than biological. (With this view of the relationship between race and culture, Locke can be compared to Claude Lévi Strauss, who as we saw in Chapter 2, analyzed race as a construction of culture.) Locke rejected ideas that biological race could determine culture, but he also thought that both race and culture were unavoidable posits for understanding human groups. Carter quotes Locke from his 1924 essay, "The Concept of Race as Applied to Social Culture":

Most authorities are now reconciled to two things,—first, the necessity of a thorough-going redefinition of the nature of race, and second, the independent definition of race in the ethnic or social sense together with the independent investigation of its differences and their causes apart from the investigation of the factors and differentiae of physical race.

It is also interesting, as Carter further notes, that Locke thought each of the major race groups of his time had multiple ethnic races within them (Carter 2012).

Because Locke was not recognized as an academic philosopher during his time, he did not leave a legacy for subsequent pragmatist African American philosophers. William Fontaine, for instance, forged his academic career as a "first" African American philosopher. Bruce Kuklick begins his biography of Fontaine with a story about a trip to the American Philosophical Association Eastern Division meeting in December, 1948. William Fontaine, who at the time was teaching at the University of Pennsylvania, got a ride to and from the conference at Charlottsville, Virginia, with his colleague Morton White and another famous philosopher, Nelson Goodman; A.J. Ayer joined them on the way back. When they arrived in Charlottsville, before going to the conference hotel, Fontaine's colleagues had to drop him off at a hotel for blacks, because the city was segregated. When Fontaine made his way to the conference hotel, a white philosopher had to tell the doorman to let him in. Fontaine's traveling companions were appalled and in 1949, the APA passed a resolution not to hold future meetings in segregated cities (Kuklick 2008, pp. 1–2). But the incident was emblematic of the pressures Fontaine continually faced, including the location of his office at the University of Pennsylvania, in a former broom closet, and his receiving tenure as an assistant professor, without promotion to associate.

Kuklick evaluates Fontaine's 1942 article, "The Mind and Thought of the Negro," and his 1944 "'Social Determination' in the Writings of Negro Scholars" as excellent contributions to sociology of knowledge and social psychology. But the work Fontaine presented to his colleagues over two decades, toward a book, *Reflections on Segregation, Desegregation, Power, and Morals* that he completed while ill with tuberculosis, was mediocre in comparison. While high ideals for racial harmony were expressed, the chapters did not connect coherently. Autobiography was intermingled with black history and public policy recommendations to desegregate housing, and Fontaine disparaged the Black Panthers as racist, throughout. Fontaine failed to appeal to a black audience whose demands for equality were intensifying, while at the same time failing to satisfy the restrictive disciplinary requirements of traditional mainstream analytic philosophers. *Reflections* was never reviewed and Fontaine died a year after it was published (Fontaine 1967; Kuklick 2008, pp. 119–24). Contemporary reviewers of Kuklick's biography tend to view Fontaine as someone who failed to measure up in a cruel, racist profession (Allen 2009). The point may be that a mediocre white philos-

opher would have had a more successful career, but there is also an implication that Fontaine lacked integrity in caving into standards he did not
whole-heartedly accept.

Between Fontaine's career and writing and the entry of African American
philosophy into academic discourse, American thought about race became
intensely politicized. To the extent that the civil rights movement and legislation have been followed by disappointing racial progress, it is now
expected that even philosophical voices will have political relevance. And
sometimes that relevance can be found in philosophical consideration of
intellectuals, such as James Baldwin, who were not academic philosophers.

Baldwin's credentials for critical cultural analysis are evident through
number of sources: his epistolary essay to his nephew, *The Fire Next Time*,
his conversation with the anthropologist Margaret Mead in *Rap on Race*, his
1965 debate with conservative William Buckley at Cambridge University,
and most recently, his reflections on race in the United States as compiled in
the 2017 documentary, "I Am Not Your Negro." As Ulf Schulenberg writes
in a 2007 essay in the *European Journal of American studies*: "[Baldwin's]
politicized version of self-creation makes it seem legitimate to advance the
argument that he is part of a left-liberal tradition of worldly pragmatism
that sees the work of the strong poet or creative redescriber as contributing
to political and social change" (Schulenberg 2007).

Baldwin expressed several major themes throughout his creative career:
White Americans, especially as depicted in Hollywood movies, live in a fan-
tasy world of effortless consumption and democracy among themselves, with
no awareness of the suffering of people of color that makes this possible (Als
2017). The American Dream for white people has been created by uncom-
pensated and unrecognized black labor (Baldwin and Buckley 1965).The
history of African Americans literally lives on in their individual lives in the
present, in their visible physical racial traits and their experience of the nor-
mality of violent expressions of racism, especially by police officers (Baldwin
and Mead 1970).

By the time of Cornel West's rise as a scholar and public intellectual,
issues of race had entered philosophy and discourse about race in the pragmatic philosophical tradition had become fully politicized. West studied
at Yale University and has taught at Union Theological Seminary, Harvard
University, and Princeton University. He has taught in departments of religion and African American Studies, but many philosophers of race have
claimed him. Although, West says about himself: "I'm a blues man in the
life of the mind. I'm a jazz man in the world of ideas" (West 2015).

West is one of the most well-known African Americans of arts and letters in his generation, regularly presenting his thought in television and radio shows and interviews, and performing with a band called "Cornel West Theory" and as "Councilor West" in the movies "Matrix Reloaded" and "Matrix Revolutions." His speech and writing are oratorical and span the history of Western humanism. West is in that sense the Du Bois of the twenty-first century, calling for hope and telling Americans, from ordinary people to President Barack Obama, how they are obligated to help the poor and "redignify human suffering." West thus preaches, as much as he teaches, based on a core commitment to altruistic socialism and Christianity, as well as a somber appreciation of human tragedy. In his first book, *Prophesy Deliverance!: An Afro-American Revolutionary Christianity*, he wrote:

> The object of inquiry for Afro-American critical thought is the past and the present, the doings and the sufferings of African people in the United States. Rather than a new scientific discipline or field of study, it is a genre of writing, a textuality, a mode of discourse that interprets, describes, and evaluates Afro-American life in order comprehensively to understand and effectively to transform it. It is not concerned with "foundations" or transcendental "grounds" but with how to build its language in such a way that the configuration of sentences and the constellation of paragraphs themselves create a textuality and distinctive discourse which are a material force for Afro-American freedom. (West 1982, p. 15)

West continually refers to black **prophecy**, not as prediction of the future, but as a critical description of the past and present that will allow for change in the future. In *Keeping Faith: Philosophy and Race in America*, West criticized academic pragmatist philosophers for failing to attend to social conditions in reality. Instead, he insisted: "[Prophetic pragmatism] analyzes the social causes of unnecessary forms of social misery, promotes moral outrage against them, organizes different constituencies to alleviate them, yet does so with an openness to its own blindnesses and shortcomings" (West 1993, p. 139).

Part of taking up prophetic pragmatism requires an understanding of what West calls "black prophetic fire" as a driving force for liberation by African Americans in the past. In *Black Prophetic Fire*, a dialogue with Christa Buschendorf, West discusses the work and activism of Frederick Douglass, W.E.B. Du Bois, Martin Luther King Jr., Ella Baker, Malcolm X, and Ida B. Wells. West gives the iconic figures—Douglass, Du Bois, King, and Malcolm X——their due, but he goes further in drawing out the contributions of Ella Baker and Ida B. Wells. He attributes Wells's courageously fiery anti-lynching campaign to the power of her Christian faith, remarking: "She said: 'We want a higher moral ground, but I'm going to hit this issue head-on'" (West and Buschendorf 2014, p. 141). In a different tone, West contrasts the steadfast, unselfish contributions of Ella Baker to those of King and narcissistic contemporary activists, describing her as "an unassuming person who helps the suppressed to help themselves" (West and Buschendorf 2014, p. 90).

West also cautions that the success of prophecy is not a smooth path. In his address to 3000 people at Riverside Church in New York City, for a 2011 event commemorating the fortieth anniversary of the 1971 riot in Attica Prison, West counseled endurance and awareness of possible defeat:

> We're going to have a new wave of truth telling. We're going to have a new wave of witness bearing. And we're going to teach the younger generation that these brothers didn't struggle in vain, just like John Brown and Nat Turner and Marcus Garvey and Martin King and Myles Horton and the others didn't. And we shall see what happens. We might get crushed, too. But you know what? Then you just go down swinging, like Ella Fitzgerald and Muhammad Ali. (Goodman and González 2011)

In concluding our discussion of pragmatism and Philosophy of Race, we turn to the connection V. Denise James draws between nineteenth century African American feminist, Anna J. Cooper and classical pragmatist William James, who also founded modern psychology as an academic discipline. James contrasts Cooper's appeal to faith with William James's, in that Cooper argued for moral grounds for belief, while James aimed to produce intellectual ones (James 2013). The way that James puts Cooper in dialogue with William James is part of a broader project of black feminist pragmatism that is visionary in engaging the social change mission of classical pragmatism (James 2009).

Existential Phenomenology and Race

Existential phenomenology has been an effective methodology for examining the experience of race from the standpoint of individuals. As such, universal structures of human consciousness are relied upon to examine relationships, reactions, and constructions of identity in societies that are already formed around pervasive racial differences and racist beliefs about them. Contemporary writers have used texts from Georg Wilhelm Friedrich Hegel (1770–1831), Jean-Paul Sartre (1905–1980), and Frantz Omar Fanon

(1925–1961) as philosophical starting points for questions about freedom. There has also been a religious tradition that resonates with the kinds of spiritual egalitarianism discussed in Chapter 2.

Hegel's description of the "master-slave" dialectic has riveted the attention of many analytic, as well as continental philosophers of race (Baur 2014; Brandom 2007; Kojève 1969; McDowell 2006; Moyar 2008; Pinkard 1994; Pippin 2010; Stern 2002; Westphal 2003, 2009). To understand this broad engagement, it helps to recall Frederick Douglass's (1818–1895) real-life encounter with the slave-breaker, Edward Covey. When he was about seventeen, Douglass was leased by his owner to work for Covey. He endured hard labor under harsh and unsympathetic conditions and after one particularly brutal beating walked seven miles to appeal to his owner to intervene. His owner sent him back to Covey, who soon after prepared to beat him, again. That was when Douglass resisted. He fought with Covey, and ended up getting the better of him. And Covey never touched him again. Douglass wrote:

> This battle with Mr. Covey was the turning-point in my career as a slave. It rekindled the few expiring embers of freedom, and revived within me a sense of my own manhood. It recalled the departed self-confidence, and inspired me again with a determination to be free… It was a glorious resurrection from the tomb of slavery to the heaven of freedom. (Douglass 1845, pp. 62–3)

What did Hegel say that gives Douglass's fight with Covey deep philosophical importance? In Chapter 4 of *Phenomenology of Spirit* or *Phenomenology of Mind*, Hegel's subject is "Lord and Bondsman," which has been interpreted as "master and slave."

> The one is independent, and its essential nature is to be for itself; the other is dependent, and its essence is life or existence for another. The former is the Master, or Lord, the latter the Bondsman. … The master is the consciousness that exists for itself … a consciousness existing on its own account which is mediated with itself through another consciousness, i.e. through another whose very nature implies that it is bound up with an independent being or with thinghood in general. … The bondsman being a self-consciousness in the broad sense, also takes up a negative attitude to things and cancels them; but the thing is, at the same time, independent for him and, in consequence, he cannot, with all his negating, get so far as to annihilate it outright and be done with it; that is to say, he merely works on it. To the master, on the other hand, by means of this mediating process, belongs the immediate relation, in the sense of the pure negation of it, in other words he gets the enjoyment.

...

In all this, the unessential consciousness is, for the master, the object which embodies the truth of his certainty of himself. But it is evident that this object does not correspond to its notion; for, just where the master has effectively achieved lordship, he really finds that something has come about quite different from an independent consciousness. ...The truth of the independent consciousness is accordingly the consciousness of the bondsman. This doubtless appears in the first instance outside itself, and not as the truth of self-consciousness. But just as lordship showed its essential nature to be the reverse of what it wants to be, so, too, bondage will, when completed, pass into the opposite of what it immediately is: being a consciousness repressed within itself, it will enter into itself, and change round into real and true independence. ... Thus precisely in labor where there seemed to be merely some outsider's mind and ideas involved, the bondsman becomes aware, through this re-discovery of himself by himself, of having and being a "mind of his own". (Hegel 1910, pp. 108–15)

In these passages (—dense, opaque, and well-mined by scholars—), Hegel describes the complexity of human recognition and domination. The lord is free but he needs the bondsman's consciousness to be aware of his freedom and that limits his freedom, because the bondsman is not free. The bondsman has the same relation to the things he works on, as the lord has to him, and he discovers his own freedom and mind, through that work.

Hegel's "master-slave analysis" is important in terms of consciousness and human relations: Consciousness of anything requires self-consciousness. Self-consciousness requires recognition from others. The lord/master requires recognition from the bondsman/slave. However, domination is not absolute, because what a dominated person does creates self-consciousness or awareness of the self. Hegel's analysis of consciousness was very influential for subsequent theorists of dominance, as well as of consciousness and human relations, more generally.

Returning to Douglass and Covey, we can see that Covey could not dominate Douglass without Douglass's cooperation—Douglass had to recognize Covey as dominating him and he had to do the work Covey ordered him to do. More than that, although Douglass describes himself as having been demoralized by his hard work and cruel treatment under Covey, he achieved enough domination over things and himself through that experience to effectively follow through with his choice to resist Covey on the day of the fight. This is not to suggest that conditions under the evils of slavery were redemptive for slaves, but it does highlight the importance of choice for psychological as well as physical freedom. Sartre constructed a philosophy of freedom in exactly that sense.

In his influential 1945 address, "Existentialism is a Humanism," Sartre presented his doctrine of absolute, universal human freedom and responsibility:

> In life, a man commits himself, draws his own portrait and there is nothing but that portrait. No doubt this thought may seem comfortless to one who has not made a success of his life. On the other hand, it puts everyone in a position to understand that reality alone is reliable; that dreams, expectations and hopes serve to define a man only as deceptive dreams, abortive hopes, and expectations unfulfilled; that is to say, they define him negatively, not positively. Nevertheless, when one says, "You are nothing else but what you live," it does not imply that an artist is to be judged solely by his works of art, for a thousand other things contribute no less to his definition as a man. . . . .[A] man is no other than a series of undertakings, that he is the sum, the organisation, the set of relations that constitute these undertakings. (Sartre 1945, p. 9)

Sartre also presented a metaphysics that supported his idea of radical freedom. In *Being and Nothingness*, he divided the world into two "regions of being," the "for-itself" or consciousness, and the "in-itself," the realm of everything that consciousness could be conscious of, including its own past states. From the standpoint of consciousness, the in-itself is inert and can have no effect on the consciousness that is conscious of it. Freedom resides in consciousness, as consciousness of something other than itself in the moment of self-awareness (Sartre 1984, 3–33). Consciousness, or the for-itself, is not a thing but a nothingness. It is this nothingness that we are, which is absolutely free and which makes us responsible for our lives. However, we are always in an historical situation that limits our choices at any given time (Sartre 1984, 127–33).

The structure of consciousness as described by Sartre allows for *bad faith*, a flight of consciousness by pretending that it is an in-itself. Failure to acknowledge our situation is one form of bad faith and pretending that our situation makes freedom impossible is another. Sartre also distinguishes between "cowards" and "swine" in types of bad faith: the coward denies and suppresses his own freedom; the swine denies and oppresses the freedom of others (Sartre 1984, 86–119). Racism exhibits bad faith, as Sartre illustrates in *Anti-Semite and Jew* with his portrait of the French anti-Semite who presents himself as "the true Frenchman":

> The true Frenchman, rooted in his province, in his country, borne along by a tradition twenty centuries old, benefiting from ancestral wisdom, guided by tried customs, does not need intelligence. His virtue depends upon the assimilation of the qualities which the work of a hundred generations has lent to the

objects which surround him; it depends on property. It goes without saying that this is a matter of inherited property, not property one buys. (Sartre 1944, p. 16)

In his 1995 *Bad Faith and Antiblack Racism*, Lewis Gordon analyzes US antiblack racism as Sartrean bad faith that constructs black people as inferior and sub-human (Gordon 1995).

Frantz Fanon approached racism from a more concrete phenomenological perspective than Sartre's, in *Black Skin, White Masks*, describing the experience of being made an object of racism by a white person:

> In the white world the man of color encounters difficulties in the development of his bodily schema.
>
> …
>
> 'Look, a Negro!' It was an external stimulus that flicked over me as I passed by. I made a tight smile.
> 'Look, a Negro!' It was true. It amused me.
> 'Look, a Negro!' The circle was drawing a bit tighter. I made no secret of my amusement.
> 'Mama, see the Negro! I'm frightened!' Frightened! Frightened! Now they were beginning to be afraid of me. I made up my mind to laugh myself to tears, but laughter had become impossible. …
> My body was given back to me sprawled out, distorted, recolored, clad in mourning in that white winter day. The Negro is an animal, the Negro is bad, the Negro is mean, the Negro is ugly; look, a nigger, It's cold, the nigger is shivering, the nigger is shivering because he is cold, the little boy is trembling because he is afraid of the nigger, the nigger is shivering with cold, that cold that goes through your bones, the handsome little boy is trembling because he thinks that the nigger is quivering with rage, the little white boy throws himself into his mother's arms: Mama, the nigger's going to eat me up. (Fanon 1952, pp. 83–6)

In these passages, Fanon discloses how his bodily freedom and agency is limited by the reaction of a white child to him—"My body was given back to me sprawled out, distorted, recolored." However, Fanon did not follow Sartre's ideal of absolute freedom in terms of black identity (a dispute that we will take up in Chapter 6).

Black religious or theological existentialism adds striving toward liberation to the black egalitarian tradition discussed in Chapter 2. As noted, in *The Philadelphia Negro*, Du Bois reported on the importance of the black church for community organization in the late nineteenth century. Black churches were centers for activism that provided refuge, through the civil rights movement. The spiritual support expressed in practical life was developed in the writings of distinctly American black existentialist philosophers. *In Black Theology and Black Power*, written after Martin Luther King Jr.'s assassination, James Cone drew on the work of both religious and atheist European existentialists to insist that God's people are all oppressed people, and in the United States, black people are oppressed. His message of revolution against white racism was based on moral teachings in the bible, but he emphasized the importance of earthly struggle:

> The free Christian man cannot be concerned about a reward in heaven. Rather, he is a man who, through the freedom granted in Christ, is ready to plunge himself into the evils of the world, revolting against all inhuman powers which enslave men. (Cone 1969, p. 125)

Dwayne Tunstall has developed religious phenomenological existentialism by engaging writings from the Christian existentialist Gabriel Honoré Marcel and from Lewis Gordon. Tunstall combines Marcel's task of participating in being and the resistance of dehumanization through Gordon's account of bad faith for an explanation of how antiblack racism results in dehumanization of blacks, globally, as well as in the United States (Tunstall 2013).

Conclusion

Both American philosophy, including pragmatism, and continental philosophy in its strain of existential phenomenology, add important dimensions of lived experience to ideas about race, which are not present in purely cognitive analyses. The American philosophical contribution is closely tied to the struggles of African American thinkers as individuals and members of a group experiencing ongoing oppression. By comparison, the continental approach in its existentialist derivation from Husserlian phenomenology may seem more theoretical, and austere in the responsibility Sartre places on individuals. However, theological existentialist perspectives have served to take up belief and faith in ways that resonate with earlier American egalitarian traditions. Thus far in our chapters, the discussion of race, overall, has either been limited to abstract social systems of race and the concrete black-white binary. To further broaden the perspective for Philosophy of Race, Chapter 5 will focus on different race-like ideas, in both the American past and other parts of the world, which nonetheless share much with the ideas dealt with thus far.

Glossary

American philosophy—work by philosophers in the United States which is nationally distinctive in **pragmatic**, method or US-related subject matter.

destiny—fate, what will necessarily happen in the future, what will happen because of some force in control of events.

existentialism—philosophical focus on human experience in existing, with attention to the structures of consciousness that enable that experience.

phenomenology—philosophical practice of describing the objects of consciousness while bracketing their existence or objectivity.

prophecy—prediction of the future, but according to Cornel West, criticism of past and present to motivate action for a better future.

pragmatism—American philosophical tradition sharing a principle that claims, concepts, and hypotheses need to be understood in terms of their consequences in reality.

rhetoric—speech of a writer or speaker aiming to educate, persuade, and motivate an audience in a particular context.

Discussion Questions

1. What do Du Bois and Husserl share in their methods and what is different?
2. What did Du Bois mean by racial destiny? Evaluate this idea.
3. How did Du Bois and Locke differ about the aims of art?
4. What does Douglass's fight with Covey mean in Hegel's terms of the master-slave relationship?
5. How do Sartre's ideas of absolute freedom apply to race?
6. Give three examples of bad faith and racism from your own experience and explain how and why they are bad faith.
7. What does Frantz Fanon's account of how others see him imply about racist societies?
8. Explain how Cornel West's idea of prophecy is about the future.
9. How is black theology different from egalitarian theology as described in Chapter 2.
10. How do you relate the treatment of race in this chapter to the scientific approaches in Chapter 3. Are they compatible?

References

Allen, Anita L. "Black Philosopher, White Academy: The Career of William Fontaine by Bruce Kuklick." *The Pennsylvania Magazine of History and Biography*, vol. 133, no. 2, Apr. 2009, pp. 213–5.

Als, Hilton. "Capturing James Baldwin's Legacy Onscreen." *New Yorker Magazine*, Feb. 13 and 20, 2017 Issue. http://www.newyorker.com/magazine/2017/02/13/capturing-james-baldwins-legacy-onscreen.

Baldwin, James, and William F. Buckley. "James Baldwin Debates William F. Buckley: Has the American Dream Been Achieved at the Expense of the American Negro?" Cambridge University, 1965, Youtube, 2012. https://www.youtube.com/watch?v=oFeoS41xe7w.

Baldwin, James, and Margaret Mead. *Rap on Race*. New York, NY: Mass Market Paperback, 1970.

Baur, Michael, editor. *G.W.F. Hegel: Key Concepts*. Abingdon: Routledge, 2014.

Brandom, Robert. 2007. "The Structure of Desire and Recognition. Self-Consciousness and Self-Constitution." *Philosophy & Social Criticism*, vol. 33, pp. 127–50.

Carter, Jacoby Adeshei. "Alain Leroy Locke." *Stanford Encyclopedia of Philosophy*, May 13, 2012. https://plato.stanford.edu/entries/alain-locke/.

Cone, James H. *Black Theology and Black Power*. Maryknoll, NY: Orbis Books, 1969.

Douglass, Frederick. *Narrative of the Life of Frederick Douglass, An American Slave: Written by Himself*, edited by Robert O'Meally. Boston: Barnes and Nobles. Published at the Anti-Slavery Office, 1845.

Du Bois, W.E. Burghardt. *The Conservation of Races*. The American Negro Academy Occasional Papers, No. 2, Washington, DC: Published by the Academy, 1897, Online Source: Project Gutenberg: www.gutenberg.org/etext/31254.

Du Bois, W.E. Burghardt. *The Souls of Black Folk: Essays and Sketches*. Chicago, IL: A. C. McClurg, 1904, 5th ed.

Du Bois, W.E.B. "The Superior Race (An Essay)." *The Smart Set: A Magazine of Cleverness*, vol. 70, no. 4, Apr. 1923, pp. 55–60. http://www.webDuBois.org/dbSuperiorRace.html.

Du Bois, W.E.B. *The Philadelphia Negro: A Social Study*, edited by E. Digby Balzell. New York, NY: Schocken Books, 1967.

Fanon, Frantz. *Black Skin, White Masks*. Translated by Charles Lam Markmann, London: MacGibbon & Kee, 1952/1968.

Fontaine, William T. "The Mind and Thought of the Negro of the United States as Revealed in Imaginative Literature, 1876–1940," Southern University Bulletin 28, Mar. 1942, pp. 5–50. See more at: http://www.blackpast.org/aah/fontaine-william-thomas-1909-1968#sthash.lMwYs3ih.dpuf.

Fontaine, William T. *Reflections on Segregation, Desegregation, Power and Morals*. Chicago, IL: Thomas, 1967.

Goodman, Amy, and Juan González. "Attica Is All of Us: Cornel West on 40th Anniversary of Attica Prison Rebellion." *Democracy Now!: A Daily Independent Global News Hour*, 2011. https://www.democracynow.org/2011/9/12/attica_is_all_of_us_cornel.

Gordon, Lewis R. *Bad Faith and Antiblack Racism*. Atlantic Highlands, NJ: Humanities Press, 1995.

Gorman, Robert A. "The Phenomenological 'Humanization' of Social Science—A Critique." *The British Journal of Sociology*, vol. 26, no. 4, Dec. 1975, pp. 389–405.

Harris, Leonard, editor. *The Philosophy of Alain Locke, Harlem Renaissance and Beyond*, Philadelphia: Temple University Press, 1989; Republished as Harris, Leonard, editor. *The Critical Pragmatism of Alain Locke*. New York: Rowman & Littlefield, 1999.

Harris, Leonard. "Looking for Alain Locke." *Oxford Handbook of Philosophy and Race*, edited by Naomi Zack, New York, NY: Oxford University Press, 2017, pp. 125–33.

Harris, Leonard, and C. Molesworth, *Alain LeRoy Locke: The Biography of a Philosopher*. Chicago, IL: Chicago University Press, 2008.

Hegel, G.W.F. *The Phenomenology of Mind*. Translated by J.B. Baillie. Mineola, NY: Dover, 1910/2003.

Husserl, Edmund. *The Crisis of European Sciences and Transcendental Philosophy*. Translated by D. Carr. Evanston, IL: Northwestern University Press, [1936/54], 1970.

James, V. Denise. "Theorizing Black Feminist Pragmatism: Forethoughts on the Practice and Purpose of Philosophy as Envisioned by Black Feminists and John Dewey." *The Journal of Speculative Philosophy*, New Series, vol. 23, no. 2, 2009, pp. 92–9.

James, V. Denise. "Reading Anna J. Cooper with William James: Black Feminist Visionary Pragmatism, Philosophy's Culture of Justification, and Belief." *The Pluralist*, vol. 8, no. 3, 2013, pp. 32–45.

Kojève, Alexandre. *Introduction to the Reading of Hegel*. Translated by J.H. Nichols, Jr., and edited by Allan Bloomed. New York: Basic Books, 1969.

Kuklick, Bruce. *Black Philosopher, White Academy: The Career of William Fontaine*. Philadelphia: University of Pennsylvania Press, 2008.

Locke, Alain, editor. *The New Negro*. New York, NY: Simon and Schuster, 1925.

Locke, Alain. "Art or Propaganda." Harlem, vol. I, no. 1, Nov. 1928, in National Humanities Center Resource Toolbox, the Making of African American Identity: Vol. III, 1917–1968. http://nationalhumanitiescenter.org/pds/maai3/protest/text10/lockeartorpropaganda.pdf.

McDowell, John. H. 2006. "The Apperceptive I and the Empirical Self: Towards a Heterodox Reading of 'Lordship and Bondage' in Hegel's Phenomenology." *Hegel: New Directions*, edited by Katerina Deligiorgi. Chesham: Acumen, pp. 33–48.

Morris, Aldon. *The Scholar Denied: W.E.B. Du Bois and the Birth of Modern Sociology*. Berkeley, CA: University of California Press, 2015.

Moyar, Dean, and Michael Quante, editors. *Hegel's Phenomenology of Spirit: A Critical Guide*. Cambridge: Cambridge University Press, 2008.

Pinkard, Terry. *Hegel's Phenomenology: The Sociality of Reason*. Cambridge: Cambridge University Press, 1994.

Pippin, Robert R. *Hegel on Self-Consciousness: Desire and Death in the Phenomenology of Spirit*. Princeton: Princeton University Press, 2010.

Sartre, Jean-Paul. "Existentialism Is a Humanism." *Existentialism and Humanism*, academia.edu, edited by P. Mairet. New Haven, CT: Yale University Press, 1945. http://s3.amazonaws.com/academia.edu.documents/4716326/sartre.pdf?AW-SAccessKeyId=AKIAIWOWYYGZ2Y53UL3A&Expires=1497380852&Signature=ddEEfmeuOiVCOtoHsuisbsJ3dBE%3D&response-content-disposition=inline%3B%20filename%3DExistentialism_is_a_Humanism.pdf.

Sartre, Jean-Paul. *Being and Nothingness*. Translated by Hazel E. Barnes, New York, NY: Gallimard, 1943/1946/1984.

Sartre, Jean-Paul. *Anti-semite and Jew*. Translated by George J. Becker. New York, NY: Schocken Books, 1944/1948.

Schulenberg, Ulf. "Speaking Out of the Most Passionate Love"—James Baldwin and Pragmatism." *European Journal of American studies* [Online], 2–2|2007, document 3, Online Since 5 November 2007, Connection on 12 June 2017. http://ejas.revues.org/1333.

Shenk, Timothy. "Booked #4: What Did Race Mean to W.E.B. Du Bois?" (Interview with Kwame Anthony Appiah About His book, *Lines of Descent: W.E.B. Du Bois and the Emergence of Identity*. Cambridge, MA: Harvard University Press, 2014.) *Dissent*, May 7, 2015.

Stern, Robert. *Routledge Philosophy Guidebook to Hegel and the Phenomenology of Spirit*. London: Routledge, 2002.

Tunstall, Dwayne. *Doing Philosophy Personally: Thinking About Metaphysics, Theism, and Antiblack Racism*. New York, NY: Fordham University Press, 2013.

West, Cornel. *Prophesy Deliverance!: An Afro-American Revolutionary Christianity*. Philadelphia, PA: The Westminster Press, 1982.

West, Cornel. *Keeping Faith: Philosophy and Race in America*. New York, NY: Routledge, 1993.

West, Cornel with Christa Buschendorf. *Black Prophetic Fire*. Boston, MA: Beacon Press, 2014.

West, Cornel. "Dr. Cornel West: Official Website." http://www.cornelwest.com/index.html#.VRjkU7l0zcs. Accessed Mar. 29, 2015.

Westphal, Kenneth R. *Hegel's Epistemology: A Philosophical Introduction to the Phenomenology of Spirit*. Indianapolis: Hackett, 2003.

Westphal, Kenneth R., editor. *The Blackwell Guide to Hegel's Phenomenology of Spirit*. Oxford: Blackwell, 2009.

5

Ethnicity and Related Forms of Race

If we put aside the polite social practice of using the word "ethnicity" as a euphemism for "race," we can begin with a distinction that ethnicity refers mainly to culture, whereas race refers to hereditary physical traits. Both ethnicity and race are passed on in families, although in different ways. People are believed to physically inherit their racial traits. By contrast, ethnic traits are taught and learned, usually from relatives and others in a community. This cultural aspect of ethnicity is both cause and effect of American **ethnic enclaves** or neighborhoods where one group has a dominant presence. Places called Little Italy, China Town, Spanish Harlem, Little Persia, or Greektown are some examples, but so are Andersonville, Illinois where Swedish immigrants settled and the Germantowns in Pennsylvania.

Ideas of race sometimes overlap with ideas of ethnicity. For instance, many Hispanic/Latinx Americans believe that despite their official classification as an ethnicity, they are treated as members of a nonwhite race. Also, historically in the United States, immigrants who were first identified as members of nonwhite races, such as Italian, Irish, Polish, and Jewish people became re-identified as racially white, over several generations of **assimilation**. There are other complexities: Jews are now considered primarily a religious group, although it is assumed that they also have a distinct ethnicity; African Americans are considered primarily a racial group, although it is assumed they also have a distinct ethnicity. Ethnicity as related to race becomes even more complex if we compare ideas of human difference globally, such as socioeconomic and mixed-race notions of race in Brazil, and

© The Author(s) 2018
N. Zack, *Philosophy of Race*, Palgrave Philosophy Today,
https://doi.org/10.1007/978-3-319-78729-9_5

caste in India. Also, indigenous identities are neither racial nor ethnic, although they resemble both.

Ethnicity is close enough to race, conceptually, to merit discussion of ideas of ethnicity in the same context as discussion of ideas of race. Therefore, to complete this Part I discussion of ideas of race, this chapter will be devoted to three interrelated topics: ethnicity and US immigration; global race-like ideas; indigenous identities.

Ethnicity and US Immigration

Diversity of Ethnic Groups

There are thousands of ethnic groups in the world, set apart by custom, appearance, language, culture, religion, history, ancestry, or geographical location. In 2003, political scientist James Fearon prepared a list of 822 ethnic and "ethnoreligious" groups that made up at least one percent of the population in 160 countries in the early 1990s (Fearon 2003). The US Census lists 92 ancestry groups for Americans in 2015, according to income (ranging from about $100,000 to $22,000) (see Table 5.1).

The international lists based on 1% of populations and the US Census lists based on income undoubtedly leave out many groups. For instance, in the New York City public school system alone, the Department of

Table 5.1 US ethnic groups (US Census 2015)

Indian, Taiwanese, Filipino, Australian, European, Russian, Greek, Lebanese, Croatian, Latvian, Lithuanian, Austrian, Iranian, Slovene, Swiss, Bulgarian, Romanian, Scandinavian, Italian, Japanese, British, Chinese, (including Taiwanese), Serbian, Belgian, Scottish, Welsh, Polish, Chinese (excluding Taiwanese), Slovak, Danish, Czechoslovakian, Swedish, Norwegian, Syrian, Czech, Hungarian, Ukrainian, Finnish, German, English, Palestinian, French Canadian, Portuguese, Irish, Albanian, Canadian, Slavic, Pakistani, Nigerian, Scotch-Irish, Indonesian, Dutch, Egyptian, French, Turkish, Armenian, Ghanaian, Vietnamese, Yugoslavian, Korean, Guyanese, British West Indian, Brazilian, Barbadian, Arab, Laotian, Thai, Cambodian, West Indian, Cajun, Trinidadian and Tobagonian, Assyrian/Chaldean/Syriac, Pennsylvania German, Jamaican, Cape Verdean, Hmong, Haitian, Jordanian, Moroccan, Nepali, Bangladeshi, Afghan, Sub saharan African, Bahamian, Ethiopian African, Arab/Arabic Burmese, Iraqi, Somali (United States Census Bureau 2015)
There are also subgroups, such as these 12 Native American tribes (again listed in order of average income ranging from about $49,000 to $29,000):
Chickasaw, Choctaw, Alaska Natives, Creek, Iroquois, Cherokee, Blackfeet, Chippewa Lumbee, Navajo, Sioux, Apache (United States Census Bureau 2015)

Education reports that in 2013, 41% of all students or 438,131 were English-Language Learners (ELLs), leading to a count of 160 different languages spoken in the K-12 population (NYC Department of Education 2013). It seems safe to assume that the ELLs in New York City come to school from homes in which languages other than English are spoken. Language is one (if not the main one) of the indicators of ethnicity.

Definitions and Constructions of Ethnicity

There are two approaches to defining "ethnic group." The first and straightforward definition is to take the reality of ethnic groups as what the term is about, which leads to the standard dictionary definition: "A community or population made up of people who share a common cultural background or descent" (Oxford English Dictionary 2017).

However, as Fearon points out about his list of 822 ethnic groups in 160 countries, most researchers continue to identify ethnic groups based on the methods used by Soviet ethnographers in the 1960s, first published as *Atlas Narodov*. In that work, language was the main factor used to define ethnic groups, but some groups had racial traits also and others, for instance, Anglo-Canadians in the United States, were defined by national origin. Subsequent researchers have identified some groups by **ethnic fractionalization**, which occurs when groups are excluded or oppressed. **Primordialist** researchers believe that ethnic groups have fixed biological traits or deeply historical cultural traits; **constructivists** or **instrumentalists** view ethnic groups as "contingent, fuzzy, and situational." Fearon also points out that without a rigid and perhaps arbitrary standard based on numbers or the percentage of a larger population, identifying ethnic groups is arbitrary. Even census categories do not solve this problem:

> If we consult official census categories, we get three "races" - white, African American, and Asian - and an additional group, Hispanic, which the government emphatically declares is "not a race." Is this the right list for the United States? Why disaggregate Hispanic into Puerto Rican Americans, Cuban Americans, Americans, and so on, or likewise for Asian? Why not distinguish between Americans, Irish Americans, Italian Americans, German Americans, and so on? And should we use the current census categories, when earlier censuses formulated categories quite differently? (Fearon 2003, pp. 196–7)

The methodological problems identified by Fearon are related to the second approach to defining ethnicity, which even goes beyond constructivism or instrumentalism or ideas that the realities of ethnic groups are relative to wider social, political, and economic factors external to the groups themselves. This is a view that the very idea of ethnicity and ethnic groups is an **invention**, a new kind of social technology, prompted by historical events and imposed on people who would not otherwise have been ethnic groups. One striking example of such an invention is the US Census Hispanic/ Latino category that includes a diversity of groups from Central and South America, but not Spaniards from Spain, although Spain is the national origin of the language spoken throughout most groups in this ethnic category. The Hispanic/Latino census category includes US residents from: Puerto Rico, Mexico, Cuba, Argentina, and Brazil and all other countries in South America. While many US residents from Cuba and Argentina might identify as racially white, those with other Hispanic/Latino backgrounds are not perceived as white and in most cases view themselves as people of color. So not only is this census category somewhat arbitrary in lumping distinct groups together, but it is not a purely ethnic category, as census forms stipulate.

Linda Alcoff has suggested that the concept of *ethnorace* is a fruitful way to understand the experience of Hispanic/Latino Americans, because it is less static than race and allows for the interchangeability of ideas of race and ideas of ethnicity (Alcoff 2000). Indeed, researchers at the Census began considering revisions of how to count the Hispanic/Latino group more accurately, thereby implicitly acknowledging that the addition of the category in 1970 was an invention (Haub 2012).

The idea of ethnic groups as invented is closely related to ideas that racial groups have been invented. (The historical account of scientific ideas of race in Chapter 3 supports that view for traditional biological racial categories.) The invention of race is not a relic of the distant past and as a contemporary process, it overlaps with inventions of ethnicity. Falguni Sheth has discussed new forms of racial identity imposed on Middle Eastern and North African (MENA) immigrants by the US government in the post-9/11 United States (Sheth 2017). The newly intense focus on members of these groups as threats to national security has been accompanied by a sense that they can be identified by physical appearance. That is a form of **racialization**, even though racist hate crimes have been triggered by articles of clothing, which are clearly forms of ethnicity, as ethnicity has been traditionally understood (Muslim Advocates 2017). Although members of MENA groups have been officially categorized as racially white, the US Census in 2015 began considering a separate classification for this population. Such reclassification would be a double-edged sword. On the one hand, it would provide a mechanism for resistance against discrimination based on a recognized identity, but on the other hand, it could draw MENA individuals further into government surveillance and record keeping, as well as intensify racism against them (Karoub 2015).

The Invention of Traditional US Ethnic Groups and Immigration

The idea that ethnicity and ethnic groups are invented applies not only to contemporary formations, but to many long-settled US immigration groups. Werner Sollers, in introducing his 1989 anthology, *The Invention of Ethnicity*, writes:

> It is not any a priori [before experience] cultural *difference* that makes ethnicity. 'The Chinese laundryman does not learn his trade in China; there are no laundries in China.' This the Chinese immigrant Lee Chew asserts in Hamilton Holt's *Life Stories of Undistinguished Americans* (1906). (Sollers 1989, p. xvi)

Ethnic groups are not identified by outsiders or themselves as mere varieties of human diversity to be neutrally united under common labels. There are always factors and social forces external to groups, which result in their being named and described as ethnic groups. And this is a more basic way in which ethnic groups are invented, because it is deeper than questions of how to divide or individuate ethnic groups and what the criteria for ethnic groups are—it brings ethnic groups into existence.

In the United States, the strongest factor in the invention of ethnicity has been immigration and social forces have included need for workers, concerns about national identity by dominant groups, concerns about job loss by established residents, outright prejudice and zenophobia, hatred and fear. These forces have influenced immigration policy and laws that have resulted in new arrivals beginning multigenerational lives in the United States, as members of ethnic groups. In their countries of origin, they were not distinguished from other residents as "ethnic groups," although they may have been persecuted on religious or political grounds. In the United States, it would not have been necessary to identify them as ethnic groups if they effortlessly blended in with more settled groups who were already considered full Americans. The invention of ethnic groups was also the invention of the value of assimilation. The great waves of immigration to the United States occurred in the nineteenth and twentieth centuries. For each new immigrant group, those groups already in residence had created the dominant and normal culture to which they were expected, and strove, to assimilate (Powell 2005).

Immigration Law and Ethnicity

The bare history of immigration law tells its own story about the invention of American ethnic groups. From the colonial period to the early nineteenth century (1620–1820), most arrivals were from Great Britain (England, Ireland, Scotland, and Wales), France, the Netherlands, and the Palatinate region of Southwest Germany. From 1820 to 1880, about fifteen million of those who came to be called "old immigrants" arrived from Sweden, Norway, Denmark, what is now the Czech Republic, and Northern Ireland. They settled in families in the rural Northeast and Midwest. A small number of single Chinese men also arrived to the West Coast, usually to hostile reception by whites. After about 300,000 Chinese men had arrived, Congress passed the Chinese Exclusion Act in 1882 and further Chinese immigration was banned. From 1880 to 1920, the largest wave yet, about twenty-five million people, arrived from Eastern and Southern Europe on great steamships from Italy, Russia, Greece, Hungary, and Poland. Most in this wave were single adults who became the labor pool for factories in urban American, through World War II.

After 1924, Congress began to limit the numbers of immigrants from Europe and new arrivals were screened for skills in manual labor and the professions or family relations to US citizens. The Immigration Act of 1924 imposed quotas of 2% of the same group already residing in the United States, for each immigrant group. The civil rights movement of the 1960s ushered in the 1965 Hart-Celler Immigration and Nationality Act. Quotas were rescinded but there was a cap of 170,000 visas a year. Occupational and familial preferences from the 1924 act were retained, but restrictions due to "race, sex, place of birth or place of residence" were outlawed. New immigrants from Korea, China, India, Pakistan, the Philippines, South and Central America, and Africa, began to arrive. From 1990 to 2000, foreign-born American residents increased almost 60%, to over 31 million. Most of the new immigrants in the late twentieth century were from Asia, South America, and the Caribbean, while the number of European immigrants markedly decreased (Cornell University 2017).

To get a sense of what has been considered successful immigration, brief accounts of the collective experiences of the dominant Anglo-population and Germans, Irish, Italians, and Jews in the United States will help flesh out the legal account.

US Immigrant Groups: White Anglo-Saxon Protestant, German, Irish-Catholic, Italian, and Jewish

White Anglo-Saxon Protestant Americans

Anglo-American Protestant groups, including those from England, Scotland, Wales, Northern Ireland, Canada, Australia, New Zealand, and the Isle of Man have dominated US culture and major institutions since colonial times. After English Puritans arrived at Plymouth Rock on the *Mayflower* in 1620, 80,000 English settled in Virginia, Maryland, Massachusetts, Connecticut, and Rhode Island, by 1742 (Klein 2000). They displaced those preceding them, the Dutch, Native Americans, and Spaniards. There were 20 indentured servants on the *Mayflower* and in 1619 the governor of Jamestown had imported twenty African slaves who had been pirated from a slave-trading Portuguese ship (Hawshaw 2007, pp. xv–xvi).

Over the next 150 years, English customs, speech, dress, and aspects of folk culture came to dominate US society in New England, the South, mid-Atlantic states, and the Southwest (Fischer 1989). English law and representative government were expressed in the US Constitution and Bill of Rights (Haft 1995, pp. 472–8). Restraint in display and recreation and the nuclear family structure were also part of the ensuing **WASP** (White Anglo-Saxon Protestant) ideal to which other immigrants or ethnic groups assimilated.

Before the Revolutionary War, Americans bought about 25% of British exports of finished goods, many of which were luxuries purchased on credit, such as fabrics, tea, fancy clothes, and fine furniture (Breen 2004, p. 185). Both the Revolutionary War and the War of 1812 with England interrupted commerce. But soon after, English foreign investment developed US land, industry, railroads, mining, and cattle ranching. Eight of the first ten American presidents were English and English Americans became a plurality (greater in number than any other group) in executive, legislative, and judicial branches of government (Haft 1995, pp. 475–6). From 1997 to

2006, 13,000 British persons immigrated to the United States each year, of which over 8000 became citizens (Klein 2000). Assimilation was never a problem for individual English immigrants. The US and the UK governments were allies during World Wars I and II, the Cold War, and the first Gulf War, as well as in post-9/11 military actions in Afghanistan and Iraq (Haft 1995, p. 476).

The Scots-Irish, or Ulster Irish descended from 200,000 Scottish lowland Presbyterians, who the English government settled in Northern Ireland, during the 1600s. Upon their first arrival in New England in 1717, they were considered "illiterate, slovenly, and filthy" and themselves "nurtured a profound hatred for the English." But they were fully assimilated by the late 1700s (McLemore and Romo 2005, pp. 63–4). Distinct from this group were the Scots, many of whom were prisoners taken during the English Civil War or criminals sent to work on tobacco plantations in South Carolina, where they were a third of the state population by the 1790 census (Dobson 1994, pp. 4–5). Scots continued to arrive throughout the nineteenth century, often in clans who settled in West Virginia, Kentucky, and Tennessee. (The Hatfield—McCoy feud in the Tug River Valley between West Virginia and Kentucky achieved national notoriety during the 1880s.) Almost 5 million Americans claimed Scots ancestry in 2000 (Rice 1982; Hess 1995, pp. 1204–5).

Welsh explorers were reported to have predated Columbus in the United States. Welsh history and myths about twelfth-century Welsh contact with American Indians motivated eighteenth-century immigration to the United States (Heimlich 1995, pp. 1408–11; Curran 2010, pp. 21–36). Since colonial times, Welsh immigrants were welcomed because they were skilled workers. By 2008, 6% of Americans claimed Welsh ancestry and almost twice as many have Welsh surnames, including African Americans (Welsh-American 2008).

Manx have immigrated from the Isle of Man, a land mass of 227 square miles, equidistant from Ireland, Scotland, and Whales. In 2006, the US resident population of Manx was about 80,000, of which 38,000 were born on the Isle of Man (Isle of Man Digest 2011). There were two major waves of Australian and New Zealand immigration, the 1849–50 California gold rush drew up to 8000 and after World War II, 11,650 immigrated, many of whom were new wives of US servicemen who had been stationed in the South Pacific (Parkin 1980, p. 163).

Canadians have immigrated and assimilated easily compared to other groups. There are at present about 500–800,000 Canadians living in the United States (Klein 2000; Fedunkiw 1995, p. 244).

German Americans

Americans with German ancestry number over 40 million, the most numerous US ethnic group, who by the twenty-first century were mostly third generation or later (US Census "Quick Facts" 2010). Until the twentieth century, German-Americans were not fully assimilated, but retained their distinct social institutions, including newspapers (almost 1000 by 1900), political groups, and singing societies (30 in San Francisco in 1890) (Bergquist 2005). But international politics intervened. Germany was a US enemy during World War I and the political fallout included anti-German propaganda in the United States, which accelerated German-American assimilation. The German-American National Alliance, representing German interests in the United States, dissolved under congressional pressure and the number of German organizations, including newspapers, quickly shrank. During the 1930s before World War II and over the war, 11,000 German Americans were **interned**, or removed from the West and East coasts and relocated to over 50 closed "camps" throughout the United States and Hawaii. But the patriotism of German Americans was generally unquestioned and many fought in the US military. Two twentieth-century US Presidents had German ancestry: Herbert Hoover, who served after World War I and Dwight D. Eisenhauer, who served after World War II (Carlson 2003; Kazal 2004; Schaefer 2011, pp. 165–6). After World War II, English-speaking German immigrants have been able to assimilate immediately, including over 100,000 who arrived to the United States from 1990 to 2010 (Homeland Security 2010; Harzig 2008).

Irish-Catholic Americans

Researchers believe that the 39 million Irish-Americans are descended from the 3.2 million Roman Catholic "potato famine Irish," who arrived in the United States from 1841 to 1890, to settle on the East Coast (US Census "Quick Facts" 2010). Many were peasants, escaping starvation and English economic and political oppression. About 40% of those who traveled below deck, in *steerage*, died enroute. There were large numbers of young single women who worked in domestic service and became school teachers throughout the country (Ireland Story 1998; Schaefer 2008).

Nineteenth-century Irish-Catholics immigrants were not accepted as white, but viewed as an inferior racial group. Samuel F.B. Morse, inventor of the telegraph, in 1834 published *A Foreign Conspiracy Against the Liberties of the United States*, vilifying the Irish as illiterate and claiming that the Pope was planning to move the Vatican to the Mississippi River Valley. In *Awful Disclosures*, Maria Monk's 1836 best seller, paranoia was combined with pornography in a fantastical account of intercourse between nuns and priests and infanticide in a Montreal convent. By the Civil War, Irish gangs or "fire companies," were attacking African Americans as their competitors for jobs; they also resisted their draft to the Union side, particularly during the "Draft Riots of 1863" (Members of some fire companies later participated in the Fenian movement for Irish independence.) (Kenny 2000, pp. 124–7).

Following Ireland's independence from Britain in 1921, Irish-Americans asserted themselves as superior to Italian, Polish, and Slovak Roman Catholic immigrants, as well as blacks (Ignatiev 1995; Schaefer 2008). Through the **patronage system** (election winners distribute the spoils of office to those who organized their victories), Irish Americans became well represented in police and fire departments in New York City, Boston, Chicago, and other places. The Irish became regarded as racially white and became more inclusive. Saint Patrick's Day is now celebrated throughout the United States, without much regard for the real "Irishness" of participants (Blessing 1980, pp. 529–39, 545).

Italian Americans

About 16 million Americans claim Italian descent, or almost 6% of the population (US Census "Quick Facts" 2010). Italians had explored the New World before Italy became a united country in 1860: In the fifteenth and sixteenth centuries, Cristoforo Colombo, Giovanni Cabotto, Amerigo Vespucci, and Giovanni de Verranzano all explored and charted parts of what would be the United States; Father Marcos da Nizza explored Arizona. There were Italian glass bead makers in Jamestown, silk producers in Georgia, and landowners in Maryland. Philippo Mazzei, a Tuscan physician, shared his interest in agricultural science with his neighbor, Thomas Jefferson. Fifty Italians fought in the Revolutionary War. The 14,000 Italians in the United States before the Civil War were artisans, artists, teachers, musicians, and political refugees. Constantino Brumidi painted frescoes in the Capitol rotunda from 1852 to 1877 and Antonio Meucci, from Florence, invented a version of the telephone 26 years ahead of Alexander Graham Bell; the first Italian church in the United States was founded in 1866, in New York City. Despite such cultural contributions, skin color discrimination against Italians was virulent in the South throughout the nineteenth century, including segregation, attempts to substitute Italian laborers for slaves, and lynchings (Parillo 2008; Candeloro 1992, pp. 1173–4).

About 5 million Italians arrived between 1880 and 1920, from Sicily and parts of the impoverished *Mezzogiorno*, east and south of Rome. They came for *pane e lavoro* (bread and work) and many were single males, who returned to Italy. After the Depression of the 1930s and the reign of Benito Mussolini in Italy, Italian immigration to the United States slowed, but it picked up again after World War II. Italians immigrants often came in clans and settled near neighbors from Italy, in Philadelphia, New Orleans, New York, and Boston. Culture was based on *famiglia* and the Church, including many festivals throughout the year. There had not been a strong tradition of education in the *Mezzogiorno* and upward mobility did not occur until the third and fourth generations. Early generations worked at unskilled jobs and in family-owned and run restaurants, shoe repair shops, barbershops, and dry and green groceries. Job security came after successful union organizing, including: the International Laborers' Union, the Amalgamated Clothing Workers Union, the Garment Workers Union, and the Teamsters Union. Italian organizations included The Order of the Sons of Italy of America, which had thousands of lodges, and many newspapers of which *It Progresso Italo-Americano* endured the longest (Parillo 2008; Klein 2008; Candeloro 1992).

The impression of America that Italian immigrants formed during such times were not optimistic about their assimilation to the mainstream. This partly accounts for the Italian American presence in organized crime and the sensationalization of those activities, in the media and popular entertainment depended on their identity as a distinctive group. However, most researchers now agree that criminal stereotyping and suspicion of Italian-Americans is unjust and impedes their progress in politics, as well as business. Third- and fourth-generation Italian-Americans are well represented in the professions and by 2000, their median family income was higher than the national median. As assimilated generations moved to the suburbs and generally assumed a white racial identity, "Little Italy" disappeared from many American cities. Italian-American marriage outside the group is 40%, the average for white European immigrant groups in the United States (Guglielmo and Salerno 2003; US Census "Qucik Facts" 2010; Klein 2008; Candeloro 1992).

Jewish Americans

Forty percent of Jews in the world live in the United States (Israel has only 20%, making up 80% of its population). Jewish Americans are now a small, religiously identified ethnic minority, who have been very successful in American secular society in politics, the arts, academia, law, medicine, and the media. Until the end of World War II, Jews were considered a racial group, although there are no uniform physical traits shared by all Jews. Most Jews in the United States have Northern and Eastern European ancestry, but there are also Jews from the Mediterranean region and North Africa. One-third of all Jewish-Americans have no religious affiliation and do not observe Jewish religious practices (The term *Judaization* refers to shared culture and history, as a basis of Jewish identity.) (Porter 2008; Shapiro 1992). After World War II, and the Nazi attempt to exterminate all Jews, suggestions that Jews are racially nonwhite have been viewed as anti-Semitic. Almost all American Jews now identify as white Americans (Brodkin 1998).

In 1654, twenty-three Jews first arrived in New Amsterdam from Brazil. Spanish- and Portuguese-speaking Jewish immigrants, known as "Sephardim," were part of a **diaspora** following the fifteenth- and sixteenth-century expulsion of Jews from Spain and Portugal. With help from "kindred congregations" in Central and South America and Europe, they built synagogues in New York and Newport. Colonial Sephardim were joined by "Ashkenazim," German-speaking Jews from central Europe and Poland, who also spread **Yiddish**, a spoken language, based on Middle High German and other European languages, Hebrew, and Aramaic. During the colonial period, Sephardic and Ashkenazi Jews intermarried and also interacted with the Anglo establishment, to tolerable degrees. For example, Mordecai Noah (1785–1851) was born in Philadelphia of a mixed Jewish family and served as US consul in Tunis. He later entered politics in support of the Anti-Catholic Native American party and published a Whig newspaper, *The Evening* Star (Goran 1980, pp. 571–4).

Ashkenazi Jews who arrived from 1830 to 1880 considered the Orthodox Ashkenazi-Sephardic alliance too lax, religiously, and they established separate congregations. German Jews who arrived before the Civil War settled throughout the United States, often working as artisans and merchants; many followed the westward demand for manufactured goods, as distributors, retailers, and peddlers. By 1859, there were 141 wholesale firms with Jewish names in New York City, alone. The mid-nineteenth century group of 100,000–200,000 German mercantile Jews quickly became middle class. By the time of the Civil War, 160 places in the United States had forms of Jewish community life, including Cincinnati, New Orleans, and San Francisco. Ordained rabbis began to arrive in the 1840s, but efforts to establish a **synod**, or general organization of clergy, with a standard prayer book, and uniform guiding principles of a religion for American Jews, failed (Goran 1980, pp. 576–8, quote cited p. 578).

From 1884 to 1924, one-third of the Jews in Eastern Europe emigrated as a result of religious persecution, political oppression, expulsion, and economic displacement; About 2 million came to the United States, from

Russia, Lithuania, the Ukraine, Galicia, Hungary, and Romania. Most were young skilled workers, often in the clothing trades. They settled in major east coast cities in crowded enclaves and thrived culturally, establishing a Yiddish theater and literary tradition, as well as the modern motion picture industry. The established German Jewish community supported them in philanthropic projects. The first generation of the Eastern European wave did not assimilate as readily as had mid-nineteenth-century German Jews. But through education, the second and further generations entered the professions and became successful entrepreneurs, labor leaders, and socialist political activists.

In the early twentieth century, some mainstream Americans reacted to Jewish financial success and political radicalism with virulent anti-Semitism that did not distinguish between Eastern European Jews and the already established German Jews. All Jews were accused of being clannish, vulgar, greedy, physically inferior, and so forth. American Jews supported the Jews remaining in Eastern Europe during World War I, who were subject to famine, expulsion, and **pogroms** (violent attacks on Jewish communities). The American-Jewish Joint Distribution Committee (JDC) raised $60 million between 1914 and 1922. As anti-Semitism increased in Germany, mirrored by the German-American Bund in the United States, 150,000 German Jews sought refuge in the United States during the 1930s, including Albert Einstein. Between 1939 and 1945, the JDC sent $80 million to Europe, but it could not stem the tide of the Nazi holocaust in which 6 million Jews were killed; 550,000 American Jews served in the US armed forces during World War II. After the war, Jewish Americans continued to prosper and by the 1970s were no longer subject to explicit, organized anti-Semitism (Goran 1980, pp. 586–97).

The Present and Future of American Ethnic Groups

This brief account of the historical experiences of American groups suggests that assimilation to dominant Anglo-American culture has involved opposition and struggle for successful groups. But dominance at one time may not be permanent. The 2016 US presidential campaign revealed economic and social dissatisfaction within the parts of the WASP group who did not have college degrees (Tyson and Maniam 2016). That same year, in *Hill Billy Elegy: A Memoir of a Family and Culture in Crisis*, J.D. Vance described contemporary descendants of the Scots-Irish population from Kentucky and Ohio, as economically marginal and pessimistic about their place in twenty-first-century society (Vance 2016).

Scholars differ about whether the new immigrant/ethnic groups who have arrived since the late twentieth century will go through the same processes of assimilation as those who immigrated earlier. Sociologists Richard Alba and Victor Nee are optimistic that past patterns will in time repeat (Alba and Nee 2005). However, new MENA immigrants face problems of post-9/11 suspicion and fears of terrorism that were not as widespread and intense, earlier. And undocumented immigrants from Central America, especially Mexico, have been targeted by changes in enforcement policy and political promises of "building a wall" under President Donald Trump's administration. In addition, Moslem religious affiliation and practice among MENA immigrants and a general racialization of Hispanic/Latino immigrants have come up against new expressions of American White Christian Nationalism, during and after the 2016 political campaign (Gidda 2016).

The other side of mainstream establishment barriers to assimilation of immigrants after 1990 is that electronic communications and air travel make it easier for them to maintain ties with relations in places of origin. Many members of these groups find it simple to send money and consumer items back to their countries of origin and ongoing contact supports retention of their original cultural identities (Rebala 2015). Their incentive to assimilate may be further weakened by hate crimes against members of their groups, US government suspicion, and general feelings of alienation outside of cosmopolitan urban centers.

Indigenous Identities

Indigenous identities throughout the world are based on perspectives and values at odds with Western ideas of race and ethnicity. This is evident in self-descriptions by contemporary Native Americans and Australian and New Zealand aboriginals.

Native Americans

The United States is commonly referred to as "a nation of immigrants," meaning that it is a nation of foreigners and their descendants, who voluntarily came here. However, Native Americans who were here well before European and Asian immigrants and blacks who were brought as slaves were not immigrants in this sense. African American ideas about human identity, race, and ethnicity have not differed radically from white ideas.

Their main ambition has not involved resisting taxonomies of race and ethnicity but demanding justice and equality within systems regulated by those taxonomies. Some of those aims and aspirations were discussed in Chapter 2 and more will be considered in Part II. However, Native Americans and other indigenous peoples have concepts of human identity and origins that are radically different from Euro-American views of both race and ethnicity. These differences are evident in the story of "Kennewick Man."

Kennewick Man

Human remains were found when the Columbia River in Kennewick, Washington, flooded in 1996. Anthropologist James Chatters identified a middle-aged man with "caucasoid" features who lived about 9300 years ago. Chatters thought that these remains, dubbed "Kennewick Man" confirmed hypotheses that a European group had arrived in the Americas before North Asians who were the ancestors of modern Native Americans. The age of Kennewick Man brought the skeleton under the jurisdiction of the Native American Graves Protection and Repatriation Act of 1990 and the Army Corp of Engineers removed it to a secure vault in the Burke Museum. Representatives of the Umatilla Indians, tribes in Oregon, Washington, and Idaho claimed Kennewick Man for reburial and Chatters and colleagues sued for possession or access to the skeleton for further research (Zimmerman and Clinton 1999).

Armand Minthorn, representing the Umatillas claimed that the age of the skeleton alone established it as Native American. He said:

> If this individual is truly over 9,000 years old, that only substantiates our belief that he is Native American. From our oral histories, we know that our people have been part of this land since the beginning of time. We do not believe that our people migrated here from another continent, as the scientists do.
>
> We also do not agree with the notion that this individual is Caucasian. Scientists say that because the individual's head measurements does not match ours, he is not Native American. We believe that humans and animals change over time to adapt to their environment. And, our elders have told us that Indian people did not always look the way we look today. (Minthorn 2014)

How does this dispute show a radical difference in ideas about human biological diversity? Although in calling Kennewick Man "caucasoid," anthropologists later clarified that they were not making a racial designation, but were applying a typology, which the Umatilla Indians regarded as irrelevant to their heritage. The scientists based lineage on **phenotypical** (visible bodily) resemblance, whereas the Umatilla Indians based lineage on place of residence. If Kennewick man had resided where they believed their ancestors had always resided, then he was their ancestor, a member of their tribal nation. The question of whether modern Native Americans had in time changed in appearance is not at odds with scientific theories of evolutionary adaptation. But the importance of place of origin for determining what scientists would consider membership in a race or population is of primary importance in the indigenous meaning of identity. Place of ancestry alone, rather than visible traits, is thus the basis for Native American group identities. Place of ancestry played an important role in the history of modern scientific ideas about race, but this was based on observable human traits of inhabitants in distinct places and not on those places alone.

There are more modern ways of determining ancestry than skeleton appearance, for instance, whether Kennewick Man's DNA more closely matches the DNA of Umatilla Indians or Europeans. Also, both groups seem to have assumed that Kennewick man was a reproducing member of the ancestral population of contemporary Umatilla Indians. But even if he were European, Kennewick man may have been an interloper and not part of the Umatilla ancestral lineage. Umatillas might have been there before he arrived.

In September 2014, Douglas Owsley, Smithsonian physical anthropologist reported his findings, based on **morphology**, that the skeleton was related to Pacific groups such as the Ainu and Polynesians. But in June 2015, Eske Willersley and colleagues from the University of Copenhagen published findings from sequencing the genome of Kennewick Man and comparing DNA from a hand bone to worldwide genomic data that included the Ainu and Polynesians. Willersley et al. concluded that Kennewick Man is most closely related to modern Native Americans. In February 2017, Kennewick Man, who the Umatillas called "The Ancient One," was returned to the Umatilla Indians by the Burke Museum, which had curated the remains, as a neutral party. Kennewick man was buried by Umatilla Indians in a private ceremony at an undisclosed place (Burke Museum 2017).

Australian and New Zealand Aboriginals

Indigenous inhabitants of Australia were called "Aboriginals," after 1830 when white settlers took their name of "Australians" for themselves. Similar to the Umatilla Indians, they do not have an internal idea of race or racial typologies, but have identified themselves based on family relations, rather than place. Contemporary aboriginals have more parents and grandparents who are not aboriginal than those who are aboriginal. However, this widespread family genealogy of mixture does not interfere with aboriginal identity, because that identity is based on kinship culture. In the early 1970s, aboriginal leaders collaborated with the Commonwealth Department of Aboriginal Affairs to define Aboriginals based on three main factors: family descent from Aboriginal ancestors, self-identification as Aboriginal, and acceptance by the Aboriginal community as an Aboriginal person. In this sense, aboriginals in both Australia and New Zealand emphasize connectedness—in contrast to Euro-American racial identities, which apply to individuals, aboriginal identities derive from being part of aboriginal collectives.

Maori people in New Zealand call the ongoing process of communication about descent and culture, "whakapapa." Reference to ancestral and contemporary places over time is an important part of what is shared, as is language and the recognition of language groups the same and different from one's own. Bill Gammage has recently shown how aboriginal Australians had complex ecological practices that contributed to the nature of the land in modern Australia (Gammage 2011). Aboriginals are aware of their culture as encompassing myth, history, dreaming, religious rituals, and stories of group relations and they refer to their cultural knowledge as "tjukurrpa" (Australian Institute of Aboriginal, and Torres Strait Islander Studies 1994; Grieves 2014).

Ainu in Japan

Native Americans, Australian Aboriginals, and New Zealand Maori all share degrees of distance from the nations that emerged after their territories were occupied. The Ainu of Japan, by contrast, have been absorbed into the Japanese notion of nation race. Tarō Asō, former Prime Minister and Deputy Prime Minister of Japan since 2012, said in 2005 that Japan was "one nation, one civilization, one language, one culture and one race. There is no other nation (that has such characteristics)" (Siddle 2003). His words echoed those of Prime Minister Yasuhiro Nakasone who referred to Japan as a "homogeneous nation" in 1986. Mitsunori Keira, head of the citizens' group Yaiyukara-no-Mori that preserves indigenous Ainu culture, protested (*Japan Times* 2005). While Japan has officially embraced indigenous culture as part of national identity, critics claim that the rights and needs of existing Ainu people have been neglected (Bukh 2010).

Race, Caste, and Class

Ideas of Race in Brazil

Eleven times as many African slaves were imported to Brazil as to the United States and both countries have large European immigrant populations. The racial history of Brazil is thus very similar to that of the United States, but ideas of race within the two countries are strikingly different. In the United States, most people with black ancestry identify as black, so that there are very few whites who also claim black ancestry. But in Brazil, many who are considered white are also known to have black ancestry. According to Edward Telles, the reason for the difference is that racial identity in Brazil is based wholly on appearance, with little regard for ancestry. Telles also argues that whereas segregation (keeping blacks and whites apart) has been the core of US racial ideology, in Brazil, the core of racial ideology is racial mixing. Brazilians have officially valued racial ambiguity, as opposed to the value of racial purity in the United States, and Brazilians believe that they are the result of a long history of such racial mixing (Telles 2014, pp. 1–23). Nevertheless, whites have remained dominant and the importance of social class for those who are mixed has been described as "money lightens." Upward socioeconomic mobility and greater education have been correlated with a tendency of mixed-race parents to classify their children as white. However, Luisa Schwartzman explains this in terms of the mixed-parents having white co-parents and notes that there is a recent countertrend among black men married to white women, since political aspects of race changed in Brazil toward the end of the twentieth century (Schwartzman 2007).

Abandoning earlier ideas of Brazil as a racial democracy, after researchers reported racial exclusion of blacks and ongoing white supremacy, the government of Brazil instituted affirmative action policies in 2001. Brazilians who appeared black or mixed race made up three-quarters of the bottom tenth of those employed and they earned about 40% less than whites. Only 13% had access to college education. The Law of Social Quotas was passed in 2012, setting aside half of all admissions in top higher education to public high school students, who were disproportionately black. After many white students began to apply for these spots, the government resorted to bio-measurement of racial features, a measure that many viewed as a return to ideas of race in effect during slavery (de Oliveira 2017).

Measurement of racial traits can theoretically be used to affirm nonwhites as Brazil has been attempting, but the practice has an oppressive history, so it is not surprising that it has caused controversy. In Nazi Germany, racial-trait measurements were performed to determine non-Aryan ancestry, for persecution and extermination (United States Holocaust Memorial Museum 2017). Contemporary exclusions and discrimination are therefore denounced by comparing them to past racial-trait measurements: In US Historically Black Colleges and Universities, admission is said to have been determined by whether an applicant's skin was lighter than a brown paper bag (Carter 2013). In South Africa under apartheid, black racial identity was determined by assessing hair with a "pencil test" (Ndlovu 2008).

Caste in India

Caste differences on the Indian subcontinent, but mainly in India, are similar to racial categories insofar as they are hereditary. They resemble the influence of class on racial identities in Brazil, but caste identities are based on only one aspect of class, namely occupation. Their cultural role aspect makes caste differences closer to ethnic than racial differences, although caste is different from ethnicity in not allowing for change. Like race and ethnicity, caste is a system throughout society. What is caste? In India, **caste** is a system that divides society into a hierarchy of hereditary groups, based on occupation. The system provides for neither individual upward social mobility nor interactions between members of different castes. India's caste system was legally abolished in 1950, but it is persistent enough to justify affirmative action for disadvantaged castes and those outside of the system.

The four main Indian castes were described in the *Vedas*, ancient Hindu religious texts: Brahmins (priests, teachers, and scholars); Kshatriyas (rulers, police, soldiers, and administrators); Vaishyas (farmers, cattle herders, traders, and bankers); and Shudras (craftsmen and professional service providers). Karma and past life actions determined an individual's caste; positions could be changed only if a group in the same caste did so (Cox 1947, pp. 3–120). Historian Oliver Cox related the following in 1947, about the Gachua Talis and Kolus, two different ancestral groups of "oil pressers" who extracted Neem oil from the fruits and seeds of the every green neem tree:

> The Gachua Talis and Kolus are both oil pressers. They became separate castes when the Kolus left the traditional practice of soaking up the pressed oil from their mortars with a rag and adopted the device of making a hole in the bottom of the container, through which the oil was drawn off. The status of the Kolus is now very much lower than that of the Gachuas. (Cox 1947, quote p. 10)

There are differences of wealth and status within each caste, although members of other castes may not recognize them.

The outsiders of the caste system included tribal groups, foreigners, and those who were "untouchables," because Hindu purity laws were violated by their occupations (butchering, cleaning public places, leatherworking, garbage disposal, and undertaking). Untouchables have encompassed a number of groups with different languages and religions. After 1950, they came to self-identify as *Dalit*, meaning "broken." K.R. Narayanan, a Dalit, was elected President of India in 1997, but Dalit have continued to experience segregation, contempt, social humiliation, and discrimination, solely because of their caste. Dalit are segregated and often prohibited from using common public amenities such as highways. Anthropologist William Haviland wrote in 2005:

> Even a Dalit's shadow is believed to pollute the upper classes. They may not cross the line dividing their part of the village from that occupied by higher castes, drink water from public wells, or visit the same temples as the higher castes. Dalit children are still often made to sit in the back of the classroom. (Haviland 2005, p. 575)

British colonial rule is believed to have made the caste system more rigid, to facilitate their administrative functions. Some contemporary scholars therefore view the caste system as a social construction (Prakash 1990, pp. 392–3). Cast has been compared to race, but many, including its strongest critics, have insisted that all Indian castes are of the same race (Ambedkar 1979, p. 49). Others have observed that higher castes are genetically closer to European populations than to other castes and hypothesized that groups from Eastern Europe and Central Asia invaded and dominated the indigenous population sometime between 3000 and 8000 BCE (Trivedi 2001).

Conclusion

Ethnicity is supposed to belong to culture, race to biology. But ethnic groups have been viewed and treated as races and racial groups have ethnicities. In the United States, Anglo-Americans have dominated since colonial times. European immigrants formed distinctive ethnic groups after arrival. But their identifications by customs, appearance, language, and religion, after several generations of assimilation, turned out to be less enduring and stigmatizing than nonwhite racial identities. And these groups became white Americans. It is perhaps too soon to determine whether that same process is at work for Hispanic/Latinx and Asian immigrants and their descendants, because these groups retain stronger racial descriptions as not white. MENA ethnic groups are further stigmatized by suspicion of terrorist association.

Indigenous identities are altogether different from both racial and ethnic identities, if they are taken on their own terms. Indigenous people are the descendants of first inhabitants in a place or they are those populations who have remained in the same places as their ancestors for much longer in time than other groups. Insofar as ideas of race claim to provide universal means for dividing all humankind, indigenous peoples do not internally have ideas of race. And neither do they see themselves as ethnicities, because the very concept of ethnicity pertains to human migration, in the modern period. If anything, the Euro-American conquerors of indigenous lands would be ethnic groups from an indigenous perspective.

Notions of race in Brazil, as influenced by social class and in India as castes determined by inherited occupations, are closer to Euro-American ideas of race, but less dependent on ideas of human biology. What they share with Euro-American ideas of race is descriptions of groups in terms of their status in systems containing other groups.

Although this chapter has provided a glimpse of ideas of human difference that resemble race, the resemblance breaks down on the presumed universal and eternal characteristic of racial divisions—those who have posited biological race in the modern period have sought to create systems that apply to all humankind, for all time. When group identities apply mainly to members of a particular group and are constructed by members of that group, although the results may be comparable to race, they are in reality closer to notions of **identity** than **identification**—how people describe themselves, rather than how others see them. Historically, there is a difference in the identities of those groups who seek assimilation into a wider racial or ethnic whole—European ethnic groups in the United States, for example—versus identities expressed for affirmation or declaration, such as indigenous identities. When contemporary scholars of race discuss identity, what they usually have in mind is the identities of groups and their members who accept external identification in a wider system of race. This sense of identity will be the main subject of Chapter 6.

Glossary

assimilation—learning and adoption of the language and customs of the country to which a group immigrates.

caste—a system that divides society into a hierarchy of hereditary groups based on occupation.

constructivist or **instrumentalist**—view of ethnic groups as having characteristics resulting from social factors external to those groups.

diaspora—scattered ethnic or racial group with a shared homeland or geographical origin.

ethnic enclaves —neighborhoods where a distinct ethnic group predominates, in residence and small service businesses.

ethnic fractionalization—formation of an ethnic group occurring when people are excluded or oppressed.

identification—how a group and its members are described by nonmembers.

identity—how a group and its members describe themselves.

invention of ethnicity—view of ethnic groups as the result of a new kind of social technology that was prompted by historical events and imposed on people who would not otherwise have been ethnic groups or viewed as ethnic groups.

morphology—form or shape of living things and relationships among structures and study of them.

patronage system—political system in which election winners distribute appointments to those who organized their victories.

phenotype—observable physical traits of living things, caused by interactions of genes with environments.

pogroms—violent attacks on Jewish communities in Eastern Europe during the early twentieth century.

primordialist—view of ethnic groups as having fixed biological traits or deeply historical cultural traits.

racialization—psychological and social process of viewing members of a group as members of a racial group.

Yiddish—a language spoken by Jews, based on Middle High German and other European languages, Hebrew, and Aramaic.

Discussion Questions

1. Why has ethnicity has been called an invention?
2. How has ethnic experience in the United States been like and unlike nonwhite racial experience?
3. In your own experience, how important is the dominance of WASP culture in twenty-first-century America?
4. What historical trends suggest that new immigrants will assimilate?
5. What trends will work against the assimilation of new immigrants?
6. In terms of the universal aspect of ideas of race, explain how indigenous self-descriptions by Umatillas and Australian Aboriginals are matters of

identity (how they see themselves) rather than identification (how others see them).

7. Explain how DNA studies settled the race of Kennewick man. Would the Umatilla claim have been valid with different DNA results?
8. Are the Brazilian government's methods to determine who qualifies for affirmative action racist? (Give reasons with reference to history or explain how this case is different.)
9. How does the history of US ethnic groups who came to be regarded as racially white compare with ideas of race in Brazil?
10. How is the Indian caste system like and unlike the US system of race?

References

Alba, Richard, and Victor Nee. *Remaking the American Mainstream: Assimilation and Contemporary Immigration.* Cambridge, MA: Harvard University Press, 2005.

Alcoff, Linda Martín. "Is Latina/o Identity a Racial Identity?" *Chapter 1 in Hispanics/Latinos in the United States: Ethnicity, Race, and Rights,* edited by Jorge J.E. Gracia and Pablo De Greiff, Routledge, 2000; "Latinos Beyond the Binary." http://www.alcoff.com/content/beyondbinary.html.

Ambedkar, B.R., The Annihilation of Caste. Dr. Babasaheb Ambekar: His Writings and Speeches, vol. 1, Maharashtra, India: Education Department, Government of Maharastra, 1979.

Australian Institute of Aboriginal, and Torres Strait Islander Studies. *The Encyclopaedia of Aboriginal Australia: Aboriginal and Torres Strait Islander History, Society and Culture,* edited by David Horton, vol. 2, Aboriginal Studies Press, 1994.

Bergquist, James M. "German-Americans." *Multiculturalism in the United States: A Comparative Guide to Acculturation and Ethnicity,* edited by John D. Buenker and Lorman A. Ratner. Westport, CT: Greenwood, 2005, pp. 53–76.

Blessing, Patrick J. "Irish." *Harvard Encyclopedia of American Ethnic Groups,* edited by Stephan Thernstrom. Cambridge, MA: Harvard University Press, 1980, pp. 524–45 and 695–7.

Breen, T.H. *The Market Place of Revolution: How Consumer Politics Shaped American Independence.* New York: Oxford University Press, 2004.

Brodkin, Karen. *How Jews Became White Folks: And What That Says About Race in America.* New York, NY: Routledge, 1998.

Bukh, Alexander. "Ainu Identity and Japan's Identity: The Struggle for Subjectivity." *Copenhagen Journal of Asian Studies,* vol. 28, no. 2, 2010, pp. 35–53.

Burke Museum. "The Ancient One, Kennewick Man," Feb. 20, 2017. http://www.burkemuseum.org/blog/kennewick-man-ancient-one.

Candeloro, Dominic. "Italian-Americans." *Multiculturalism in the United States: A Comparative Guide to Acculturation and Ethnicity*, edited by John D. Buenker and Lorman A. Ratner. Westport, CT: Greenwood Press, 1992, pp. 173–92.

Carlson, Allan C. "The Peculiar Legacy of German-Americans." *Society*, Jan./Feb. 2003, pp. 77–99.

Carter, Jarrett L. "Bringing Back the Brown Paper Bag Test to HBCUs." *HuffPost*, June 11, 2013. http://www.huffingtonpost.com/jarrett-l-carter/bringing-back-the-brown-p_b_3059700.html.

Cornell University. "Immigration." Legal Information Institute, 2017. https://www.law.cornell.edu/wex/immigration.

Cox, O.C., Class, Caste, and Race: A Study of Social Dynamics. New York, NY: Monthly Review Press, 1947.

Curran, Bob. *Mysterious Celtic Mythology in American Folklore*. New York, NY: Penguin, 2010.

Dobson, David. *Scottish Emigration to Colonial America, 1607–1785*. Athens, GA: University of Georgia Press, 1994.

Fearon, James D. "Ethnic and Cultural Diversity by Country." *Journal of Economic Growth*, vol. 8, no. 2, June 2003, pp. 195–222.

Fedunkiw, Marianne, and Canadian Americans. *Gale Encyclopedia of Multicultural America*, edited by Judy Galens, Anna Sheets, and Robyn V. Young. Detroit, MI: Gale Research, Inc., 1995, pp. 238–51.

Fisher, David Hackett. *Albion's Seed: Four British Folkways in America*. Cambridge, MA: Oxford University Press, 1989.

Gammage, William. *The Biggest Estate on Earth: How Aborigines Made Australia*. Crows Nest, NSW: Allen & Unwin, 2011.

Gidda, Mirren. "How Donald Trump's Nationalism Won Over White Americans." *Newsweek*, Nov. 15, 2016. http://www.newsweek.com/donald-trump-nationalism-racism-make-america-great-again-521083.

Goran, Arthur A. "Jews." *Harvard Encyclopedia of American Ethnic Groups*, edited by Stephan Thernstrom. Cambridge MA: Harvard University Press, 1980, pp. 571–88.

Grieves, Victoria. "Culture, Not Colour, Is the Heart of Aboriginal Identity." The Conversation, Australian Research Council, University of Sidney, Sept. 17, 2014. http://theconversation.com/culture-not-colour-is-the-heart-of-aboriginal-identity-30102.

Guglielmo, Jennifer, and Salvatore Salerno, editors. *Are Italians White? How Race Is Made in America*. New York: NY, Routledge, 2003.

Haft, Sheldon, and English Americans. *Gale Encyclopedia of Multicultural America*, edited by Judy Galens, Anna Sheets, and Robyn V. Young, pp. 471–85. Detroit, MI: Gale Research, Inc, 1995.

Harzig, Christiane. "German Americans." *Encyclopedia of Race, Ethnicity and Society*, edited by Richard T. Schaefer. Thousand Oaks, CA: Sage, 2008, vol. 1, pp. 540–4.

Haub, Carl. "Changing the Way U.S. Hispanics Are Counted." Population Reference Bureau, 2012. http://www.prb.org/Publications/Articles/2012/us-census-and-hispanics.aspx.

Haviland, W.A., Anthropology: The Human Challenge, Belmont, CA: Thomson Wadsworth, 2005.

Hawshaw, Tim. *The Birth of Black America: The First African Americans and the* US *Pursuit of Freedom at Jamestown.* New York, NY: Caroll and Graf, 2007.

Heimlich, E., "Welsh Americans," in J. Galens, A. Sheets, and R.V. Young, eds. Gale Encyclopedia of Multicultural American, Detroit, MI: Gale Research, 1995, 1408–1419.

Hess, Mary A. Scottish, and Scotch-Irish Americans. *Gale Encyclopedia of Multicultural America*, edited by Judy Galens, Anna Sheets, and Robyn V. Young. Detroit, MI: Gale Research, Inc, 1995, pp. 1198–210.

Homeland Security. "Yearbook of Immigration Statistics," 2010. http://www.dhs.gov/files/statistics/publications/LPR10.shtm.

Ignatiev, Noel. *How the Irish Became White.* New York, NY: Routledge, 1995.

Ireland Story. 1998. http://www.wesleyjohnston.com/users/ireland/; http://www.irelandstory.com.

Japan Times. "Aso Says Japan Is Nation of 'One Race,'" Oct. 18, 2005. http://www.japantimes.co.jp/news/2005/10/18/national/aso-says-japan-is-nation-of-one-race/#.WUr4yMap7cs.

Karoub, Jeff. "Census Bureau May Count Arab-Americans for the First Time in 2020." *PBS NewsHour*, Associated Press, Jan. 30, 2015. http://www.pbs.org/newshour/rundown/census-bureau-considering-new-category-arab-americans-2020-count/.

Kazal, Russell A. "The Interwar Origins of the White Ethnic: Race, Residence, and German Philadelphia, 1917–1939." *Journal of American Ethnic History*, Summer, 2004, pp. 78–131.

Kenny, Kevin. *The American Irish: A History.* Harlow, UK: Pearson, 2000.

Klein, Jennifer M. "United Kingdom, Immigrants and Their Descendants in the United States." *Encyclopedia of Race, Ethnicity, and Society.* Thousand Oaks, CA: Sage, 2000. http://sage-ereference.com/view/ethnicity/n565.xml; http://sage-ereference.com/view/ethnicity/n435.xml.

Klein, Jennifer M. "Sicilian Americans." *Encyclopedia of Race, Ethnicity, and Society.* Thousand Oaks, CA: Sage, 2008. http://sage-ereference.com/view/ethnicity/n511.xml.

McLemore, S. Dale, and Harriet D. Romo. *Racial and Ethnic Relations in America.* Boston, MA: Pearson Education, 2005.

Minthorn, Armand. "Ancient One/Kennewick Man: Human Remains Should Be Reburied." Confederated Tribes of the Umatilla Indian Reservation,

Sept. 1996. Archived from the Original, 2014. https://web.archive.org/web/20140812090048/http:/ctuir.org/kman1.html.

Muslim Advocates. "Map: Recent Incidents of Anti-Muslim Hate Crimes," June 18, 2017. https://www.muslimadvocates.org/map-anti-muslim-hate-crimes/.

Ndlovu, Nosimilo. "The 21-st Century Pencil Test." *Mail & Guardian*, May 24, 2008, 06:00. https://mg.co.za/article/2008-05-24-the-21st-century-pencil-test.

Office of English Language Learners 2013 Demographic Report, NYC Department of Education. http://schools.nyc.gov/NR/rdonlyres/FD5EB945-5C27-44F8-BE4B-E4C65D7176F8/0/2013DemographicReport_june2013_revised.pdf.

Oliveira, Cleuci de. "Brazil's New Problem with Blackness." *Foreign Policy*, Apr. 5, 2017. http://foreignpolicy.com/2017/04/05/brazils-new-problem-with-blackness-affirmative-action/.

Oxford English Dictionary. "Ethnicity," 2017. https://en.oxforddictionaries.com/definition/ethnic_group.

Parillo, Vincent, N. "Italian-Americans." *Encyclopedia of Race, Ethnicity, and Society*. Thousand Oaks, CA: Sage, 2008. http://sage-ereference.com/view/ethnicity/n307..xml.

Parkin, Andrew. "Australians and New Zealanders." *Harvard Encyclopedia of American Ethnic Groups*, edited by Stephan Thernstrom. Cambridge MA: Harvard University Press, 1980, pp. 163–4.

Porter, Jack Nusan. "Jewish Americans." *Encyclopedia of Race, Ethnicity, and Society*. Thousand Oaks, CA: Sage, 2008. http://sage-ereference.com/view/ethnicity/n314.xml.

Powell, John. *Encyclopedia of North American Immigration*. New York, NY: Facts on File, 2005.

Prakash, Gyan. "Writing Post-Orientalist Histories of the Third World: Perspectives from Indian Historiography." *Comparative Studies in Society and History*, vol. 32, no. 2, 1990, pp. 383–408.

Rebala, Pratheek By Pratheek Rebala. "This Map Shows Where Immigrants Send the Most Money Home." *Time Labs*, Sept. 9, 2015. http://labs.time.com/story/where-immigrants-send-the-most-money-home/.

Rice, Otis, K. *The Hatfields and the McCoys*. Lexington, KY: University Press of Kentucky, 1982.

Schaefer, R.T. "Irish Americans," Encyclopedia of Race, Ethnicity, and Society, Thousand Oaks, CA: Sage Publications, VOL. 1, 2008, 758–9.

Schaefer, Richard T. *Race and Ethnicity in the United States*. Upper Saddle River, NJ: Prentice Hall, 2011.

Schwartzman, Luisa Farah. "Does Money Whiten? Intergenerational Changes in Racial Classification in Brazil." *American Sociological Review*, vol. 72, no. 6, 2007, pp. 940–63.

Shapiro, Edward. "Jewish-Americans." *Multiculturalism in the United States: A Comparative Guide to Acculturation and Ethnicity*, edited by John D. Buenker and Lorman A. Ratner. Westport, CT: Greenwood Press, 1992, pp. 149–72.

Sheth, Falguni. "The Racialization of Muslims in the Post-9/11 United States." *The Oxford Handbook of Philosophy and Race*, edited by Naomi Zack. New York, NY: Oxford University Press, 2017, pp. 342–51.

Siddle, Richard. "The Limits to Citizenship in Japan: Multiculturalism, Indigenous Rights and the Ainu." *Journal of Citizenship Studies*, vol. 7, no. 4, 2003, June 2010, pp. 447–62. http://www.tandfonline.com/doi/abs/10.1080/13621020320 00134976.

Sollers, Werner, The Invention of Ethnicity, New York, NY: Oxford University Press, 1989.

Stable URL: http://www.jstor.org/stable/40215943.

Telles, Edward E. *Race in Another America: The Significance of Skin Color in Brazil*. Princeton, NJ: Princeton University Press, 2014.

Trivedi, B.P., "Genetic Evidence suggest European migrants may have influenced the origins of India's caste system." Genome News Network, J. Craig Venter Institute, May 14, 2001.

Tyson, Alec, and Shiva Maniam. "Behind Trump's Victory: Divisions by Race, Gender, Education," Fact Tank—Our Lives in Numbers. *Pew Research Center*, Nov. 9, 2016. http://www.pewresearch.org/fact-tank/2016/11/09/behind-trumps-victory-divisions-by-race-gender-education/.

United States Census Bureau. "Median Household Income in the Past 12 Months (in 2015 Inflation-Adjusted Dollars)." American Community Survey, 2015. https://factfinder.census.gov/faces/nav/jsf/pages/index.xhtml.

United States Holocaust Memorial Museum. "Nazi Racism." The Holocaust: A Learning Site for Students, 2017. https://www.ushmm.org/outreach/en/article. php?ModuleId=10007679.

US Census. "Quick Facts," 2010. http://quickfacts.census.gov/qfd/states/00000. html.

Vance, J.D. *Hillbilly Elegy: A Memoir of a Family and Culture in Crisis*. New York, NY: HarperCollins, 2016.

Welsh-American. 2008. http://www.facebook.com/pages/Welsh-American/14298530 5715399.

Zimmerman, Larry J., and Robert N. Clinton. "Case Notes: Kennewick Man and Native American Graves Protection and Repatriation Act Woes." *International Journal of Cultural Property*, vol. 8, no. 1, 1999, pp. 212–28.

Part II

Relations, Practices, and Theories of Race in Society

Introduction

The ideas about race discussed in Part I have a messy relationship to the construction and reality of race in society. These ideas and theories are by no means blueprints. If one believes that ideas shape reality, then reality can be seen as the result of those ideas, but there is little evidence that the world works that way. Typically, ideas of race are formed after the facts in reality, so that it is important to consider reality directly and revise settled ideas, come up with new ones, or consider what the settled ideas have failed to take into account.

Chapter 6 provides an examination of the social construction of race, with accounts and analyses of how race has been socially constructed through colonialism and global development; social technologies of race and racism; individual racial identities, including mixed race, and models for resisting and deconstructing race. Behavior and institutional practices that harm racial minorities are broadly recognized to be morally wrong and the term for that is *racism*.

The late twentieth century academic study of racism began with individuals and legal structures. It was assumed that racist actions and exclusions were carried out because individuals had certain beliefs, and that people of color experienced discrimination because the law did not explicitly prohibit it. After the civil rights movement, when experiences of racism continued, new theoretical tools were developed: Individual versus structural or institutional racism; white privilege, micro-aggression, and epistemic oppression.

Chapter 7 provides analyses of these ills. Chapter 8 provides analyses of how race and ethnicity intersect with social goods such as marriage rates and health. As a social construction, race is attached to family genealogy, creating intergenerational groups and identities for individuals. Marriage rates vary with race, although more due to external social and economic factors than ethnic or racial culture or the preferences or values of individuals. In a racially striated society, class includes cultural capital as tastes and preferences and those of whites may determine power structures within institutions, to the disadvantage of racial minorities. Racial and ethnic health disparities are not the result of group cultures or biology but of environmental restrictions on opportunities, as well as stress. Health varies according to race and ethnicity, because health, education, and wealth/income are positively correlated and mutually interactive.

In Chapter 9, political philosophy, law, and public policy are considered in terms of nonwhite race. Written law in democratic societies has been egalitarian, but there has often been a gap between promulgated law and societal practice. Public policy consists of principles and their applications that may either be consistent with egalitarian law or closer to custom as structured by dominant groups. As we have seen in Chapter 1, historically, the philosophical tradition has not been racially egalitarian and anti-nonwhite racism was explicitly expressed by writers such as Hume, Kant, Hegel, and even John Stuart Mill. Nevertheless, there is a consensus about racial equality among contemporary political philosophers. The first part of Chapter 9 takes up several contemporary philosophical/ theoretical approaches to justice and injustice; the second part addresses issues of public policy in Affirmative Action and racial profiling by police officers.

Chapter 10 concludes the book with discussion of race and gender. Philosophical feminism has been welcoming toward diversity but the demographics and history of feminism as political and social movements, have not been racially inclusive. There is, as well, a tension between African American philosophy as practiced by men and Black Feminist philosophy as developed by women. The book closes with discussion of a recent controversy about whether philosophers have an ethical obligation to use scholarly sources written by members of underrepresented groups in philosophy.

6

Social Construction and Racial Identities

Before the construction of race in science, there were ideas of different human groups but no conceptual system of difference applying to all humankind. The construction of race in science drew on existing societal ideas and created abstract typologies that in turn became the cognitive element of race in society. However, at this time, after typologies of race have been discarded in the biological sciences, racial constructions in society endure and continue to be reconstructed. Socially constructed race has a momentum of its own that people live out, and social scientists, scholars, and those in the creative arts continue to study and suggest ways to change.

The construction and reconstruction of race in society has legal, social, economic, and cultural components, all of which taken together, in different combinations, or in isolated experience, make it seem to individuals that race is natural and inevitable, instead of human-made and historically and geographically contingent. Individuals have different physical traits that have already been selected as racial traits before their birth and that prior selection forms a reality to be experienced—lived with compliance or resistance, or both. Such compliance *reproduces* or maintains and furthers preexisting social race, over time. Resistance has the potential to change the background of racial construction, although any particular act of resistance has unpredictable consequences, because it has to be interpreted, supported, and duplicated by other people, in order to be effective.

Individuals belong to or are associated with racial groups that are imagined to have general traits and the individual herself comes to have patterns of behavior, expectations, and beliefs that pertain to how she regards

© The Author(s) 2018
N. Zack, *Philosophy of Race*, Palgrave Philosophy Today,
https://doi.org/10.1007/978-3-319-78729-9_6

and presents herself in racial terms. That is, although race is already present in the social world that a child and adult live in, the child and then the adult has the task of forming a racial aspect of the self and presenting that racial identity to others. Society identifies people racially and people come to have racial identities, both as single units and as parts of the groups with which they identify and to which they belong. Thus, to say that race is *socially* constructed may refer to only one side of the process of social construction. Society, which is to say, other people, have constructed ideas about race and systems regulating behavior based on race. But human individuals are not mere mirrors of social institutions and the thoughts and actions of other individuals. A complete account of the social construction of race, therefore, includes its construction on the level of individual identities.

The **social construction** of race and racial identities affect many aspects of human life in societies with racial systems, often in profound, unintended, and unpredictable ways. There are social constructions that are benign or neutral, for example, the money system and weather reports. Such benign and neutral social constructions usually do not purport to be caused by different underlying physical facts about members of distinct groups, which determine their nature. Race, however, is not a benign social construction, because it purports to be based on real biological differences that do not exist. Human aptitudes and capabilities are randomly distributed within different social racial groups, so that differences in achievement are not caused by those traits that society continues to consider racial traits— there are no biological racial traits in the scientific sense and no differences in human value or moral worth based on biological race. Rather, differences in achievement between racial groups are the result of the fact that social racial systems are hierarchical. Racial identities come with predetermined social status and differences in power. Another way of describing this is to say that disadvantaged racial groups and their members are oppressed by more advantaged racial groups and their members.

Oppression is unjust treatment or control and when the objects of oppression are racial groups and their members, it is usually called *racism*. Racism will be the subject of Chapter 7, but it can be difficult to separate racism from the construction of race itself. One clear difference is that even though racial hierarchy is in itself oppressive, not everyone who benefits from a system of constructed race or racial hierarchy is necessarily a racist person. There are also aspects of oppression that do not begin from within positions of racial hierarchies, but originate in other hierarchies, such as wealth or gender. In order to account for the emergence of race as an idea and system in modernity, it is necessary to understand the non-racial forms of oppression that preceded race and led to the construction of race. Because racial systems are not caused by natural aspects of race—which do not exist—the underlying motivations for constructing those systems may be masked to participants, by ideology. **Racial ideology** is a false system of claims and beliefs about racial differences and racial groups that justifies racial oppression, as well as racial disadvantage. After systems of race have been constructed, racial ideology may be used to justify the actions of oppressive groups and individuals. But racial ideology is psychic and symbolic, a form of discourse. To implement racial ideology and serve underlying powerful economic and political interests, **social technologies of race** are necessary (for example, new racial identifications). Ideology and social technologies of race may lead to new constructions of race and with them, new racial identities.

The sections of this chapter address several aspects of the social construction of race and identity. First, racial construction for economic reasons will be explored in terms of colonialism and global development. This will be followed by subjects pertaining to processes that occur inside of functioning systems of race: social technologies of race and racism; individual racial identities; models for resisting and deconstructing race.

Colonialism and Global Development

Colonization of Africa, Asia, and South America by European nations spanned the sixteenth to the twentieth centuries (Essential Humanities, 2008–2013). The period from the 15th through the seventeenth centuries, called the "Age of Exploration" or the "Age of Discovery," was initially financed by Spain and Portugal. There were earlier voyages during the Middle Ages, including land travel to the Middle East and China by Italian traders, Catholic missionaries, and members of the Russian royal family. Muhammad al-Idrisi (1100–1165), an Arab geographer, created a detailed map of the known world, "Tabula Rogeriana," for King Roger II of Sicily. A Moroccan scholar traveled to Africa and China in the mid-1300s and in the early 1400s, Arab and Chinese traders went to India, Thailand, East Africa, Arabia, and Southeast Asia (World Atlas 2017). Not all early exploration made it into the big historical record (as noted in Chapter 5, there are accounts of twelfth century Welch contact with American Indians).

The Age of Colonization is more or less officially past. European colonies became *mandates* after World War I and decolonization was almost complete after World War II. Portugal gave up Macau to China in 1999. As of 2008, there were 16 remaining colonies in the world, populated by 1.2 million people, including tourist destinations such as the British Virgin Islands, Bermuda, and the Caymen Islands (Lange 2008). Colonization was made official by political domination, taking over preexisting sovereignty, or creating new political structures—all backed up by force. The stronger the political domination, the greater imposed economic changes, and with that, social upheaval in colonized populations (Ziltener et al. 2017).

Colonization has been succeeded by **development**, the expansion of the Western market economy and infrastructure supporting it to parts of the world that were, for the most part, former colonies. The emphasis by international corporations (backed up by governments) on natural resource extraction—including **outsourced labor** for wages much lower than what workers are paid in developed countries—trade, and distribution for final consumption, exhibit further economic continuity with colonialism. And in purely economic terms, global prosperity has generally increased with development (Agénor and Montiel 2008). Yet no one doubts that there are tragic casualties of these economic changes: internal ethnic wars and massacres, civilian deaths in wars supported by external national powers, malnutrition, famine, and environmental degradation, including water shortages and disaster-level fallout from human contributions to climate change (Center for Global Development 2017).

The age of colonization was sufficiently at odds with Enlightenment ideals, especially in its enablement of chattel slavery, to have occasioned the need for anti-nonwhite racial science and white supremacist racial ideologies. Global development, by contrast, is not as explicit about racial difference, although it is not entirely coincidental that the poorest nations in the world, in Asia, Africa, and South America, are populated by nonwhite people. Furthermore, although slavery is both officially illegal and no longer has ideological justification, there are more slaves alive in the twenty-first century than at any time in the past.

Observers and activists estimate that there are 12–45 million slaves at present. Many are women and children who are sexually exploited through "human trafficking." They are often entrapped through schemes and scams that lure them from their homes with promises of attractive employment that turn out to require prostitution and drudgery. They are then coerced into incurring unpayable debt for the cost of their transportation and lodging and the lives of their family members may be jeopardized if they escape. Other forms of trafficking involve outright sale of adolescents and children for whatever purposes their buyers determine. Contemporary slaves are extremely poor and most are nonwhite (Free the Slaves 2017).

Some progressive scholars study development as both the legacy of colonialism and a continuation of it, via **postcolonial studies** or **postcolonial critical theory of international relations (IR)** (Bayliss et al. 2011). Along these lines, it could be said that if specific racial traits and the system of race were constructed during the age of colonization, then the results of those constructions have contributed to further constructions of race that associate global nonwhiteness with technological backwardness and poverty. Alternatively, it could be claimed that the process works in the other direction, so that global poverty results in the construction of new racial taxonomies on international levels.

It is also important to understand that colonialism, with its constructions of race, was not a smooth preconceived plan carried out by Europe against the rest of world. Europe was often the site of internal wars and there were fits and starts in developing the ideologies to justify colonial practices. For instance, the Dominican friar Bartolomé de Las Casas (1484–1656), shocked the conscience of the Catholic Church with *A Short Account of the Destruction of the Indies* (1542) that chronicled the conquistadors' atrocities against indigenous people in the West Indies. Las Casas dedicated his life to the rights of the Indians, basing his arguments on Church law (Las Casas 1992). Against pro-slavery advocates, he argued that Indians were rational and merited conversion to Christianity (Pennington 1970). By 1607, Spain was bankrupted through inflation caused by a flood of gold into a static economy with no infrastructure to produce goods that the gold could be used to buy (Cavendish 2007). Portugal had the oldest and longest foreign empire but during its alliance with Spain, Portugal was attacked by Spain's enemies and Brazil, its richest colony, gained independence in 1822 (Pedreira 2000). These obstacles to the colonial process and its eventual fall are evidence of the historical unevenness of racial oppression, although successful revolution by the oppressed was rare. Haiti was an early exception.

The slave revolution in Haiti (1791–1803) victoriously gained independence from France for her richest colony. Toussaint l'Overture, a former slave, led forces to defeat the French and repel an English invasion. He took over the Spanish colony of Santo Domingo (later the Dominican Republic) to rule over the entire island, newly named Hispaniola. Napoleon tried to re-enslave Haiti and captured l'Overture, but General Jean-Jacques Dessalines, also a former slave, conclusively defeated the French (Sutherland 2007–2017; Ott 1973.)

Compared to anti-colonial rebellion or revolution there are more institutionalized forms of resistance to the unjust results of development, both internationally through the United Nations and other humanitarian organizations and from within developing nations and communities within them. But there may at times be external moral paralysis in the face of internal genocide, as in the 1994 war in Rwanda, which was largely the result of the legacy of colonialism.

Within Rwanda, Tutsis were an Ethiopian group who conquered the Hutus during the 1300s. Hutus and Tutsis both speak Bantu and French, they shared the same cultural traditions, and practiced Christianity. They lived in peace, with mutual assimilation until Belgium colonized Rwanda in 1916. Belgium colonizers favored the Tutsis, most of whom were lighter in skin color than most Hutus. Tutsis became the dominant ethnic group until Rwandan independence in 1962, when the Hutus, who were the majority, gained control and held the Tutsis responsible for economic problems. Ethnic violence erupted and Tutsi refugees fled to Uganda and formed the Rwandan Patriotic Front (RPF). In 1994, the Hutu president's plane was shot down. Hutu government soldiers and civilian militias attached Tutsis with machetes and blew up the churches where civilians had taken refuge. This widespread massacre was the Rwandan Genocide, in which 800,000 Rwandans were killed over three months. United Nations forces tried to restore peace but withdrew after ten soldiers were killed. Tutsis, through the RPF and support from Uganda, then embarked on a civil war that resulted in taking over the Rwandan government. Two million Hutus fled to Zaire (The Democratic Republic of Congo), where they were believed to engage in conflicts between Zaire and Rwanda, in addition to their own confrontations with Rwandan forces. The result was 5 million deaths. The Tutsi government of Rwanda repeatedly invaded Zaire in attempts to eradicate the Hutus there (BBC Africa 2012). For reasons still not widely understood or agreed upon, the international community continues to stand by while the Hutu-Tutsi violence continues. In 2008, a Hutu commander told the press, "We are fighting every day because we are Hutu and they are Tutsis. We cannot mix, we are always in conflict. We will stay enemies forever" (Johnson 2012).

Of course, as a sovereign nation, Rwanda is responsible for its own internal affairs. And if the seeds of the ongoing Hutu-Tutsis war were planted during colonialism, that does not mean those who continued to nurture them are not responsible for the discord they create. Nevertheless, from an historical perspective, the 1994 Tutsis-Hutu civil war is continuous with the change in the relations between these groups under Belgium rule. But history goes on. The new 2003 constitution under President Kagame, leader of the Tutsis RFP outlawed the formation of political parties based on race or ethnicity. Toward preventing further genocide, Kagame amassed unprecedented power and was reelected for another 7-year term in 2010.

International observers closely watched Kagame's reelection in August 2017, because the stability of Rwanda is considered crucial for the stability of the entire region of sub-Saharan Africa. Kagame has brought important changes in health, education, and prosperity, but it is feared that his continuance in power will reduce the prospects for democratic rule in Rwanda and beyond (Mbaku 2017).

Social Technologies of Race and Racism

There have been many social technologies of race that pick out racial groups lower in status. Some, such as segregation, was explicit. Others, such as control over human reproduction through marriage restrictions, began by being explicit but continue as implicit matters of custom. There have also been legal doctrines, for instance *terra nullius* and *territorium nullius* and *separate but equal* that were used to support specific practices and then retired when their associated practices were abolished. More difficult to address are indirect social technologies, such as preferential residential segregation and racial differences in educational opportunities.

Terra Nullius and Territorium Nullius

Jeremy Bentham (1748–1832), the founder of philosophical **utilitarianism** (the principle that moral good is the greatest pleasure for the greatest number), thought that there were no natural rights and that all rights are created by government and are legal rights. He accordingly had a jaundiced view of Australian aborigines before 1788, because he presumed them to be without government:

> We know what it is for men to live without government, for we see instances of such a way of life—we see it in many savage nations, or rather races of mankind; for instance, Among the savages of New South Wales, whose way of living is so well known to us: no habit of obedience, and hence no government—no government, and thence no laws—no laws, and thence no such things as rights—no security—no property, liberty, as against regular control, the control of laws and government—perfect; but as against all irregular control, the mandates of stronger individuals' none. (Bentham 1816/1998, p. 6)

Here is what an official travel website wrote in 2010 about the inhabitants of New South Wales in the time frame relevant to what Bentham wrote.

At the time of British settlement at Sydney Cove it is estimated that 300,000 aboriginal people, speaking around 250 languages inhabited Australia. On arrival, finding no obvious political structure, the Europeans took the land as their own. The Indigenous people were driven out of their homes and many killed. Various new European diseases spread rapidly amongst the indigenous people, killing many. The introduction of feral and domestic animals contributed to the destruction of natural habitats. Fighting wiped out the Aboriginal population in Tasmania and greatly reduced the numbers in the rest of Australia. (Australian Explorer 2017)

In other words, Bentham, as many of his generation, assumed that without evident government according to European standards, there could be no human civilization or civility. That extremely legalistic thinking was part of an approach to the world during the age of colonization, which derived from a long tradition of **natural law** (law that upheld basic or God-given order in the world). The justification for dispossession of indigenous lands has in retrospect been called the doctrine of **terra nullius** or the right of first taker to what is owned by no one. But at the time Bentham wrote, he was implicitly relying on **territorium nullius**, a doctrine holding that a territory without government jurisdiction can be seized by a society with an established government (Fitzmaurice 2007). Bentham and other educated Englishmen of his day could not conceive of non-western forms of government even when they encountered them. For instance, the Iroquois Indians in New York State had a complex system of representative government, in existence to this day, but not recognized by European settlers as valid sovereignty (Mohawk Nation Office, Kahnawà:ke Branch 2017).

Human Reproduction, Segregation, and Education

State control over which people are legally permitted to marry and as a result, legitimately have children with, is a biological form of social technology. Like other animals, people inherit observable traits from their parents and ancestors. They will resemble their parents and ancestors in hereditary traits of skin color, hair texture, and physical structure, if their parents and ancestors resemble each other. Control of human reproduction over generations has amounted to a physical construction of race. A key idea in US racial reproductive history was **white racial purity**. Given the assumption that the white race was superior, it became important to control who could be white. The simplest way to do this was to regulate the parentage and ancestry of white people. Looking toward the future, only white people could have white children and grandchildren. Looking back, although the past cannot be controlled, it could be stipulated that only those with all white ancestry qualified as white. By about 1900, any known degree of nonwhite ancestry was sufficient for a person not to be considered white. Before then, varied US state law allowed for whites to have one nonwhite grandparent or great grandparent (Zack 1993, pp. 19–41).

Marriage was important as a secondary article of social technology, because it legitimized new births. People whose parents were not married were illegitimate, which was a social stigma until the late twentieth century when the rate of illegitimate births peaked. (Births outside of marriage increased 5% a year from 89,500 to 1.7 million, from 1940–1990 (Ventura and Bachrach 2000)). White families could have no nonwhite members and in a society placing a high value on families, as well as whiteness, white families constituted by white people were more highly valued than any other kind of racial family. Whites could and did have children with nonwhites but until recently, those children were not recognized as members of the white person's official family (Zack 1993, pp. 43–50).

Anti-miscegenation laws, regulating marriage among people of different races were more than simple matters of the rights of any couple getting married. Such laws assumed there had been control over human breeding in the past so that members of the existing white race were already racially pure. The antimiscegenation laws were assumed to protect such white racial purity, over time. But the legal practice of protecting white racial purity was disrupted by new law in 1967, in *Loving v. Virginia*, when the US Supreme Court struck down all remaining antimiscegenation laws prohibiting marriage between blacks and whites in sixteen states: Virginia, Arkansas, Delaware, Florida, Georgia, Kentucky, Louisiana, Mississippi, Missouri, North Carolina, Oklahoma, south Carolina, Tennessee, Texas, and West Virginia (Sickels 1972, pp. 1–10).

Segregation was another important social technology for maintaining racial hierarchy, because it kept the races apart in public facilities, including and especially public schools, which maintained differences in class, as well as racial separation. Nonwhite segregated facilities, including schools, were not of the same quality as white facilities, but the US Supreme Court maintained the fiction of equality through its doctrine of **separate-but-equal** in *Plessy v. Ferguson*, 163 US 537 (1896) (see Chapter 2). Segregation in housing was originally mandated by law in many parts of the United States. Until 1950, The Federal Housing Administration maintained racially discriminatory mortgage finance policies that supported restrictive agreements to support property values in white neighborhoods. But even after those laws were struck down by the 1965 Fair Housing Act (see Chapter 2), residential segregation persisted (Trifun 2009; Logan 2017).

In the United States, public school education is locally financed by property taxes and supported by community involvement. The more expensive the property, the more money collected in property taxes, and the better the schools in that district—insofar as monetary resources make schools better. Where people live and the race of their neighbors is now officially a private social matter, left to individual choice based convenience, taste, and affordability that includes available funding by corporate mortgage lenders. But residential segregation is not merely a private social and economic matter. A number of institutional factors contribute to ongoing residential segregation: white aversion to living in racially integrated neighbors; *red lining* by banks (refusing to fund mortgages in minority neighborhoods); *steering* by real estate agents (minorities are not shown properties in white neighborhoods); income and wealth inequalities that correlate with race. As a result, in 2008, 75% of poor whites lived in predominantly middle-income neighborhoods, while 75% of poor African Americans lived in neighborhoods with a 20% household poverty rate (Trifun 2009). Neighborhoods mostly populated by minorities have drastically less resources than white neighborhoods, for K-12 education. For decades, Jonathan Kozol and others have documented this disparity and there is little reason to expect that the situation will improve, soon (Kozol 1991, 1995–2017).

Individual Racial Identities

Individual racial identities are partly the result of how the racial groups to which individuals belong are related to each other in society. The other part involves individual thought and action. A child can be assumed to begin life without awareness of race as such, as something that pertains to her, even though she may react to human traits that others consider racial. Adults may reconfigure their racial identities toward greater well-being through more positive self-images. Insofar as personal racial identity is not a permanent quality or thing, it may be a process of internal dialogue, as first described by W.E.B. Du Bois in his idea of "double consciousness." Mixed-race people do not fit into the monoracial system and they may need to negotiate their racial identities with others and reflect more on those identities than those who are monoracial.

Childhood and Conversion

Children learn the basics for their racial identities while quite young (Banks and Rompf 1973). In their 2002, *The First R: How Children Learn Race and Racism*, Debra Van Ausdale and Joe Feagin recount the results of spending 11 months in a racially integrated preschool. They found that contrary to earlier sociological assumptions, young children do show racial bias, they understand adult ideas of race, and they use derogatory race words to shun and insult their peers. Even three and four year olds understand that racial identity is based on skin color and ancestry. There are also differences between black, white, and mixed-race children: black children insist that mixed black and white children are black and are more aware of skin color differences within racial groups; white children insist that skin colors are permanent and seem to understand that "white" has a social meaning; mixed children are aware of being mixed black and white (Ausdale and Feagin 2002). In a research review compiled a decade later, Lawrence Hirschfeld provided broader support of Ausdale and Feagin's findings, with discussion of studies showing that 6-month-old infants showed greater recognition of own-race faces than those of races different from their care givers. Cross-cultural studies also suggested that infants preferred own-race faces in societies where that race was dominant (Hirschfeld 2012).

The studies of very young children and infants show that individuals recognize racial traits in themselves and others. But that does not mean they understand the system of race that gives full meaning to those traits and to racist behavior. This raises the question of how older children in subordinate racial groups view themselves and what their level of awareness of race, is. In Toni Morrison's 1970 novel, *The Bluest Eye*, eleven year old Pecola Breedlove longs for blue eyes. Pecola's life is grim, due to poverty, incest, violence, and racism. (Morrison relates in the novel's Afterward that she knew a black little girl who also wanted blue eyes.) While *The Bluest Eye* dramatizes **internalized racism**, it can also be interpreted as a poor black child's realization that her life would have been better had she been white, that is, as an impulse for self-preservation. Just as younger children may think and act with elements of race and racism, without a unified understanding of racial difference, Pecola may have experienced racial oppression in the difference between the lives of blacks and whites, without conscious knowledge of race, as such.

Contemporary researchers and practitioners in education and counseling now believe that academic success and psychological health require positive racial self-acceptance by black, mixed race, and racial minority children, in general (Equity 2017; Wanless and Crawford 2017).

Positive racial self-image is considered important for adolescents and adults, also. In the early 1970s, William Cross developed his highly influential Nigrescence Theory, which by 2000 led other researchers to construct scales for measuring stages of nigrescence (Vandiver and Fhagen-Smith 2001). The leading idea behind this program is that well-being requires black individuals to have a positive racial identity, which they reach in stages of psychological and social exploration that constitute a kind of *conversion* to a black-centered perspective, in opposition to the perspective that centers whites in US society. (Cross himself experienced this conversion.) There are five stages: In the Pre-encounter stage, blacks might be self-hating, not view black identity as important, or reject being black. Black identities are intensified and then relaxed in the immersion-emersion stage, and stabilized in the Internalization stage, when a person's blackness is integrated with their gender, religion, work, and other aspects of life (Cross 1991, 2001; Gayden 2015).

Overall, two strains in social science identity theory are evident in the early twenty-first century: internal processes of self-valuation and the relation between the individual and her environment (Stryker and Burke 2000). In the present philosophical context, especially given the relevance of phenomenological approaches, as discussed in Chapter 4, our focus has been on internal processes concerning the self. Neither reports of the racism of children, nor interventions in racial self-image reveal what racial identity is, in or for the self. Why does the infant pay more attention to those who are the same race as she is? Do we know that she has not also focused on other physical traits that her primary caregiver has? How does the child know where she places in the racial system and what kind of thing is her race to her? Is it a description that she comes to recognize as a true description of her, or is it something more like her name, that is, an *ascription*, a proper name that she answers to? Does the child imagine that others are ascribing race to her, when she ascribes a racial identity to herself or does she independently ascribe a racial identity to herself? Perhaps these are not the right questions to ask about individual racial identity, because they assume that racial identity is a thing or quality inside a person.

On a theoretical level, insofar as some theorists have claimed that the self is a series of silent dialogues or conversations, perhaps individual racial identity is more like that, a kind of open-ended internal dialogue about race (Yan and Wong 2005; Haste and Abrahams 2008). Reading is also a form of dialogue between writer and reader, based on what the writer has written and what the reader reads. Much of the American self-help and self-advancement movements have been available in print throughout the nation's history. This is especially true of the vast progressive literature on race, including nineteenth century **racial uplift** writings for African Americans (Gaines 2010).

Du Bois's Idea of Double Consciousness

The term **double consciousness** became very well-known by scholars of race after Du Bois's used it twice, first in an 1897 *Atlantic Monthly* article and second on the first and second pages of "Our Spiritual Strivings," the first chapter of his 1903 book, *The Souls of Black Folk*. After recounting a conversation with a white person asking his views about violence against blacks, Du Bois wrote:

> To the real question, How does it feel to be a problem? I answer seldom a word.
> And yet, being a problem is a strange experience,—peculiar even for one who has never been anything else, save perhaps in babyhood and in Europe. ... After the Egyptian and Indian, the Greek and Roman, the Teuton and Mongolian, the Negro is a sort of seventh son, born with a veil, and gifted with second-sight in this American world,—a world which yields him no true self-consciousness, but only lets him see himself through the revelation of the other world. It is a peculiar sensation, this double-consciousness, this sense of always looking at one's self through the eyes of others, of measuring one's soul by the tape of a world that looks on in amused contempt and pity. One ever feels his two-ness,—an American, a Negro; two souls, two thoughts, two unreconciled strivings; two warring ideals in one dark body, whose dogged strength alone keeps it from being torn asunder. (Du Bois 1903, pp. 1, 2)

As John Pittman points out in his comprehensive entry on Du Bois's notion of double consciousness in the *Stanford Encyclopedia of Philosophy*, this passage is echoed in another passage written by Du Bois in Chapter 10 of *Souls of Black Folk*, "Of the Faith of the Fathers":

> From the double life every American Negro must live, as a Negro and as an American, as swept on by the current of the nineteenth while yet struggling in the eddies of the fifteenth century,—from this must arise a painful self-consciousness, an almost morbid sense of personality, and a moral hesitancy which is fatal to self-confidence. The worlds within and without the Veil of Color are changing, and changing rapidly, but not at the same rate, not in the same way; and this must produce a peculiar wrenching of the soul, a peculiar sense of doubt and bewilderment. Such a double life, with double thoughts, double duties, and double social classes, must give rise to double words and double ideals, and tempt the mind to pretence or revolt, to hypocrisy or radicalism. (Pittman 2016; Du Bois 1903, pp. 155–6)

The passage from Chapter 1 of *The Souls of Black Folk* describes the reflexive nature of consciousness in terms that might not be unique to African American experience. The general insight that the self-reflecting on itself has an object different from itself goes at least as far back as Shakespeare: The eye sees not itself

> but by reflection, by some other things. . . .
> And since you know you cannot see yourself
> So well as by reflection, I, your glass,
> Will modestly discover to yourself
> That of yourself which you yet know not of.
> –William Shakespeare, Julius Caesar (1.2.55–55; 69–72)

However, Du Bois's passage from Chapter 10 of *Faith of the Fathers* more emphatically refers to the experience of African Americans, because he there talks about the double lives and double social roles that African Americans live among whites and among other African Americans. Du Bois does not explicitly say that the double lives and roles are contradictory, but he does imply that the condition is unique and problematic for African Americans. Still, others who are in some ways outcasts or despised members of dominant society, and who also belong to groups in which they are full members and not despised, might have the same structure of double consciousness when they reflect on their contradictory lives and roles. DuBois himself wrote, decades later, in his 1940 *Dusk of Dawn*, "the majority of mankind has struggled through this inner spiritual slavery" (Pittman 2016). If there is a general human process of self-reflection, the process of self-reflection pertaining to race can be viewed as one form of dialogic self-identity.

Mixed-Race Identities

If self-identities generally share certain very widespread psychological processes, those processes become more complicated and intense if a person's racial identity within a taxonomy of races is contested or ambiguous. American mixed black and white self-identity is complex in this way and it also reveals the constructed nature of all racial differences. A person's monoracial identity is already socially constructed in the background of race in a society with a racial system. Because people have been mistaken about the existence of biological race, their ideas, and actions in the past and present concerning race constitute the *social construction* of race. But "race" means "races" and not all racial possibilities have been constructed in the United States. Rather, tradition has it that those with any black ancestry, especially if they do not have an appearance that conforms to expectations of how someone belonging to another race should look, are black. But many mixed black and white Americans who identify as black are also aware of white parentage or ancestry. So, since racial identities are determined by the race of the family of which one is a member, the racial self-identity of a mixed black and white person is more complicated than even the double consciousness described by Du Bois.

Births of American mixed-race people increased since *Loving v. Virginia* in 1967. According to the 2010 census, 9 million people checked more than one box for race, which was 30% more than the 2000 census when that option was first offered. About 1.8 million respondents who checked more than one box, checked black and white (U.S. Census 2010). Mixed black and white race is a logical contradiction insofar as whiteness in the United States is defined as having no nonwhite, especially black, ancestry. That is, a person cannot be both a member of the group that has no black ancestry and a member of the group that does have black ancestry. But 1.8 million chose that option. So one subject for an inner dialogue toward the construction of a racial self-identity by a mixed black and white person might be the question, Why doesn't society count my white ancestry as part of my racial identity and should I personally count it?

In her famous 1993 Bill of Rights for People of Mixed Heritage, Maria P.P. Root asserted 12 rights that pertain to mixed-race self-identity.

I HAVE THE RIGHT…

1. Not to justify my existence in this world.
2. Not to keep the races separate within me.
3. Not to justify my ethnic legitimacy.
4. Not to be responsible for people's discomfort with my physical or ethnic ambiguity.
5. To identify myself differently than strangers expect me to identify.
6. To identify myself differently than how my parents identify me.
7. To identify myself differently than my brothers and sisters.
8. To identify myself differently in different situations.
9. To create a vocabulary to communicate about being multiracial or multiethnic.
10. To change my identity over my lifetime—and more than once.
11. To have loyalties and identification with more than one group of people.
12. To freely choose whom I befriend and love. (Root 1993)

All of Root's asserted rights could be affirmed in internal dialogue pertaining to the construction of mixed black and white racial self-identity. However, proclaiming such rights to oneself or in concert with other mixed-race people is not sufficient to change social tradition. In that sense, it is not possible for individuals to settle mixed racial identities, themselves, without participation by monoracial people. However, the same can be said about other many other self-identities that are not recognized by the dominant culture in which a person lives. Again, we are left with a dialogic process of racial self-identity construction, although now with undetermined resolution (Zack 2017).

Models for Resisting and Deconstructing Race

There have been four major models for resisting and deconstructing race in societies with oppressive racial systems: Pragmatism, Accommodationism, Racial Eliminativism, and Politicized Racial Identities. Accommodationism is a form of pragmatism in a practical sense and racial eliminativism immediately comes up against the need for politicized identities, so it makes sense to discuss these models in pairs.

Pragmatism and Accommodationism

Pragmatic approaches to deliberate or unintended unjust consequences of the construction of race share a desire to correct situations, without blame, in the face of such injustice. Affirmative action initiatives to correct past discrimination were an example of this approach. People of color would get new opportunities for admission or employment, without any direct address of past discrimination or exclusion (see Chapter 9). Onlookers who recognize injustice but do not wish to incur the cost of direct involvement act pragmatically, in this sense. The international community's noninvolvement in the 1994 massacre and attempted genocide in Rwanda is an example of such pragmatism. While members of that community might have an ongoing interest in political stability in sub-Saharan Africa and react with moral abhorrence to the facts of genocide, there is sufficient economic, political, and moral distance to make noninvolvement the most prudent reaction.

However, **accommodationism** is a reaction by those oppressed to their oppressors which seeks to avoid confrontation in words or action, usually out of fear of violent defeat. There were long periods of accommodation by African Americans, during and after slavery and historical exceptions are striking. For instance, Nat Turner's Rebellion was the only slave rebellion on US soil. In Southampton County, Virginia, Nat Turner (1800–1831), a slave and self-proclaimed Baptist minister, led an attack on August 21,

1831, which left 55 or 61 white men, women, and children, dead. Turner and sixteen of his followers were captured and executed and black slaves were killed throughout the area, their heads left on roads to caution others (History Matters 2017). Turner was vilified until the 1960s. He had written "Confessions" that were interpreted as sexually and diabolically deranged and the aftermath of his rebellion caused hysteria among slave owners and other whites, throughout the world (Aptheker 2006). The white reaction to Nat Turner's rebellion was an abiding source of fear among African Americans that made general accommodationism understandable. If whites were not accommodated, their fear could motivate them to more oppressive antiblack racism and violence.

Still, accommodationism has not been universally endorsed by African American leaders. Du Bois disparagingly called Booker T. Washington "the Great Accommodationist." Booker T. Washington (1856–1915) was born a slave, and secured an education despite great poverty. He founded Tuskegee Institute, a boarding school for African Americans where they were taught manual trades and domestic management, under highly disciplined conditions. Washington's main idea was that Negroes ought not to confront whites or demand political equality (it was the age of lynching) but should instead contribute needed goods and services to the economy and make the best of their segregated second-class lives. Washington became the main representative of African Americans, meeting with heads of state and business leaders, all over the world, from the 1890s until his death. He was famous and highly praised by the white establishment for his 1895 address, known as the "Atlanta Compromise," at the Cotton States and International Exposition in Atlanta. Washington said:

> To those of my race who depend on bettering their condition in a foreign land or who underestimate the importance of cultivating friendly relations with the Southern white man, who is their next-door neighbor, I would say: "Cast down your bucket where you are"— cast it down in making friends in every manly way of the people of all races by whom we are surrounded.
>
> Cast it down in agriculture, mechanics, in commerce, in domestic service, and in the professions. ... Our greatest danger is that in the great leap from slavery to freedom we may overlook the fact that the masses of us are to live by the productions of our hands, and fail to keep in mind that we shall prosper in proportion as we learn to dignify and glorify common labour, and put brains and skill into the common occupations of life. ... It is at the bottom of life we must begin, and not at the top. Nor should we permit our grievances to overshadow our opportunities. ... .

To those of the white race who look to the incoming of those of foreign birth and strange tongue and habits for the prosperity of the South, were I permitted I would repeat what I say to my own race, "Cast down your bucket where you are." … .

In all things that are purely social we can be as separate as the fingers, yet one as the hand in all things essential to mutual progress. (Washington, 1901, pp. 111–4)

Washington's accommodationism involved acceptance of inequality, but went beyond that through a program of education, hard work, and self-discipline. Still, throughout *Up From Slavery*, Washington claimed that white society was a meritocracy and he frequently and lavishly praised whites who had helped Tuskegee Institute.

Racial Eliminativism and Politicized Identities

Racial eliminativism is an extreme position that has been attributed to philosophers who have emphasized the lack of a foundation in the human biological sciences for common sense racial taxonomy (Appiah 1995, 1996; Zack 1993, 2002). The eliminativist position would be that we should "get rid of race," because the idea of race is based on now-discarded science and that idea has been a source of great human misery and injustice. Educated individuals can understand the scientific situation regarding race, but beyond them, it is not evident what getting rid of race would mean or entail. Race has become embedded in human life and tradition and it has positive emotional and liberatory meanings for nonwhite people in their daily lives, as well as for whites who benefit from high-status positions and those who have inherited past benefits from those positions. Overtime, nonwhite racial identities have become important unifying symbols for resistance against oppression and demands for justice. This suggests that it might be ineffective to get rid of race in any cognitive or intellectual sense, without also eliminating racism, which would require substantial social change. Finally, even if everyone would be better-off without race, there is no clear path to that end except continual education and reeducation about the facts of race. But in a country with local educational systems and strong free speech rights, such as the United States, there would be no democratic way to implement the elimination of race from public speech and classrooms.

As discussed in Chapter 3, since the early 1990s, philosophers of race have been engaged in what has been called "The Race Debates," a series of discussions about how to react to the fact that race does not have the biological foundation so many previously assumed it had. Insofar as there is a consensus about the lack of biological foundation according to biologists, all participants in these debates are modified eliminativists to one degree or another, depending on what about "race" they advocate eliminating. Thus, *racial constructivists* emphasize the social, institutional and political constructions of race within society, insisting on their reality, while suspending questions about underlying biology. And *racial population naturalists* seek to preserve a stripped-down scientific version of race by picking out the human populations to which ordinary language racial taxonomy might refer (James 2017). In neither of those cases is there an attempt to resurrect older ideas of **racial essences** as real spiritual or physical entities, shared by all members of race in social racial taxonomies, as primary causes of the traits associated with that race. Thus, both sides of the race debates in philosophy are eliminativists about racial essences.

Racial identities, especially for people of African descent, have been politicized as a means for resisting racial oppression and achieving racial justice. The question of racial eliminativism, discussed above, arrived relatively late to US Philosophy of Race. In the early 1960s, there was a race debate between Frantz Fanon and Jean-Paul Sartre regarding the necessity of essentialism for the liberation of Africans who, although French, faced racial discrimination when they claimed their nationality. Both Sartre and Fanon generally agreed that racial identities would not be necessary after the end of racism, but Fanon expressed misgivings about Sartre's right to proclaim that on his (Fanon's) behalf (Bernasconi 2002). Apart from the literary and political complexities of its time, the Fanon-Sartre dispute highlights the political and moral importance of the racial identity of who advocates racial eliminativism, those who belong to the group of the racially advantaged or those who belong to the group of the racially oppressed. That is, it is one thing for people of color to be racial eliminativists. But they are likely to be suspicious of whites who want to eliminate race without a deep understanding of racism, the subject to which we now turn, in Chapter 7.

Conclusion

Constructions of race are evident historically through the present. Globalism is continuous with colonialism in that the same disadvantaged populations are not white Europeans. Social technologies of race such as segregation and same-race marriage customs reproduce racial taxonomies by preserving the racial identities of status groups. Individual racial identities, including nonconventional ones, such as mixed black and white race, may be constructed through constant internal dialogue. Pragmatic and accommodationist approaches to racism allow nonwhites to live within these systems by minimizing conflict. Most participants in the so-called race debates are eliminativists about racial essences, although wholesale racial eliminativism is unlikely at this time.

Glossary

anti-miscegenation laws—state regulation of whether people of one race could marry people of another race.

accommodationism—a reaction by those oppressed, which seeks to avoid confrontation with oppressors, in words or action, usually out of fear of violent defeat.

colonization—political annexation or takeover of a territory or nation by a stronger national power, historically backed by aggressive force, with different degrees of economic, social, and political involvement following.

development—economic and political projects by governments and international business in countries or regions that are relatively poor and lack the same infrastructure as the countries of developers.

postcolonial studies or **postcolonial critical theory of IR (International Relations)**—theoretical and practical analyses of populations and countries in areas of the world that were previously colonized and believed to undergo the effects of colonization.

double consciousness—W.E.B. Du Bois's idea that African Americans view themselves both as they are in their own communities, and as whites view them; idea of the selfreflecting on itself, going back to Shakespeare in "Julius Caesar."

eliminativism—position that the idea of race should be discarded based on what is known about its lack of a foundation in the human biological sciences.

internalized racism—an individual's application to herself of societal racism against the racial group to which she belongs.

miscegenation—term for racial mixing, especially in marriage, as in **antimiscegenation laws** that prohibited interracial marriage.

natural law—tradition of European and English law that upheld basic or God-given order in the world.

oppression—unjust treatment and control.

racial ideology—false system of claims and beliefs to justify racial hierarchy and racial oppression.

racial essence—posit of a spiritual or physical "something" that members of each distinct human race shared and which caused the traits associated with that race.

racial identity—description that places an individual, racially, as a member of a group within social system of race.

racial hierarchy—an abstract or real system of distinct races that ranks them with regard to one another with regard to status and social power, as based on posited traits.

racial uplift—nineteenth century projects, undertaken by more successful African Americans to support and bring about racial progress for the wider group of African Americans.

segregation—legally imposed or socially supported separation of people by race in the use of public facilities and amenities.

separate-but-equal—US legal doctrine permitting segregation under the fiction that racially separate facilities were equal, which they never were.

social construction of race—beliefs and practices pertaining to racial traits and the hierarchy of racial groups, which usually claims to have a biological foundation.

social technology of race—social and institutional mechanism to provide for the functioning of a societal system of race.

terra nullius—the justification of the ownership of first taker to what is owned by no one.

territorium nullius—the doctrine that collectives without government did not own the land they occupied.

utilitarianism—moral system based on the principle that moral good is the greatest pleasure for the greatest number.

white racial purity—idea that white people have no nonwhite ancestry.

Discussion Questions

1. Give examples from your own experience of how people encounter race in society as already constructed.
2. How is development continuous with colonialism? Does race construct development or does development construct race? (Explain both perspectives.)
3. What are the lessons from Rwanda in terms of competition among nonwhite groups under oppression?

4. Explain the difference between *terra nullius* and *territorium nullius*.
5. What is your assessment of Cross's idea of Nigrescence?
6. How might a racial self be a dialogue in terms of Du Bois's idea of double consciousness? Explain how that situation may not be unique to black Americans.
7. How is mixed black and white race a logical contradiction?
8. What are some examples of social technologies of race not mentioned in the text?
9. How is accommodationism pragmatic?
10. Explain how racial eliminativism is a more widespread position than the "race debates" indicate.

References

Agénor, Pierre-Richard, and Peter J. Montiel. *Development Macroeconomics*. Princeton, NJ: Princeton University Press, 2008.

Appiah, K.A. "The Uncompleted Argument: DuBois and the Illusion of Race." *Overcoming Racism and Sexism*, edited by L. Bell and D. Blumenfeld, Lanham, MD: Rowman & Littlefield, 1995, pp. 59–75.

Appiah, K.A. "Race, Culture, Identity: Misunderstood Connections." *Color Conscious*, edited by Anthony Appiah and Amy Gutmann. Princeton, NJ: Princeton University Press, 1996, pp. 30–105.

Aptheker, Herbert. *Nat Turner's Slave Rebellion*. Mineola, NY: Dover, 2006.

Australian Explorer. "Australian History," 2017. www.australianexplorer.com/australian_history.htm.

Banks, W. Curtis, and William James Rompf. "Evaluative Bias and Preference Behavior in Black and White Children." *Child Development*, vol. 44, no. 4, 1973, pp. 776–83. https://doi.org/10.2307/1127723.

Bayliss, John, Steve Smith, and Patricial Owens. *The Globalization of World Politics: An Introduction to International Relations*, 5th ed. New York, NY: Oxford University Press, 2011.

Bentham, Jeremy. *Anarchical Fallacies*, edited by William Atkins Edmunson, Cambridge, MA: Cambridge University Press, 1998.

Bernasconi, Robert. "The Assumption of Negritude: Aimé Césaire, Frantz Fanon, and the Vicious Circle of Racial Politics." *Parallax*, vol. 8, no. 2, 2002, pp. 69–83.

BBC Africa. "Rwanda: How the Genocide Happened," 2012. http://www.bbc.co.uk/news/world-africa-13431486.

Cavendish, Richard. "Spanish Bankruptcy." *History Today*, vol. 57, no. 11, Nov. 2007.

Center for Global Development. "Climate Change," 2017. https://www.cgdev.org/topics/climate-change.

Cross, William. *Shades of Black*. Philadelphia, PA: Temple University Press, 1991.

Cross William. "Encountering Nigrescence." *Handbook of Multicultural Counseling*, Thousand Oaks, CA: Sage, 2001, pp. 3–44.

Du Bois, W.E.B. *The Souls of Black Folk*. Atlanta, GA, Chicago: A.C. McClurg & Co.; [Cambridge]: University Press John Wilson and Son, Cambridge, U.S.A., 1903, http://www.wwnorton.com/college/history/give-me-liberty4/docs/WEBDuBois-Souls_of_Black_Folk-1903.pdf.

Essential Humanities. "European Colonialism," 2008–2013. Accessed June 24, 2017. http://www.essential-humanities.net/history-supplementary/european-colonialism/.

Equity: Supporting Positive Racial Identity Development. "Resources for Supporting Positive Racial identity Development," June, 2017. https://sites.google.com/a/chccs.k12.nc.us/racialid/.

Fitzmaurice, Andrew. "The Genealogy of Terra Nullius." *Australian Historical Studies*, vol. 38, no. 129, 2007, pp. 1–15.

Free the Slaves. 2017. http://www.freetheslaves.net/.

Gaines, Kevin, K. "Racial Uplift Ideology in the Era of 'the Negro Problem'." *Teacher Serve*, National Humanities Center, 2010. http://nationalhumaniti-escenter.org/tserve/freedom/1865-1917/essays/racialuplift.htm.

Gayden, Rashad. "Comparison of Two Theories of Racial Identity: Nigrescence Theory and Cultural Ecology Theory." MA thesis, 2015, Education Leadership Department, Winona University.

Haste, Helen, and Salie Abrahams. "Morality, Culture and the Dialogic Self: Taking Cultural Pluralism Seriously." *Journal of Moral Education*, vol. 37, no. 3, 2008, pp. 377–94. http://www.tandfonline.com/doi/abs/10.1080/03057240802227502.

Hirschfeld, Lawrence A. "Seven Myths of Race and the Young Child." *Du Bois Review: Social Science Research on Race*, vol. 9, no. 1, 2012, pp. 17–39. https://doi.org/10.1017/s1742058x12000033.

History Matters. "The Nat Turner Rebellion," 2017. http://historymatters.gmu.edu/d/6811/.

James, Michael. "Race." The Stanford Encyclopedia of Philosophy Spring 2017 Edition, edited by Edward N. Zalta. https://plato.stanford.edu/archives/spr2017/entries/race/.

Johnson, B. 2012. "A History of the Hutu-Tutsi Conflict." *About.com World News*. http://worldnews.about.com/od/africa/a/hutututsiconflicthistory.htm.

Kozol, Jonathan. *Savage Inequalities*. New York, NY: Random House, 1991; Jonathan Kozol.com. http://www.jonathankozol.com/.

Kozol, Jonathan, Interview, 1995–2017. YouTube, https://www.youtube.com/watch?v=p2KEErZwQhg.

Lange, Karen E. "Last Colonies." *National Geographic Magazine*, June 26, 2008. http://ngm.nationalgeographic.com/geopedia/Last_Colonies.

Las Casas, Bartolomé de. *The Devastation of the Indies: A Brief Account*. Baltimore, MD: Johns Hopkins University Press, 1992.

Logan, John R. "The Persistence of Segregation in the 21st Century Metropolis." *City & community*, vol. 12, no. 2, 2013. https://doi.org/10.1111/cico.12021. PMC. Web. 26 June 2017. https://www.ncbi.nlm.nih.gov/pmc/articles/PMC3859616/.

Mbaku, John Mukum. "Foresight Africa 2017: Election Spotlight on Rwanda." Africa in Focus, Brookings, Jan. 30, 2017. https://www.brookings.edu/blog/africa-in-focus/2017/01/30/foresight-africa-2017-election-spotlight-on-rwanda/.

Mohawk Nation Office, Kahnawà:ke Branch, 2017. http://www.kahnawakelonghouse.com/index.php?mid=1.

Ott, Thomas O. *The Haitian Revolution 1789–1804*. Knoxville, TN: University of Tennessee, 1973. http://www.pbs.org/wgbh/aia/part3/3p2990.html.

Pedreira, Jorge Miguel Viana. "From Growth to Collapse: Portugal, Brazil, and the Breakdown of the Old Colonial System, 1750–1830." *Hispanic American Historical Review*, vol. 80, no. 4, Nov. 2000, pp. 839–64.

Pennington, Kenneth. Bartolomé de Las Casas and the Tradition of Medieval Law, *CUA Law Scholarship Repository*, The Catholic University of America, Columbus School of Law, 1970. http://scholarship.law.edu/cgi/viewcontent.cgi?article=1652&context=scholar.

Pittman, John, P. "Double Consciousness." *Stanford Encyclopedia of Philosophy*, 2016. https://plato.stanford.edu/entries/double-consciousness/#TrajConc.

Root, Maria, P.P. "Bill of Rights for Racially Mixed People," 1993. https://multiracialnetwork.files.wordpress.com/2012/09/billofrights.png and https://multiracialnetwork.wordpress.com/2012/09/10/revisiting-roots-bill-of-rights/Root.

Sickels, Robert J. *Race, Marriage, and the Law*. Albuquerque, NM: University of New Mexico Press, 1972.

Stryker, Sheldon, and Peter J. Burke. "The Past, Present, and Future of an Identity Theory." *Social Psychology Quarterly*, vol. 63, no. 4, Special Millennium Issue on the State of Sociological Social Psychology, Dec. 2000, pp. 284–97.

Sutherland, Claudia E. "Haitian Revolution, 1791–1804." African American History, Black Past.org v.2. 02., 2007–2017. http://www.blackpast.org/gah/haitian-revolution-1791-1804.

Trifun, Natasha M. "Residential Segregation After the Fair Housing Act." *Human Rights Magazine, American Bar Association*, vol. 36 no. 4, 2009. https://www.americanbar.org/publications/human_rights_magazine_home/human_rights_vol36_2009/fall2009/residential_segregation_after_the_fair_housing_act.html.

U.S. 2010. Census Briefs, "The Two or More Races Population, 2010." https://www.census.gov/prod/cen2010/briefs/c2010br-13.pdf; "Overview of Race and Hispanic Origin." http://www.census.gov/prod/cen2010/briefs/c2010br-02.pdf.

Van Ausdale, Debra, and Joe R. Feagin. *The First R: How Children Learn Race and Racism*. Lanham, MD: Rowman & Littlefield, 2002.

Vandiver, B.J., Fhagen-Smith, P. E., Cokley, K.O., Cross, W.E., and Worrell, F.C. 2001. "Cross's Nigrescence Model: 'From Theory to Scale to Theory.'" *Journal of Multicultural Counseling and Development*, vol. 29, pp. 174–200. https://doi.org/10.1002/j.2161-1912.2001.tb00516.xMiu.

Ventura, Stephanie J.M.A., and Christine A. Bachrach. "Nonmarital Childbearing in the United States, 1940–99," vol. 48, no. 6. National Vital Statistics Reports, National Center for Health Statistics, Centers for Disease Control and Prevention, Oct. 18, 2000. https://www.cdc.gov/nchs/data/nvsr/nvsr48/nvs48_16.pdf.

Wanless Shannon B., and Patricia A. Crawford. "Supporting Positive Racial Identity Development in Early Childhood Classrooms." *PittEd-School of Education Magazine*, University of Pennsylvania, 2017.

Washington, Booker T. *Up from Slavery: An Autobiography by Booker T. Washington*, Project Gutenberg, 1901. http://www.gutenberg.org/ebooks/2376.

World Atlas. "What Was the Age of Exploration or the Age of Discovery?" 2017. http://www.worldatlas.com/articles/what-was-the-age-of-exploration-or-the-age-of-discovery.html.

Yan, Chung, and Yuk-Lin Renita Wong. "Rethinking Self-Awareness in Cultural Competence: Toward a Dialogic Self in Cross-Cultural Social Work." *Families in Society: The Journal of Contemporary Social Services*, vol. 86, no. 2, 2005, pp. 181–8. http://familiesinsocietyjournal.org/doi/abs/10.1606/1044-3894.2453?code=afcf-site.

Zack, Naomi. *Race and Mixed Race*. Philadelphia: Temple University Press, 1993.

Zack, Naomi. *Philosophy of Science and Race*. New York: Routledge, 2002.

Zack, Naomi. "How Mixed Race Is not Constructed: US Identities and Perspectives." *Oxford Handbook of Philosophy and Race*, edited by Naomi Zack, New York, NY: Oxford University Press, 2017, pp. 380–91.

Ziltener, Patrick, Künzler, Daniel, and Walter, André, "Research Note: Measuring the Impacts of Colonialism: A New Data Set for the Countries of Africa and Asia." *Journal of World-Systems Research*, [S.l.], vol. 23, no. 1, Feb. 2017, pp. 156–90. Available at http://jwsr.pitt.edu/ojs/index.php/jwsr/article/view/683. Accessed June 25, 2017. https://doi.org/10.5195/jwsr.2017.683.

7

Racism and Neo-racisms

The word "racism" was not always in use along with beliefs in the existence of human races. During the age of racial essentialism and explicit white supremacy based on posits of racial hierarchy, what is called "racism" today was built into the idea of race. As ideas that human races were morally equal gained credibility, names came into use for those who retained inegalitarian beliefs and the practices associated with those beliefs. According to the *Oxford English Dictionary* the first recorded use of the word "racism" in English derives from Richard Henry Pratt's (1840–1924) criticism of government policy that segregated Native Americans:

> Segregating any class or race of people apart from the rest of the people kills the progress of the segregated people or makes their growth very slow. Association of races and classes is necessary to destroy racism and classism.

Pratt had been Second Lieutenant in charge of the Buffalo Soldiers, the sole African–American unit during the Civil War. He persuaded Congress to fund a boarding school for Native American children, the Carlisle Indian Industrial School at Carlisle, Pennsylvania, with a mission to extinguish their language and culture so that they could assimilate to white society (Demby 2013). The irony is that today, Pratt would be considered a cultural racist for his goal of eliminating Native American culture.

At first, the word "racism" came into broad intellectual use to describe Nazi propaganda against Jews in the 1930s (Fredrickson 2002, p. 5). According to the United Nations High Commission in 1969, racial discrimination is about ethnicity as well as race:

© The Author(s) 2018
N. Zack, *Philosophy of Race*, Palgrave Philosophy Today,
https://doi.org/10.1007/978-3-319-78729-9_7

In this Convention, the term "racial discrimination" shall mean any distinction, exclusion, restriction or preference based on race, colour, descent, or national or ethnic origin which has the purpose or effect of nullifying or impairing the recognition, enjoyment or exercise, on an equal footing, of human rights and fundamental freedoms in the political, economic, social, cultural or any other field of public life. (United Nations, Part I, Article 1, 1, 1969)

The word "racism" was in ordinary usage by the 1970s and it played a prominent role in the new wave of progressive academic scholarship that began at the end of that decade. Anthony Appiah in 1990 distinguished between *racialists*, or those who believe there are races with essences, and two kinds of *racists*: *extrinsic racists* believe that racial essences determine morally relevant differences such as character traits; *intrinsic racists* believe that races are morally different, regardless of their essences (Appiah 1990, pp. 5–6).

In the early twenty-first century, when ordinary people in US society and those in the mass media talk about "race"—talk that many believe does not happen often enough—they are usually talking about racism. But the two are different, conceptually: "racism" refers to attitudes and actions toward people; "race" is about the taxonomy of human races. (Chapters 1–6 addressed race and this chapter is about racism.) Part of the widely recognized reluctance of people to talk about race in the early twenty-first century is related to agreement that racism is unjust and morally bad. **Racism**, as we will consider it in this chapter, consists of **prejudice** or negative beliefs about people because of their race, and **discrimination** or unfavorable treatment of people because of their race. Prejudice and discrimination are the two components of racism, but that in itself doesn't tell us very much. To add content to these abstractions, we need to understand what specific kinds of speech and action in reality are racist. And we need to understand how they work, to what extent they are illegal, and who or what is to blame for them. It's also important to understand whether racism can be changed and to consider how that could come about.

The late twentieth-century academic study of racism began with individuals and legal structures. It was assumed that racist actions and exclusions were carried out because individuals had certain beliefs, and that people of color experienced discrimination because the law did not explicitly prohibit it. After the civil rights movement, the number of people identifying as white supremacist or segregationist rapidly decreased, but the effects of racism continued. Scholars then realized that racism was still observable, but without known individual prejudice or intentional individual discrimination. That insight led to ideas of structural or institutional racism or racism without individual intent. However, individuals still participate in those racist structures and institutions that harm nonwhites but not whites. Therefore, ideas of implicit racism arose, including *white privilege, micro-aggression* and *epistemic oppression*. The first part of this chapter is about racism as something done by individuals—hearts-and-minds racism and racist action. This will be followed by discussion of contemporary institutional or structural racism and the chapter will conclude with analyses of implicit racism.

Racism by Individuals

Racism by individuals consists of unexpressed racist thoughts and feelings and explicit and deliberate racist speech and action. Racist action ranges over many forms of human behavior, including crime.

Racist Thought and Speech

Hearts-and-minds racism (HMR) is racism in, of, or by individuals, consisting of the beliefs of individuals and their reactions, emotions, impressions, and dispositions to act in racist ways. Prejudice, as judgment made before experience, plays an important role in this kind of individual racism. The racist has a closed mind and cold heart regarding groups and their members who are the objects of her racism. Such racism is often based on limited personal experience and interaction with people of races different from one's own, or it is simply adopted from others, such as friends and family members, who are already racists. HMR may be limited to a person's private life or socially and politically expressed. Most HMR racists are intrinsic racists according to Appiah's definitions—just the race of a person who is member of a group they are racist against is enough to evoke their racism.

Philosophers have addressed HMR with ethical analyses pertaining to moral responsibility in terms of individual virtue/vice and praise/blame. To be responsible for racism, it must be true that an individual could have not become a racist. J.L.A. Garcia has put forth a *volitional* or willed account of racism, as a vice in the heart of a racist that affects or infects her actions. Garcia claims that beliefs are secondary to racism, because racism is primarily motivated by emotions and attitudes and need not logically follow from beliefs (Garcia 1996). Tommy Shelby has responded to Garcia by insisting that the racist must have some beliefs associated with her racism and suggesting that racism more closely resembles an ideology or false view of the world, than either emotions or isolated beliefs (Shelby 2002).

Public racist speech was linked to politics after the 2016 US presidential election. Richard B. Spencer addressed the National Policy Institute, self-described as "an independent organization dedicated to the heritage, identity, and future of people of European descent in the United States, and around the world." Spencer proclaimed, "America was until this past generation a white country designed for ourselves and our posterity. It is our creation, it is our inheritance, and it belongs to us." Spencer's white audience cheered, applauded, and raised Nazi salutes in homage to President-Elect Donald Trump (Lombroso and Appelbaum 2016). They were expressing a political ideology of HMR as Shelby suggests, but also expressing individual emotions and attitudes as intrinsic racists.

The question naturally arises of whether some people of color are HMR racists. Insofar as people of color may react in racist ways against whites who have directed racist discourse and action against them, they are not intrinsic racists. That they are reacting to the racism of others suggests that they would not be racist against whites if whites had not been racist against them. When people of color engage in antiwhite racist discourse in the absence of immediate white racist discourse or action, they are often referring to past white racist action, such as slavery and lynching under Jim Crow, not so much in prejudice as postjudice. **Postjudice** is an attitude of judging people based on their race, because members of that same race perpetrated racist harms in the past. It goes beyond claiming that those past actions have ongoing effects in the present, because it holds contemporary people responsible for what ancestors of the racial group they belong to, did in the past.

Insofar as HMR by white people expresses white superiority, contempt for nonwhites, and an attitude by those of higher status based on race, it draws on ideas of racial hierarchy that value whites over all other racial groups. There is no such historical or contemporary background of higher status for people of color, especially African Americans. Those who may be intrinsic racists against whites do not have the same ability to express superiority, contempt, or any attitude from higher status. In an immediate context, people of color may at times be properly charged with antiwhite HMR, but when broader societal status contexts are considered, the charge is difficult to back up.

There are milder versions of non-racist defenses among people of color that may look like racism to a casual observer. Within racially integrated schools and colleges, students of color tend to segregate. Part of that self-segregation is a reaction to the aversion and avoidance of interactions with students of color, by white students; another part is a desire of students of color to associate with one another. In a 2007 qualitative study of nine high-achieving black students in a predominantly white high school,

Dorinda Carter concluded that meeting and talking within their racial and achievement group supported their academic success and gave these students opportunities to affirm their own racial identities, as well as cope with non-supportive aspects of their environment (Carter 2007). Research on first-generation college student success suggests that students of color (many of whom are the first in their families to attend college) benefit from structured Living-Learning programs for both academic and social resources (Inkelas et al. 2007; University of Oregon 2017).

As private or public discourse, HMR is still speech and not yet action. In the United States, such discourse is constitutionally protected as a First Amendment right to free speech. Other countries are not as permissive about racist speech. After World War II, in reaction to the Holocaust, there was legislation throughout Europe against anti-Semitic discourse, as a means to prevent recurrence of genocide. This legal policy expanded through the European Convention on Human Rights (ECHR), the International Convention on the Elimination of All Forms of Racial Discrimination (CERD), and the International Covenant on Civil and Political Rights (ICCPR). In Article 10, the ECHR imposes restrictions on freedom of expression, to protect "the reputation and rights of others." The CERD in Article 4(a) requires signatory nations to enact punishment for "all dissemination of ideas based on racial superiority or hatred." In Article 20, the ICCPR requires signatory nations to have laws against "any advocacy of national, racial, or religious hatred that constitutes incitement to discrimination, hostility, or violence" (The Middle East Forum 2017).

Between US Free Speech permissiveness and European restrictions, Canada restricts racial and ethnically discriminatory free speech. Canadian law also covers electronic communication. Section 13 of the Canadian Human Rights Act warns that it is a "discriminatory practice" to send hate messages via telecommunications equipment, including the internet (CBC News, Canada 2011). But there are strict standards for prohibition and punishment, as well as loopholes. Prohibited speech must be severe, targeted, public, and deliberate. Religious interpretation and rhetoric such as irony are permissible (Butt 2015).

Racist Action and Hate Crimes

Racist action is anything harmful done to, with, or about members of a racial group, from racist motives. Not all such actions are crimes. In US law, only individual racist action that is categorized as a hate crime is punishable.

The requirements for action to count as hate crime are detailed and stringent. Here is how the FBI, relying on definitions provided by Congress, defines hate crimes:

> A hate crime is a traditional offense like murder, arson, or vandalism with an added element of bias. For the purposes of collecting statistics, Congress has defined a hate crime as a "criminal offense against a person or property motivated in whole or in part by an offender's bias against a race, religion, disability, ethnic origin or sexual orientation." Hate itself is not a crime—and the FBI is mindful of protecting freedom of speech and other civil liberties. (FBI 2017)

The FBI has also made a public commitment to investigating and prosecuting hate crimes, "as the highest priority of its Civil Rights Program," based on racist history that is recounted on its website:

> The FBI investigated what are now called hate crimes as far back as World War I. Our role increased following the passage of the Civil Rights Act of 1964. Before then, the federal government took the position that protection of civil rights was a local function, not a federal one. However, the murders of civil rights workers Michael Schwerner, Andrew Goodman, and James Chaney, near Philadelphia, Mississippi, in June 1964 provided the impetus for a visible and sustained federal effort to protect and foster civil rights for African Americans. MIBURN, as the case was called (it stood for Mississippi Burning), became the largest federal investigation ever conducted in Mississippi. On October 20, 1967, seven men were convicted of conspiring to violate the constitutional rights of the slain civil rights workers. All seven were sentenced to prison terms ranging from three to ten years. (FBI 2017)

Hate is not a crime in the United States and hating a racial group is not a crime. In the FBI definition of hate crimes and the description of the historical background to its commitment against them, the victims as well as the perpetrators of hate crimes are perceived by the FBI to be individuals and not racial groups. This legal focus on individuals, which is in accord with the 1960s civil rights and immigration legislation wording, makes it difficult to secure legal remedies for racist actions that go beyond harm to individuals and affect many more members of a larger racial group. The FBI does have a category of "crimes against society" but these are "so-called" victimless crimes such as prostitution and drug use (FBI: NIBRS 2015).

There are other gaps in the FBI's definition of hate crimes. If an individual is racist toward a racial group and its members and commits a crime against one of its members for an immediate motive different from his or her racism, that crime would not qualify as a hate crime. For example, imagine a situation of road rage caused by a minor accident between a black motorist and a racist white motorist. The white motorist pulls out a gun and kills the black motorist because he is enraged by the damage to his bumper. That would not qualify as a hate crime, even if the white motorist would not have killed another white motorist in the same situation, although it would be racist action. To qualify as a hate crime, racist action has to be mainly or solely motivated by the race of the victim.

Hate crimes meeting the FBI criteria and recorded as such are relatively rare in the United States. For 2015, the FBI reported for "Victims of Hate Crime Incidents," that there were 5818 single-bias incidents involving 7121 victims; 59.2% of victims (about 4200) were targeted because of the offenders' race/ethnicity/ancestry bias (FBI 2016, 2017). By comparison, in 2015, there were an estimated 1,197,704 violent crimes in the United States and an estimated 7,993,631 property crimes (FBI: UCR 2017). Thus, out of about 1.2 million crimes against individuals, about 7000 or 7% were reported as hate crimes associated with race/ethnicity/ancestry/bias (which include intimidation). Either hate crimes are underreported or the requirements for what constitute hate crimes exclude racist crimes that in common sense would be considered hate crimes—or both. In a report from the Bureau of Justice Statistics, it was estimated that between 2003 and 2011, over 250,000 hate crimes occurred each year (Sandholtz et al. 2003). That would average out to about 35 times the FBI hate crimes reported for 2015.

Although relatively rare as reported, racial and ethnic hate crimes receive intense media coverage and alarm many members of the group to which targeted victims belong. As related by Human Rights Watch, University of California researchers reported that hate crimes against Muslims increased 44% in 2016, going from 180 incidents in 2015 to (an estimated) 260 in 2016 (Pitter 2017). There were also reports of increased hate crimes against Muslims after the 2016 elections. Thus, *Slate* staff reported in June 2017:

> Since the election of President Donald Trump, news outlets and social media accounts have swelled with reports of swastikas at schools, racist taunts, and other hate-fueled attacks and acts of intimidation. The Southern Poverty Law Center, which has aggregated media reports and gathered submissions from its website, catalogued 1064 such incidents, 13 of which were later debunked as false reports, in the first month after Trump won the presidency. (Twenty-six of those incidents were perpetrated against Trump supporters.) (*Slate* Staff 2017)

Overall, the United States does not have a legal apparatus to punish or deter hate speech against nonwhites or crimes that may arise from hearts-and-minds racism. Institutions such as universities may have their own internal policies to curb such expression and action by individuals, and the general impression is that they are more stringent than outside government entities. However, in Spring 2017, five progressive African–American tenured professors, who exercised their free speech rights to criticize violence by whites or refer to black self-defense, were aggressively attacked in conservative media, which led to death threats and disruption of their lives. The professors received either lukewarm support from their administrations or disciplinary action (Creeley 2017). This suggests that First Amendment rights are not fully protected against those who use them abusively against other individuals who are using them and that they have become a weapon against academic freedom.

Institutional Racism

Institutional racism or **structural racism** is a form of discrimination that affects large numbers of nonwhites. It is racist, because the effects of the discrimination on nonwhites by or within public and private institutional procedures and social practices, amounts to treatment worse or more unjust than how whites are treated. There may be no intentional bias by individuals who carry out institutional racism. The instruments of institutional racism need not mention race explicitly in order to have unequal racial effects. Institutional racism does not require an HMR component.

The US Criminal Justice System

From arrest to imprisonment, to life after release from prison, the US criminal justice system functions as a form of institutional racism against African Americans, Hispanic/Latinos, and other nonwhites. Disproportionate numbers of nonwhites are incarcerated. A paraphrase of Peter Wagner and Bernadette Rabuy's report on US mass incarceration in 2016, on behalf of The Prison Policy Initiative, provides a general picture: Over 2.3 million people are incarcerated in 1719 state prisons, 102 federal prisons, 901 juvenile correctional facilities, 3163 local jails, and 76 Indian Country jails. Others are held in military prisons, immigration detention facilities, civil commitment centers, and prisons in US territories.

On a yearly basis, 641,000 people are released from prison, but 11 million people are jailed. Nonviolent drug offenses involve 20% of those arrested, with most of those arrests occurring at the federal level.

(African Americans represent 12.5% of illicit drug users, but they constitute 29% of those arrested for drug offenses and 33% of those incarcerated in state facilities for drug offenses (National Association for the Advancement of Colored People (NAACP) 2017.) Almost all convictions are the result of *plea bargains* when defendants, including those who are innocent, plead guilty for a lesser offense in order to avoid the uncertainty of a trial. Federal prisons hold 16,000 people for criminal convictions of violating federal immigration laws and 41,000 are civilly detained by US Immigration and Customs Enforcement (ICE). All together, 840,000 people are on parole (conditional release) and 3.7 million are on probation (as an alternative sentence) (Wagner and Rabuy 2017).

Wagner and Rabuy also note that at 13% of the whole population, African Americans are 40% of the prison population; at 64%, whites are 39% of the prison population, and at 14%, Hispanics are 19% of the prison population (Wagner and Rabuy 2017). There are other figures related to these disparities according to the NAACP's. "Criminal Justice Factsheet:" From 1980 to 2015, the US prison population grew from half a million to over 2.2 million. One in 37 adult Americans or 2.7% are under correctional supervision. African American adults are incarcerated five times the rate of whites; African American children are 32% of children arrested, 42% of children detained, and 32% of arrested children who are sent to criminal court (NAACP 2017).

Although the United States contains 5% of the global population, it makes up 21% of the global incarcerated population. If African Americans and Hispanics were arrested at the same rate as whites, the prison population would be reduced by 40% (NAACP 2017). If that were to happen, the United States would make up about 12% of the world's prison population compared to being 5% of its total population. The use of prison itself to discipline or oppress nonwhites might be based on a more general social and political commitment to control minority populations. There is also a partly private prison industry that provides jobs for contractors and staff, as well as profits for corporations. One cause of so many nonwhites in prison may be that they are already a vulnerable part of the population, economically and socially.

The US prison system is to an extent self-perpetuating regarding minorities. The processing of people of color into prison, the effects of their incarceration on family members, and the nature of their lives after release, are integral parts of the prison system. Michelle Alexander in *The New Jim Crow* describes the increase in the US prison population, together with the War on Drugs begun during the Reagan administration, as a conservative reaction to the success of the civil rights movement. Felons face permanent obstacles to employment and lose the right to vote, after their release. While relatives are incarcerated, family members are not only separated from fathers, sons, and husbands, but often forced to go onto various government aid programs and/or suffer extreme poverty, which predisposes the next generation to poverty and prison (Alexander 2011). Moreover, there is reason to believe, as we will discuss in Chapter 9, that racial profiling is part of the wide net that disproportionately charges people of color with crimes that put them in prison—and part of the justification for racial profiling is the high rates of minority imprisonment (Zack 2015, pp. 54–6). There is also long-standing evidence that prosecutors and juries may be racially biased (Equal Justice Initiative (EJI) 2017). The result of all this is that preexisting racism and preexisting punitive tendencies in US culture, the poverty of prison families, and high rates of minority incarceration, all work together to perpetuate high rates of minority incarceration.

Public K-12 Education

In their introduction to *No Excuses: Closing the Racial Gap in Education*, Abigail Thernstrom and Stephan Thernstrom write:

> Today at age 17 the typical black or Hispanic student is scoring less well on the nation's most reliable tests than at least 80 percent of his or her white classmates. In five of the seven subjects tested by the National Assessment of Education Project (NAEP), a majority of black students perform in the lowest category—Below Basic. The result: By twelfth grade black students are typically four years behind white or Asian students, while Hispanics are doing only a tad better than black students. These students are finishing high school with a junior high education. (Thernstrom and Thernstrom 2003, p. 2)

Success in the US public school system is officially based on merit. But merit at any given age depends on resources available for the child to develop and those resources include funds available to public schools and intangible resources such as support for student motivation to achieve. In Chapter 6, we mentioned the correlation between residential property values and resources for public schools. Affluent neighborhoods that have disproportionately lower numbers of minority residents generally have better schools. Racial differences in home ownership and mortgage debt are also well-known. After the Great Recession of 2007–2008, US homeowners lost 7 trillion in equity (home value minus mortgage debt). Black-white gaps increased and Latino-white gaps were the greatest, because blacks and Hispanic/Latinos tend to own property in poorer neighborhoods that are not as resilient in economic downturns (Faber and Ellen 2016). Although home values went down in those neighborhoods, erosion of local tax revenue for K-12 education was offset by higher tax rates. States typically provide 45% of school funding, the federal government provides 46% and the rest is provided by local taxes. However, cuts in state spending affected gaps in school funding that were already underway, with significant effects on most of the 52 million K-12 students in 50 states and 14,000 school districts (Leachman et al. 2016).

Not only do poor nonwhite children have less available educational resources when they attend school, but their residential backgrounds result in deficits in cognitive skills when they begin school (Lee and Burkam 2002). There is a high likelihood that poor neighborhoods, poor preparation for school, and poor schools form intergenerational life cycles for poor people of color. Among African American children in grades 7–12, 35% have been suspended or expelled, compared to 20% of Hispanics and 15% of whites (NAACP 2017).

African Americans are less upwardly mobile economically than whites; upward economic mobility rates are highest for white men, followed in order by white women, black men, and black women. However, both black and white children with higher academic test scores in primary and middle school are more likely to experience substantial upward socioeconomic mobility than those with lower scores (Mazumder 2008). Those results suggest what anecdotal information confirms—success in school is a path to success in life, and there is a race gap in both forms of success.

Why do disproportionate numbers of minority children not succeed in school? Poor performance in poor schools together with nonwhite racial identities may affect student attitudes in self-confirming ways. *Oppositional Culture Theory*, as developed by John Ogbu, holds that minority children resist school because it represents white culture, which they oppose based on their life experience. His theory has been popularized as resistance to "acting white," but he emphasizes the experience that supports minority student attitudes. Although "success in school may be a path to success in life," minorities have few role models who have succeeded in life based on their educational achievements (Ogbu 2008). Ogbu's theory has been controversial. Garvey Lundy, for example, claims that black students do not resist school as part of resisting white behavior, but rather resist white behavior in favor of their own cultural agency (Lundy 2003).

A racial gap in school performance and motivation for academic achievement is evident. Conservatives have raised questions about race-based differences in intelligence and individual responsibility. There has consistently been a 15 point difference in IQ scores between whites and blacks. However, Richard E. Nesbitt writing in the *New York Times* points out several problems with the assumptions of *hereditarians* (those who believe IQ is inherited):

> The hereditarians begin with the assertion that 60 percent to 80 percent of variation in I.Q. is genetically determined. However, most estimates of heritability have been based almost exclusively on studies of middle-class groups. For the poor, a group that includes a substantial proportion of minorities, heritability of I.Q. is very low, in the range of 10 percent to 20 percent, according to recent research by Eric Turkheimer at the University of Virginia. This means that for the poor, improvements in environment have great potential to bring about increases in I.Q. (Nesbitt 2007)

Other researchers have criticized the validity of IQ tests, on the grounds that a white middle-class cultural context is assumed for correct answers to some questions. In 1984 the US Court of Appeals for the 9th Circuit upheld a lower court ruling that IQ tests used to place black students in California school classes for the "educable mentally retarded" were culturally biased (Foster 1984).

The critic of the claim that the race gap in education is an instance of institutional racism might insist that individual children or their parents are responsible for success in school. So how is the racial gap in education an instance of institutional racism? Part of the answer has already been provided in discussion of less resources for predominantly nonwhite schools in poor neighborhoods. There is a smaller racial gap in educational achievement in middle-class racially integrated schools. Researchers report that school integration improves the academic performance of all students and that supports the environmentalists on the subject of racial differences in IQ. The Century Foundation posted in 2016:

> Integrated schools help to reduce racial achievement gaps. In fact, the racial achievement gap in K–12 education closed more rapidly during the peak years of school desegregation in the 1970s and 1980s than it has overall in the decades that followed—when many desegregation policies were dismantled. More recently, black and Latino students had smaller achievement gaps with white students on the 2007 and 2009 NAEP when they were less likely to be stuck in high-poverty school environments. The gap in SAT scores between black

and white students continues to be larger in segregated districts, and one study showed that change from complete segregation to complete integration in a district could reduce as much as one quarter of the current SAT score disparity. (The Century Foundation 2016)

Other researchers confirm that poor students who attend better funded schools have higher rates of high school graduation and better income and less poverty as adults (Kirabo et al. 2015; Baker 2012).

Public education is itself a primary institution in US society. The combination of poor schools and social racism is beyond the ability of individual children to change. The racial gap in education has been accepted as normal. Academic success is important for all children to advance socioeconomically, especially those who are poor. Therefore, present racial disparities in the US educational system are an important instance of institutional racism.

Implicit Racism

Implicit racism is neither overtly negative discourse about people based on their race, nor harmful action, nor wide-scale social structures that obviously and statistically have unjust consequences for nonwhites. Rather, implicit racism occurs one-on-one or with small groups as its audience, and from the standpoint of implicit racists, it is often not easily recognized as racist. But, like institutional racism, implicit racism is racist because of its harmful effects on people of color. Not all people of color may identify the same incidents as implicitly racist, but respect for those who describe their experience of it entails that implicit racism is not "just subjective" and that it should not be dismissed. The concept of implicit racism has many instances in societies with systems of race where there is also both hearts-and-minds and institutional racism and we will consider micro-aggression, white privilege, and epistemic oppression.

Micro-aggression

A **micro-aggression** is something a person says, does, or causes to happen that members of racial or ethnic minority groups experience as indirect or covert prejudice or discrimination. Micro-aggression is socially acceptable and may not be noticed by people who are not its targets and it may even be unintentional or accidental. Micro-aggressions tend to project stereotypes onto people of color, doubt their specific racial identities if they do not conform to stereotypes, or belittle them as human beings because of their race or ethnicity. They are often present in casual banter (Nigatu 2013). But their effects may be quite insulting and alienating in making people of color feel as though they do not belong in certain contexts, are not really members of groups to which they belong, or are socially, professionally, or academically, unacceptable (Runyowa 2015). Researchers believe that the effects of micro-aggression are cumulative and in a process called *weathering*, can lead to problems in both physical and mental health (Ho 2015, p. 221).

Some writers have claimed that white teachers may be implicitly racist toward students of color, even though most white teachers are now committed to racial egalitarianism. Writing for the magazine *Everyday Feminism*, Jamie Utt suggests ten ways in which white teachers might be implicitly racist—and how they can be corrected: (1) Basing achievement expectations on students' race or ethnicity—avoid cultural bias in assessing student capability; (2) Insisting they are "color blind"—become culturally responsive; (3) Using racially coded language, such as "ghetto" or "tiger mom" and talking about students' poverty and harrowing experiences to get attention—develop solidarity with students' families and communities; (4) Mispronouncing student names—apologize and get their names right; (5) Practicing disciplinary procedures with greater impact on students of color—organize with other teachers and the community; (6) Valuing whiteness—diversify curriculum, pay attention to students of color in the classroom; (7) Tokenizing aspects of students' cultures, as in dress, music, or speech, in order to connect with them—listen to what students want to learn; (8) Appropriating students' cultures to connect with them—understand your own ethnic culture and create classroom space for authentic cultural expression; (9) Devaluing contributions of non-teachers—listen to parents, staff, and community members and invite them into the classroom; and (10) Not advocating for teachers and employees of color—organize for more diverse hiring practices (Utt 2015).

The teacher behavior described by Utt is an important form of micro-aggression, because teachers are respected and respectable representations of authority, to whom people entrust the development of children's minds. The teachers' harmful behavior and more casual instances of micro-aggression share a superficial approach to other human beings that does not take their humanity and dignity seriously. All of Utt's correctives call for deeper and more serious approaches to racial difference.

White Privilege

Not everyone in a system of race is in a position to commit micro-aggression and to do so with impunity. Whites can not only commit micro-aggressions with the authority of their status in a background system of racial hierarchy, but it is difficult for people of color to effectively accuse them of it and other whites are often indifferent. The idea of a privilege refers to something desirable, such as an extra perk or reward, which is not officially a right, but an expected benefit from something else. Thus, **white privilege** refers to many benefits of being white in a hierarchical system of race. In 1989, Peggy MacIntosh brought the term "white privilege" into broad popular and academic use by referring to the contents of an invisible knapsack or backpack. After realizing that she benefitted from a large unseen/invisible system of race, MacIntosh wrote:

> I decided to try to work on myself at least by identifying some of the daily effects of white privilege in my life. I have chosen those conditions that I think in my case attach somewhat more to skin-color privilege than to class, religion, ethnic status, or geographic location, though of course all these other factors are intricately intertwined. As far as I can tell, my African American coworkers, friends, and acquaintances with whom I come into daily or frequent contact in this particular time, place and time of work cannot count on most of these conditions.

MacIntosh describes 50 privileges of being white, in this sense of whites simply taking their status for granted (See Table 7.1).

Some of McIntosh's backpack contents are social amenities, while others, such as "25. If a traffic cop pulls me over… I can be sure I haven't been singled out because of my race," refer to safety and security, which are rights, rather than privileges.

African American cultural critics, from James Baldwin (1924–2987) to contemporary journalist Ta-Nehisi Paul Coates (1975–) have discussed the advantages of whites in the United States, as intergenerational wealth and power accumulated at the expense of African Americans, who have been neither recognized nor compensated for their work and cultural contributions (Baldwin 1963; Coates 2015). Baldwin, in "My Dungeon Shook - Letter to my Nephew on the One Hundredth Anniversary of Emancipation" the first essay in his *The Fire Next Time*, and throughout his 1965 Cambridge University debate with conservative writer William Buckley, insists that

Table 7.1 Peggy McIntosh's Invisible Backpack (*Source From* McIntosh, Peggy, "White Privilege: Unpacking the Invisible Backpack," 1989. http://www.deanza.edu/faculty/lewisjulie/White%20Privilege%20Unpacking%20the%20Invisible%20Knapsack.pdf (This excerpted list is from the Winter 1990 issue of Independent School))

1. I can if I wish arrange to be in the company of people of my race most of the time
2. I can avoid spending time with people whom I was trained to mistrust and who have learned to mistrust my kind or me
3. If I should need to move, I can be pretty sure of renting or purchasing housing in an area which I can afford and in which I would want to live
4. I can be pretty sure that my neighbors in such a location will be neutral or pleasant to me
5. I can go shopping alone most of the time, pretty well assured that I will not be followed or harassed
6. I can turn on the television or open to the front page of the paper and see people of my race widely represented
7. When I am told about our national heritage or about "civilization," I am shown that people of my color made it what it is
8. I can be sure that my children will be given curricular materials that testify to the existence of their race
9. If I want to, I can be pretty sure of finding a publisher for this piece on white privilege
10. I can be pretty sure of having my voice heard in a group in which I am the only member of my race
11. I can be casual about whether or not to listen to another person's voice in a group in which s/he is the only member of his/her race
12. I can go into a music shop and count on finding the music of my race represented, into a supermarket and find the staple foods which fit with my cultural traditions, into a hairdresser's shop and find someone who can cut my hair
13. Whether I use checks, credit cards or cash, I can count on my skin color not to work against the appearance of financial reliability
14. I can arrange to protect my children most of the time from people who might not like them
15. I do not have to educate my children to be aware of systemic racism for their own daily physical protection
16. I can be pretty sure that my children's teachers and employers will tolerate them if they fit school and workplace norms; my chief worries about them do not concern others' attitudes toward their race
17. I can talk with my mouth full and not have people put this down to my color
18. I can swear, or dress in second-hand clothes, or not answer letters, without having people attribute these choices to the bad morals, the poverty, or the illiteracy of my race
19. I can speak in public to a powerful male group without putting my race on trial
20. I can do well in a challenging situation without being called a credit to my race
21. I am never asked to speak for all the people of my racial group

(continued)

Table 7.1 (continued)

22. I can remain oblivious of the language and customs of persons of color who constitute the world's majority without feeling in my culture any penalty for such oblivion

23. I can criticize our government and talk about how much I fear its policies and behavior, without being seen as a cultural outsider

24. I can be pretty sure that if I ask to talk to the "person in charge," I will be facing a person of my race

25. If a traffic cop pulls me over or if the IRS audits my tax return, I can be sure I haven't been singled out because of my race

26. I can easily buy posters, post-cards, picture books, greeting cards, dolls, toys and children's magazines featuring people of my race

27. I can go home from most meetings of organizations I belong to feeling somewhat tied in, rather than isolated, out-of-place, out-numbered, unheard, held at a distance or feared

28. I can be pretty sure that an argument with a colleague of another race is more likely to jeopardize her/his chances for advancement than to jeopardize mine

29. I can be pretty sure that if I argue for the promotion of a person of another race, or a program centering on race, this is not likely to cost me heavily within my present setting, even if my colleagues disagree with me

30. If I declare there is a racial issue at hand, or there isn't a racial issue at hand, my race will lend me more credibility for either position than a person of color will have

31. I can choose to ignore developments in minority writing and minority activist programs, or disparage them, or learn from them, but in any case, I can find ways to be more or less protected from negative consequences of any of these choices

32. My culture gives me little fear about ignoring the perspectives and powers of people of other races

33. I am not made acutely aware that my shape, bearing or body odor will be taken as a reflection on my race

34. I can worry about racism without being seen as self-interested or self-seeking

35. I can take a job with an affirmative action employer without having my co-workers on the job suspect that I got it because of my race

36. If my day, week or year is going badly, I need not ask of each negative episode or situation whether it had racial overtones

37. I can be pretty sure of finding people who would be willing to talk with me and advise me about my next steps, professionally

38. I can think over many options, social, political, imaginative or professional, without asking whether a person of my race would be accepted or allowed to do what I want to do

39. I can be late to a meeting without having the lateness reflect on my race

40. I can choose public accommodation without fearing that people of my race cannot get in or will be mistreated in the places I have chosen

(continued)

Table 7.1 (continued)

41. I can be sure that if I need legal or medical help, my race will not work against me

42. I can arrange my activities so that I will never have to experience feelings of rejection owing to my race

43. If I have low credibility as a leader I can be sure that my race is not the problem

44. I can easily find academic courses and institutions which give attention only to people of my race

45. I can expect figurative language and imagery in all of the arts to testify to experiences of my race

46. I can choose blemish cover or bandages in "flesh" color and have them more or less match my skin

47. I can travel alone or with my spouse without expecting embarrassment or hostility in those who deal with us

48. I have no difficulty finding neighborhoods where people approve of our household

49. My children are given texts and classes which implicitly support our kind of family unit and do not turn them against my choice of domestic partnership

50. I will feel welcomed and "normal" in the usual walks of public life, institutional, and social

the American racial system has benefitted whites at the cost of treating non-whites unjustly (Baldwin and Buckley 1965). Coates, in *Between the World and Me* that is written as a letter to his 15-year-old son, makes a similar argument and also takes up Du Bois's idea of the difference between how whites view blacks and how blacks know themselves. Coates, like Baldwin, shares a bleak perspective of the physical dangers posed by racism against African Americans. The conditions described by Baldwin and Coates are hardly a lack of privileges, but are instead point to more serious violations and denials of rights—to be discussed in Chapter 9.

Epistemic Oppression

The adjective "epistemic" means "pertaining to knowledge and its violation. Kristie Dotson defines **epistemic oppression** as exclusion from knowledge production that prevents some knowers from participating in knowledge communities. Not only are those excluded harmed, but epistemic oppression results in deficiencies of knowledge itself. Dotson posits three forms of epistemic oppression: (1) Testimonial injustice occurs when the testimony of some is not accepted as credible, due to prejudice; it can be remedied by adjusting the criteria for assessing credibility; (2) Hermeneutical injustice arises when members of some cultures are unable to contribute to collective knowledge without a change in the conceptual schemes involved, so that their experience can be described. Drawing on Miranda Fricker's work, Dotson refers to an inability of victims to describe sexual harassment in the workplace, before the concept of inappropriate and nonconsensual sexual behavior toward women in the workplace was understood and accepted (Fricker 2007); and (3) Contributory injustice occurs when there is willed ignorance of contributions that could be made by those who are excluded (Dotson 2012). Alison Bailey has suggested that "affective, aesthetic, or mystical resources" should be added to Dotson's idea of contributory injustice, which is primarily cognitive (Bailey 2014).

Epistemic oppression has an additional characteristic of seeming normal and benign to authorities within knowledge communities. Some white teachers, administrators, and college professors may not only be unaware that certain exclusions are unjust, but they may also be unaware that they are excluding knowers and their contributions from cultures different from their own. Dotson writes that such ignorance "follows from one's social position and/or epistemic location, which works to institute epistemic differences, while obscuring those same differences" (Dotson 2011, p. 248).

This raises a question of whether people can be held responsible for not knowing what they ought to know. It could be argued that those in positions of authority and power in educational institutions are obligated to represent a full human constituency, across all identities. In terms of epistemic justice, they are thereby obligated to have open minds and broad conceptual schemes.

The position of **colorblindness** with regard to race, in a society where some continue to suffer from racism, is an example of epistemic ignorance. When people say they are colorblind, the rationale may be that ignoring race is the best way to solve existing problems and injustice concerning race. However, it is implicitly racist for a white person to hold that position, because, as noted at the beginning of this chapter, ignoring what most people mean by "race" means ignoring racism. The white person proclaiming a colorblind position also has the privilege of not being a victim of what she is ignoring (Fryberg 2010).

Conclusion

The word "racism" was coined long after races were posited and what we now consider racism was practiced. There is racism in discourse and in action. Hearts-and-minds racism pertains to individuals. Racist action is more widespread than hate crimes, which requires intent in specific instances. Institutional racism, which affect millions of people in a society with a system of race does not require the element of individual intent. Nevertheless, its victims, such as poor nonwhite school children and minorities incarcerated for minor crimes or crimes they did not commit, may be harmed as much or more than if there were racist intentions to harm them. Implicit racism is behavior with racist effects but without awareness that it is racist. All three forms of racism contribute to the ways that a system of race functions in the early twenty-first century. We will see in Chapter 8 how these different forms of racism and positive ideas, constructions, and practices play out in different segments of contemporary American society.

Glossary

colorblindness—perspective that a person is unaware of racial differences effects of on minorities.
discrimination—harmful action against others based on their race.
hearts-and-minds racism (HMR)—racism of individuals.

micro-aggression—speech or behavior experienced by members of racial or ethnic minority groups as indirect or covert prejudice or discrimination.
postjudice—an attitude of judging people based on their race, because members of that same race perpetrated racist harms in the past.
prejudice—negative beliefs about others based on their race.
racism—prejudice and discrimination practiced by individuals or embedded in institutional practices.
white privilege—benefits to whites of living in a society with a history and present practice of racism against nonwhites.

Discussion Questions

1. What are the advantages to free speech when racist hate speech is permitted? What are some arguments against it?
2. Can people who belong to groups that have experienced racism themselves be racist? Explain what is meant by "racism" if they can or cannot be racists.
3. How is postjudice different from prejudice?
4. Does the prosecution of hate crimes in the United States accomplish the deterrence of racism? Why or why not?
5. How is the US prison system a system of institutional racism?
6. What are some claims or arguments that the US K-12 educational system is, or is not, a system of institutional racism? What is your assessment?
7. Give some examples of micro-aggression from your own experience.
8. Does the idea of white privilege trivialize the violation of rights of nonwhites?
9. Is epistemic injustice real injustice in your view?
10. Compare the wrongs of individual racism with institutional racism, in general or theoretical terms.

References

Alexander, Michelle. *The New Jim Crow: Mass Incarceration in the Age of Colorblindness*. New York, NY: New Press, 2011.
Appiah, Anthony. "Racisms." *The Anatomy of Racism*, edited by David T. Goldberg. Minneapolis: University of Minnesota Press, 1990, pp. 21–37.

Bailey, Alison. "The Unlevel Knowing Field: An Engagement with Dotson's Third-Order Epistemic Oppression." *Social Epistemology Review and Reply Collective*, vol. 3, no. 10, 2014, pp. 62–8.

Baker, Bruce. *Does Money Matter in Education?* Albert Shanker Institute, 2012. http://www.shankerinstitute.org/resource/does-money-matter.

Baldwin, James. *The Fire Next Time*. New York, NY: Dial Press, 1963.

Baldwin, James, and William F. Buckley. Debated at the Cambridge Union Debating Society for and Against the Following Motion: "The American Dream is at the Expense of the American Negro," 1965. http://backstoryradio. org/2016/10/09/baldwin-v-buckley/; Youtube video, July 2016. https://www. youtube.com/watch?v=UdDGFtJXlfQ.

Butt, David. "Canada's Law on Hate Speech Is the Embodiment of Compromise." Special to *The Globe and Mail*, Jan. 19, 2015, 2:06PM EST. https://www. theglobeandmail.com/opinion/canadas-law-on-hate-speech-is-the-embodiment-of-compromise/article22520419/.

Carter, Dorinda J. "Why the Black Kids Sit Together at the Stairs: The Role of Identity-Affirming Counter-Spaces in a Predominantly White High School." *The Journal of Negro Education*, vol. 76, no. 4, 2007, pp. 542–54. JSTOR. www.jstor. org/stable/40037227.

CBC News, Canada. "What Is a Hate Crime?" June 15, 2011. http://www.cbc.ca/ news/canada/story/2011/06/15/f-hate-crimes.html. Consulted July 1, 2017.

Century Foundation. "The Future of Racially and Socioeconomically Integrated Schools and Classrooms." *Facts—School Integration*, Feb. 10, 2016. https:// tcf.org/content/facts/the-benefits-of-socioeconomically-and-racially-integrat-ed-schools-and-classrooms/.

Coates, Ta-Nehisi Paul. *Between the World and Me*. New York, NY: Spiegel and Grau, 2015.

Creeley, Will. "Disturbing Trend Continues: Trinity College Professor Faces Threats." *FIRE, Foundation for Individual Rights in Education*, June 23, 2017. https://www. thefire.org/disturbing-trend-continues-trinity-college-professor-faces-threats/.

Demby, Gene. "The Ugly, Fascinating History of the Word 'Racism'." *Code Switch: Word Watch*, National Public Radio, 2013. http://www.npr.org/sections/code-switch/2014/01/05/260006815/the-ugly-fascinating-history-of-the-word-racism. Posted Jan. 6, 2014, 11:55AM ET.

Dotson, Kristie. "Tracking Epistemic Violence, Tracking Practices of Silencing." *Hypatia*, vol. 26, no. 2, 2011, pp. 236–57.

Dotson, Kristie. "A Cautionary Tale: On Limiting Epistemic Oppression." *Frontiers: A Journal of Women Studies*, vol. 33, no. 1, 2012, pp. 24–47. http://www.jstor. org/stable/10.5250/fronjwomestud.33.1.0024. Accessed June 28, 2017, 17:26 UTC.

Equal Justice Initiative, EJI. "Illegal Racial Discrimination in Jury Selection: A Continuing Legacy," 2017. https://eji.org/reports/illegal-racial-discrimination-in-jury-selection.

Faber, Jacob W., and Ingrid Gould Ellen. "Race and the Housing Cycle: Differences in Home Equity Trends Among Long-Term Homeowners." *Housing Policy Debate*, vol. 26, no. 3, 2016, pp. 456–73.

FBI:NIBRS. Federal Bureau of Investigation, National Incident-Based Reporting System, Uniform Crime Reporting Program, U.S. Department of Justice, Fall 2016 Crimes Against Persons, Property, and Society. https://ucr.fbi.gov/nibrs/2015/resource-pages/crimes_against_persons_property_and_society-2015_final.pdf.

Federal Bureau of Investigation. "Hate Crimes." What We Investigate. http://www.fbi.gov/about-us/investigate/civilrights/hate_crimes/overview. Consulted June 29, 2017; Federal Bureau of Investigation. "Hate Crime Statistics, 2015," 2016. https://ucr.fbi.gov/hate-crime/2015. Consulted June 29, 2017.

Foster, Susan G. "Court Finds I.Q. Tests Racially Biased for Black Pupils' Placement." *Education Week*, Feb. 8, 1984. http://www.edweek.org/ew/articles/1984/02/08/05320018.h03.html.

Fredrickson, George M. *Racism: A Short History*. Princeton, NJ: Princeton University Press, 2002.

Fricker, Miranda. *Epistemic Injustice: Power and the Ethics of Knowing*. New York: Oxford University Press, 2007.

Fryberg, S.M., and Nicole M. Stephens. "When the World Is Colorblind, American Indians Are Invisible: A Diversity Science Approach." *Psychological Inquiry*, vol. 21, no. 2, 2010, pp. 115–19.

Garcia, J.L.A. "The Heart of Racism." *Journal of Social Philosophy*, vol. 27, 1996, pp. 5–45.

Ho, Evelyn Y. "Socio-Cultural Factors in Health Communication." *Health Communication: Theory, Method, and Application*, edited by Nancy Grant Harrington. New York, NY: Routledge, 2015, pp. 212–39.

Inkelas, K.K., Z. Daver, and K. Vogt, et al. "Living–Learning Programs and First-Generation College Students' Academic and Social Transition to College." *Research in Higher Education*, vol. 48, 2007, p. 403. https://link.springer.com/article/10.1007/s11162-006-9031-6.

Jackson, C. Kirabo, Rucker C. Johnson, and Claudia Persico. "The Effects of School Spending on Educational and Economic Outcomes: Evidence from School Finance Reforms." *Quarterly Journal of Economics*, Oct. 1, 2015. http://webcache.googleusercontent.com/search?q=cache:WMuG-9VScsnQJ:socrates.berkeley.edu/~ruckerj/QJE_resubmit_final_version.pdf+&cd=1&hl=en&ct=clnk&gl=us.

Leachman, Michael, Nick Albares, Kathleen Masterson, and Marlana Wallace. "Most States Have Cut School Funding, and Some Continue Cutting." Center on Budgeting and Policy Priorities, Jan. 25, 2016. https://wagner.nyu.edu/files/faculty/publications/Faber_Ellen_2016_Race_and_the_Housing_Cycle.pdf.

Lee, Valerie E., and David T. Burkam. *Inequality at the Starting Gate: Social Background Differences in Achievement as Children Begin School*. Educational Resource Information Center, Washington, DC: Economic Policy Institute, 2002.

Lombroso, Daniel, and Yoni Appelbaum. "'Hail Trump!' White Nationalists Salute the President Elect." *The Atlantic*, Nov. 21, 2016. https://www.theatlantic.com/politics/archive/2016/11/richard-spencer-speech-npi/508379/.

Lundy, Garvey F. "The Myths of Oppositional Culture." *Journal of Black Studies*, vol. 33, no. 4, 2003, pp. 450–67.

Mazumder, Bhashkar. Upward Intergenerational Economic Mobility in the United States. Economic Mobility Project, Pew Charitable Trusts, 2008. http://www.pewtrusts.org/~/media/legacy/uploadedfiles/pcs_assets/2012/empreportsupward20intergen20mobility2008530pdf.pdf.

McIntosh, Peggy. "White Privilege: Unpacking the Invisible Backpack," 1989. http://www.deanza.edu/faculty/lewisjulie/White%20Priviledge%20Unpacking%20the%20Invisible%20Knapsack.pdf.

Middle East Forum. "European Hate Speech Laws." *The Legal Project*, 2017. http://www.legal-project.org/issues/european-hate-speech-laws.

National Association for the Advancement of Colored People (NAACP). "Criminal Justice Fact Sheet," 2017. http://www.naacp.org/criminal-justice-fact-sheet/.

Nesbitt, Richard E. "All Brains Are the Same Color." *New York Times*, Dec. 9, 2007. http://www.nytimes.com/2007/12/09/opinion/09nisbett.htmlOgbu.

Nigatu, Heben. "21 Racial Microaggressions You Hear On a Daily Basis." BuzzFeed. BuzzFeed, Inc., 9 Dec. 2013. https://www.buzzfeed.com/hnigatu/racial-microagressions-you-hear-on-a-daily-basis.

Ogbu, John, editor. *Minority Status, Oppositional Culture, and Schooling*. New York, NY: Routledge, 2008.

Pitter, Laura. "Hate Crimes Against Muslims in US Continue to Rise in 2016." *US Program, Human Rights Watch*, May 11, 2017. https://www.hrw.org/news/2017/05/11/hate-crimes-against-muslims-us-continue-rise-2016.

Runyowa, Simba. "Micro-aggression Matter." *The Atlantic*, Sept. 18, 2015. https://www.theatlantic.com/politics/archive/2015/09/microaggressions-matter/406090/.

Sandholtz, Nathan, Lynn Langton, and Michael G. Planty. "Hate Crime Victimization, 2003–2011." *Bureau of Justice Statistics*, Mar. 21, 2013. http://www.bjs.gov/index.cfm?ty=pbdetail&iid=4614.

Shelby, Tommie. "Is Racism in the 'Heart'?" *Journal of Social Philosophy*, vol. 33, no. 3, 2002, pp. 411–20.

Slate Staff. "Hate in America: An Updating List." *Slate*, June 23, 2017. http://www.slate.com/articles/news_and_politics/politics/2016/12/hate_in_america_a_list_of_racism_bigotry_and_abuse_since_the_election.html.

Thernstrom, Abigail, and Stephan Thernstrom. *No Excuses: Closing the Racial Gap in Education*. New York, NY: Simon and Schuster, 2003.

United Nations. "International Convention on the Elimination of All Forms of Racial Discrimination," Human Rights, Office of the High Commissioner, Adopted and Opened for Signature and Ratification by General Assembly Resolution 2106 (XX), Dec. 21, 1965, Entry into Force Jan. 4, 1969, in

Accordance with Article 19. http://www.ohchr.org/EN/ProfessionalInterest/Pages/CERD.aspx.

University of Oregon. "What Is the Umoja Pan-African Scholars Community?" Umoja Pan-African Scholars, University Housing, 2017. https://housing.uoregon.edu/umojascholars.

Utt, Jamie. "10 Ways Well-Meaning White Teachers Bring Racism into Our Schools." *Everyday Feminism*, Aug. 26, 2015. http://everydayfeminism.com/2015/08/10-ways-well-meaning-white-teachers-bring-racism-into-our-schools/.

Wagner, Peter, and Bernadette Rabuy. *Mass Incarceration: The Whole Pie 2017: The Prison Policy Initiative*, Mar. 14, 2017. https://www.prisonpolicy.org/reports/pie2017.html?gclid=Cj0KEQjw7dfKBRCdkKrvmfKtyeoBEiQAch0egTJL-MA0s0ZRhHwuZkX5tCLoHKezPq3Ck1tnoNrIxzbIaAvS78P8HAQ.

Zack, Naomi. *White Privilege and Black Rights: The Injustice of US Police Racial Profiling and Homicide*. Lanham, MD: Rowman & Littlefield, 2015.

8

Race in Contemporary Life

Ideas and feelings about race are part of the perspectives of all individuals who are aware of racial difference. More than that, although race no longer has the backing in biological science it once did, it is so robust as a social construction tied to human kinship that individuals live out their racial identities in most or all of their relationships and social roles. Consider marriage, for example. Any married person either has a spouse of the same race or of a different race. If the person is married to someone of the same race, the couple is described as a white, black, Asian, Native American, Hispanic, or Middle Eastern couple. If the person is married to someone of a different race, the couple is described as a mixed or interracial couple. A same-race couple will likely have friends, relatives, and neighbors, who are mostly of their race. A mixed-race couple may have more diversity in relations, but they will be distinct in not being of the same race. In either case, the couple's race or races will affect where they live, the socioeconomic quality of their lives (in most cases), and their children's racial identities.

Race is not the most important thing in life in a society with a system of race—some would say money was, others moral character—but it is a substantial social "factor." If an individual ignores race, especially her own racial identity—other people will remind her of it, directly or indirectly. Race is more than a matter of ideas, feelings, and identity. Racial difference maps onto differences in social status and power. **Social status** is a person's position or rank in any given pecking order or hierarchy and it has to do with how others view one. **Power** is an ability to do something, influence others, or make things happen. **Authority** is recognition of power. People who have

© The Author(s) 2018
N. Zack, *Philosophy of Race*, Palgrave Philosophy Today,
https://doi.org/10.1007/978-3-319-78729-9_8

more power than others in institutions also have greater authority than those with less power. It's important to remember that institutional power is not the power of a person but power granted her by the rules of an institution or conferred on her by someone who has more power in the same institution. Institutional power and authority range over a larger number of contexts than social status, which varies from group to group and situation to situation. Given formal equality among races, social status associated with racial identity ought not to carry over into institutional power and authority. But in reality, it does. Social status associated with racial identity creeps into institutions, along with the racial identities of individuals.

In this chapter, we will consider only several ways in which race determines, influences, or is in other ways related to life in society. The idea is not to provide a comprehensive description of race in life, but to show how race is a substantial factor of life in society. Unless a person is isolated on a desert island or in a remote mountain cabin, we all live in society. We will begin with the institution of marriage, and then proceed through discussions of social class and medicine and health.

Marriage

Marriage is a basic social institution. *Psychology Today* offers this definition: "Marriage is the process by which two people make their relationship public, official, and permanent. It is the joining of two people in a bond that putatively lasts until death, but in practice is increasingly cut short by divorce" (Psychology Today 2017). Marriage confers tax, legal, residence, medical, social security, and insurance benefits, as well as resources for social interactions and connections (NOLO 2017). Marriage also confers positive benefits in wealth and income, access to and use of health care, longevity, psychological well-being, and the mental and physical health of children (Wood et al. 2007). However, opportunities to marry may be unequal, according to race.

Marriage Rates

According to the National Longitudinal Survey of Youth 1979 (NLSY79) that collected data in 2010 on Baby Boomers, born 1957–1964, most married before age 28 and 85% had married by age 46. African Americans married later and at one-third the rate of white Americans; Hispanics married earlier. About one-third of African Americans had never married, compared to one-tenth of white Americans and one-sixth of Hispanics. The divorce rate of about 43% did not vary by race and ethnicity, although college graduates were less likely to divorce (Auginbaugh et al. 2013).

Marriage statistics for African Americans at least 35 years old began to change in the 1960s. After 1890, African Americans were more likely to be married than white Americans. But by 2010, African Americans who had never married increased from about 10 to 25% (compared to about 10% for white Americans) and those who did marry divorced more and did not remarry as much, as other groups. By 2014, only 29% of African Americans were married, compared to 48% of all Americans. Also, 50% of African Americans had never been married, compared to 33% of all Americans (Black Demographics.com 2017).

Although marriage rates for all racial and ethnic groups have declined in recent decades, there has been specific concern about the black rate. Some observers associate the decline in black marriage with high rates of incarceration after the War on Drugs (Black Demographics.com 2017). Others have blamed black women. Senator Daniel Patrick Moynihan (1927–2003) in *The Negro Family: The Case for National Action*, his 1965 research report when he was Assistant Secretary of Labor, claimed that black women preferred **matriarchy** to **patriarchy**. Moynihan was an academic sociologist before and during his political career. His claims that black women were responsible for the breakdown of the black family, because of their high rate of children born outside of marriage, were very influential (Moynihan 1965). He wrote:

> The fundamental problem, in which this is most clearly the case, is that of family structure. The evidence—not final, but powerfully persuasive—is that the Negro family in the urban ghettos is crumbling. A middle-class group has managed to save itself, but for vast numbers of the unskilled, poorly educated city working class the fabric of conventional social relationships has all but disintegrated. …

Moynihan ended his report by quoting the African American sociologist, E. Franklin Fraser (1894–1962):

> As the result of family disorganization a large proportion of Negro children and youth have not undergone the socialization which only the family can provide. The disorganized families have failed to provide for their emotional needs and have not provided the discipline and habits which are necessary for personality development. Because the disorganized family has failed in its function as a socializing agency, it has handicapped the children in their relations to the institutions in the community. Moreover, family disorganization

has been partially responsible for a large amount of juvenile delinquency and adult crime among Negroes. Since the widespread family disorganization among Negroes has resulted from the failure of the father to play the role in family life required by American society, the mitigation of this problem must await those changes in the Negro and American society which will enable the Negro father to play the role required of him. (Blackpast.org 2017)

Moynihan's assumption that in the United States only patriarchal family structures could thrive and successfully socialize children, is ironic, because he himself grew up in a female-headed household after he was nine years old (Wattenberg 2004).

Over half a century after Moynihan's report, scholars continue to consider the problems of black poverty and reject his model of pathology. In 1965, Moynihan was able to point to black women's high levels of birth outside of marriage. But in 2017, the Center for Disease Control reported that in 2015, 40.3% of all US births were outside of marriage, compared to 18.4% in 1980 (CDC 2017a, 2017b). Further studies have shown that among parents without college degrees, ages 26–31, 74% of mothers and 70% of fathers had children outside of marriage. Unwed birthrates are highest in areas of income inequality with high unemployment and few job opportunities (Cherlin et al. 2016).

Dwane Mouzon refers to current studies that debunk myths about black women's aversion toward marriage: In terms of values about marriage expectation and its importance for children, blacks were found to value marriage more than whites did; blacks and whites were equally critical of having children outside of marriage; 57% of whites compared to 65% of blacks and 72% of Latinos thought that a child needs two parents to grow up happily; more blacks than any other group thought that earning ability was important in husbands. Mouzon pinpoints the high value black women place on socioeconomic status, together with the disproportionately low earnings and wealth of black men, as the main cause of low rates of black marriage compared to white. Moreover, in 2012, there were only 91 black men for every 100 black women. (About 94% of married black women have black husbands and about 86% of married black men have black wives (Black Demographics.com 2017).) High unemployment and undereducation, as well as higher mortality and illness rates, reduce the marriageability of many black men. Mouzon's analysis and the underlying data support a structural or institutional perspective on the white–black marriage gap (Mouzon 2014). If marriage does continue to confer the benefits claimed by many, then African Americans are disadvantaged by factors beyond their control as individuals. Also, insofar as other racial groups now share high birthrates outside of marriage, the idea of individual preference for remaining unmarried loses credibility.

However, as most people inside and outside of the academy know, the idea that marriage is desirable and beneficial is not a simple, universally accepted claim, so much as a ready-made rhetorical tool. The lower marriage rate for African Americans has been a basis for moral criticism of that group. But for Mexican Americans, a higher marriage rate and earlier marriage ages for women have been the basis for criticism on the grounds that Mexican American women are thereby deprived of educational opportunities and self-development. Familial cultural values emphasizing the traditional role of women are sometimes given, not as pathologizing forces, but as obstacles to higher education and greater earning power.

Working within a life cycle framework that relates marriage to migration and periods of transition. R. Kelly Raley, T. Elizabeth Durden, and Elizabeth Wildsmith, compared Mexican American marriage patterns to those of women in Mexico. Their results showed that Mexican immigrant women marry earlier than those who live in Mexico. But if family background influences associated with early marriage, such as parental education and school leavings, are kept constant, Mexican American immigrants married later than white Americans. Also, Mexican American women born in the United States do not marry earlier than Anglo-women (Raley et al. 2004).

Thus, differences in marriage rates for African Americans and marriage age for Mexican American immigrant women cannot plausibly be assigned to ethnicity or culture. In both cases, job and educational opportunities shaped by external social conditions influence the occurrence of marriage. The ongoing assumption throughout society that cultural deviance causes minority groups to fall short of statistical white norms depends on a superficial understanding of how race and ethnicity function in society. This superficial view of race as human variety or difference, rather than a social system based on status and power, also obscures how social class works.

Interracial Marriage

Many observers and scholars view mixed-race marriages and their acceptance as a barometer of race relations, generally. While mixed-race marriage rates do not mirror institutional or structural inequalities of race, they do indicate **racial climate**, the degree and extent of hearts-and-minds racism on individual-to-individual levels, in specific contexts. Attitudes toward racial and ethnic intermarriage have been changing toward tolerance since 1967, when the US Supreme Court struck down so-called Anti-miscegenation laws in *Loving v. Virginia*. In 2015, 14% of nonblacks said they would oppose a close relative marrying a black person, compared to 63% in 1990. Also in 2015, one in six Americans married someone of a different race, five times the rate in 1967 before antistate miscegenation laws were abolished. Nonblack minority statistics mainly support the trend: 29% of Asians and 27% of Hispanics are married to someone of a different race or ethnicity. Among 2015 interracial newlyweds, 42%, the most common couples, consist of one Hispanic person and one white person. Still, between 1980 and 2015, black intermarriage increased from 5 to 18% and white intermarriage from 4 to 11%. Overall, one in seven newborns were born to interracial couples in 2015 (Bialik 2017).

Mid-twentieth century opposition to public school integration was accompanied by forceful rhetoric that such early interaction would lead to **miscegenation** (Godfrey 2003). The growing rate of interracial marriages not only fulfills that fearful prediction but the generally peaceful acceptance of interracial couples suggests that hearts-and-minds racism has drastically changed in this regard. However, contemporary interracial couples are more likely to be college educated and live in cities than rural areas. The combination of college degrees and urban lifestyles indicates middle-class status (Bialik 2017). This association of middle-class status with progress in race relations may be an important aspect of how racial difference functions in society, at this time.

Social Class

Historically, Americans have preferred to believe that the United States is a society without important distinctions based on social class. Compared to monarchies with royal families, or societies with caste systems, there are no hereditary distinctions associated with class in the traditional sense. Neither is a standard Marxist analysis that views society as a struggle of workers against owners, relevant, because there is no longer a self-conscious working class organized to advance its interests. Although most Americans are also aware of great income inequalities and new accounts of widespread stagnation and poverty, at the same time a new billionaire group rises with little or no opposition. There was a weak widespread complaint against those in the financial industry who had caused the bubble and collapse in real estate prices in 2008. But there was scarcely revolutionary or even rebellious protest, unless one counts the newly emergent populism that culminated in the 2016 presidential election. Upward socioeconomic mobility is still believed to be available to everyone.

The question of whether there are broad economic differences associated with race is not only a matter of social science methodology or progressive versus conservative perspectives. In 2015, a staff writer for *Forbes* a premier US business publication (its motto is "The Capitalist Tool") wrote the following about racial differences in wealth and income, citing government and independent sources:

> The typical black household now has just 6% of the wealth of the typical white household; the typical Latino household has just 8%, according to a recent study called 'The Racial Wealth Gap: Why Policy Matters,' by Demos, a public policy organization promoting democracy and equality, and the Institute on Assets and Social Policy.
>
> In absolute terms, the median white household had $111,146 in wealth holdings in 2011, compared to $7,113 for the median black household and $8,348 for the median Latino household. (All figures come from the U.S. Census Bureau Survey of Income and Program Participation.)….
>
> In 2011, 34% of whites completed a four-year college degree, whereas just 20% of blacks and 13% of Hispanics did ….
>
> The typical white family earns $50,400, while the typical black family earns $32,038, and the typical Latino family, $36,840. (Shin 2015)

Whether or not a person of working age is employed is a fundamental indicator of their income, and income varies by race. Despite individual upward mobility, there seem to be broad patterns of employment and unemployment, correlated with race, which persist over time. One way to confirm that is by looking at how unemployment rates change, according to educational level, and whether racial gaps in those changes remain constant. After the Great Recession of 2007–2009, unemployment among college graduates reached all-time highs of 4.7, compared to 15% for those without a high school degree. Unemployment for minorities also increased, on top of high unemployment rates before the recession (Hout and Cumberworth 2012). There was, in time, an economic recovery. For recent young college graduates in 2016, the unemployment rate was 5.6% (compared to 5.5% in 2007, before the recession began), and the underemployment rate was 12.6% (compared with 9.6%, before the recession began). There were also differences related to race and ethnicity, in 2016. Young Hispanic and African-American graduates had higher unemployment than white non-Hispanics (9.4% for young black college graduates). There were also higher rates of those unemployed and without further schooling, for both African Americans and Hispanics (Kroeger et al. 2016).

In 1978, sociologist William Julius Wilson argued in *the Declining Significance of Race* that because the civil rights legislation created opportunities for higher education and employment for African Americans, there was a black middle class, with greater social and economic distance from poor blacks than from middle-class whites. Wilson concluded that social class was a more important indicator of well-being than race (Wilson 1978). The persistence through the business cycle (times of prosperity-recession-prosperity), of a racial gap in employment, including college graduates, suggests that the effects of differences in race may be stronger than differences in social class, of which educational level is otherwise a key component. To put it simply, African-Americans and Hispanics with college degrees do not do as well economically as non-Hispanic whites with college degrees. This in turn suggests that although there are class differences within nonwhite groups, race is a more persistent indicator of economic well-being than class. Differences in race do not cancel out differences in class, such as income, wealth, and education, but they qualify them. In their 1997 *America in Black and White*, conservative analysts Abigail Thernstrom and Stephan Thernstrom argue over 700 pages that within any social class—as defined economically—African Americans are worse off in education, health, living circumstances, and many other factors of well-being (Thernstrom and Thernstrom 1997).

There is upward economic mobility on individual levels, but there is also downward mobility and both are influenced by race. Half of African Americans born into poverty remain poor by age 40, compared to less than a quarter of white Americans (Rodrigue and Reeves 2015). Moreover, a 2014 study from the Federal Reserve Bank of Chicago suggests that among middle-class families, 60% of African Americans become worse off economically than their parents, compared to 36% of whites (Mazumder 2014).

There is a puzzle here, because the popular association of social class with money and education suggests that once African Americans attain a level of income and degrees equal to those of whites, they should have the same class advantages. However, class is more complicated than economics and education. Instead of using traditional ideas of classes, Wendy Bottero and other contemporary sociologists work with the idea of stratification, in showing "how where we start in life affects where we end up." The positions of parents affect their children, but there also are other influences, involving both individual choice and external social structures (Bottero 2005, pp. 4–6). The French sociologist Pierre Bourdieu has provided an idea of social class that includes different kinds of "capital"—economic (the usual wealth/income), social (who a person knows), and cultural (tastes in a consumer economy) (Holt 1998). Bottero writes of a new notion of class as "an individualized process of hierarchical distinction":

> 'Class' processes have become more implicit and less visible, but the effects of class are no less pervasive in people's lives. This is a radical shift in how class is seen to operate. Rather than the polar terms of 'class in itself' giving rise to 'class for itself' in which inequality triggered consciousness and action, this new model sets out a reverse process, where explicit class identification and awareness dissolve, leaving behind a hierarchical version of 'class', implicitly encoded in identity through practice…The importance of this theoretical change cannot be over-emphasized, since it offers a fundamentally different way of thinking about how inequality works. (Bottero 2004, p. 1001)

Both Bourdieu and Bottero provide theories of class that depend on individual choices and behavior, rather than group goals. The **cultural capital** of individuals may identify them in class terms as elite or nonelite, but such capital is not entirely the result of socioeconomic group membership, as in earlier theories of class. Choices of food, clothing, habits of travel, including foreign travel, knowledge about art, music, and even popular culture, and hobbies requiring special skills, as well as many other matters of taste, are components of an individual's cultural capital. Individuals are naturally drawn to those with similar kinds and amounts of cultural capital and achieve social status on the basis of the recognized rarity of their cultural capital (Holt 1998).

In an apparently classless society, when and where class does in fact still operate through individual taste and implicit judgments and assessments, racial difference can be a barrier to full class equality, even when requirements of income and education are in place. Job opportunities and job security occur within institutions, where in most cases white Americans have more power and authority than nonwhites. Their subtle preferences, inclusions, and exclusions may depend on cultural capital rather than direct racial sameness and difference. From the standpoint of nonwhites within such institutions or in contact with them, issues of racial climate will be experienced that do not amount to either institutional or hearts-and-minds racism, but which nevertheless impede their access or success, as individuals, in very specific ways. That is, race can be an obstacle to real and lasting upward socioeconomic mobility for nonwhites, because individual functioning on all socioeconomic levels requires that individuals interact with other individuals. In most institutions and organizations where nonwhites might rise socioeconomically, white individuals are already dominant and have more power than nonwhites. Insofar as the cultural capital related to their racial identity determines how those whites with power shape institutions, they may choose to share power with only some other whites and fewer nonwhites. For example, whites who play tennis or regularly travel abroad may have higher status than people of color, as well as other whites who do not have those interests or resources.

Health and Medicine

There are significant disparities in health according to race. In 2013, in its second minority health report after 2011, the Director of the CDC (Center for Disease Control), issued this overview:

> Cardiovascular disease is the leading cause of death in the United States. Non-Hispanic black adults are at least 50% more likely to die of heart disease or stroke prematurely (i.e., before age 75 years) than their non-Hispanic white counterparts (5).
>
> The prevalence of adult diabetes is higher among Hispanics, non-Hispanic blacks, and those of other or mixed races than among Asians and non-Hispanic whites. Prevalence is also higher among adults without college degrees and those with lower household incomes
>
> The infant mortality rate for non-Hispanic blacks is more than double the rate for non-Hispanic whites. Rates also vary geographically, with higher rates in the South and Midwest than in other parts of the country. (Frieden 2013)

There are also differences in health care by race, ethnicity, and language. A 2002 study of a national sample of insured Americans between the ages of 18–64 found differences in physician or mental health visits, influenza vaccines, and mammograms, during the past year. English-speaking Hispanic patients did not differ significantly from non-Hispanic white patients. But Spanish-speaking Hispanic patients were significantly less likely to have physician visits, mental health visits, or influenza vaccines. Black patients had lower health care use across all measures (Fiscella et al. 2002). The following may or may not be related to such lower rates of health care: African Americans have higher incidence and mortality rates from many cancers that are amenable to early diagnosis and treatment. African-American are underrepresented in cancer trials and less likely than whites to survive prostate cancer, breast cancer, and lung cancer. Only 68% of Hispanics are insured, compared to 88% of whites and 78% of blacks. Hispanic women contract cervical cancer at twice the rate of white women. Overweight and obesity in American Indian and Alaska Native preschoolers, school-aged children, and adults is higher than that for any other racial or ethnic group. American Indian and Alaska Native women have twice the rate of stroke than white women. In a group with the highest rate of posttraumatic stress disorders, Asian-American women have the highest suicide rate of all women over age 65 in the United States (Russell 2010).

It is not surprising that life expectancy differs according to race and ethnicity, as illustrated in (Fig. 8.1) from the Center for Disease Control.

In popular thought, health differences according to race are often associated with older ideas of ethnicity or race, according to which certain ancestral backgrounds predispose members of racial and ethnic groups to some ills rather than others. This situation is analogous to the assumption discussed in the foregoing section on marriage (e.g., that Hispanic American women marry earlier for cultural familial reasons, instead of in reaction to their educational and economic circumstances as immigrants).

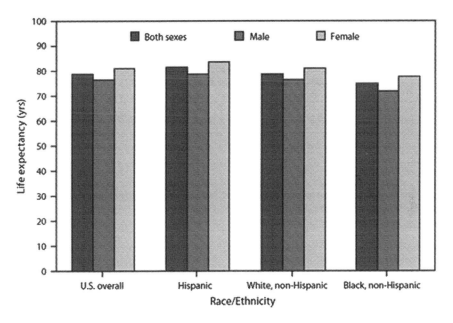

Fig. 8.1 *QuickStats*: Life expectancy at birth, by sex and race/ethnicity—United States, 2011. In 2011, life expectancy at birth was 78.7 years for the total US population, 76.3 years for males, and 81.1 years for females. Life expectancy was highest for Hispanics for both males and females. In each racial/ethnic group, females had higher life expectancies than males. Life expectancy ranged from 71.7 years for non-Hispanic black males to 83.7 years for Hispanic females (Minino 2014)

There are three analogous examples for thinking about race and health: The so-called Black heart drug, BiDil, the evolutionary account of sickle cell anemia, and obesity among the Pima Indians in Arizona.

BiDil

There was a sensationalistic report in *The New York Times* on June 13, 2005, "U.S. to Review Heart Drug intended for One Race" (Saul 2005a), with a follow-up on June 24, "F.D.A. Approves a Heart Drug for African-Americans" (Saul 2005b). About five million Americans, including 450,000 African Americans, have heart failure, an often fatal condition in which the heart does not pump enough blood. In the 1980s, NitroMed Inc. conducted a study of heart failure patients at veterans hospitals using BiDil, a drug that combined the existing drugs isosorbide and hydralazine in a fixed dose. The results were inconclusive but the African American subjects did better than others. BiDil was rejected by the FDA in 1997, because the results were inconclusive and because it went against its policy to not approve existing drugs in new combinations—that is, BiDil was not a new drug. NitroMed did not have funds to conduct a broader study.

However, in 2001, the FDA told NitroMed that BiDil could be approved as a treatment for African Americans if a study confined to African Americans showed it was effective. NitroMed contacted several African American political and scientific groups and it paid the Association of Black Cardiologists $200,000 to help organize further clinical research. NitroMed then conducted a new "African-American Heart Failure Study" on 1050 African Americans. BiDil reduced deaths by 43%.

BiDil is believed to work by increasing levels of nitrous oxide, a naturally occurring compound in the body. Many who suffer from heart failure have nitric oxide deficiency, which is more common in African Americans. But heart failure is also associated with high blood pressure and diabetes, as underlying causes which are not addressed by BiDil. Before BiDil was approved, many cardiologists noted that nitric oxide deficiency is not limited to African Americans and some said they would prescribe BiDil to any patients with the deficiency. (Once a drug is FDA approved, it can be prescribed for other purposes in "off-label" use.) (Brody and Hunt, 2006).

NitroMed's stock went up, quadrupling during pending and actual FDA approval of BiDil. It was able to extend its patent by 13 years, to 2020, on the basis of the drug's racially specific approval (Kahn 2014). Contemporary ads for BiDil show an African American father and son, with a sentimental caption (BiDil 2017). Critics have been astute at showing how BiDil was brought on the market in a racially exploitative spirit. NitroMed freely admitted that it had not used any scientific methods besides self-reporting for selecting the race of its subjects and knew that the effects of BiDil were not limited to African Americans (Blacker 2010; Kahn 2014). Relevant here is Ian Hacking's distinction between race-based and race-targeted medicine (Hacking 2005). **Race-based medicine** is based on distinct physical characteristics of a specific racial group and there is no evidence for its foundation. **Race-targeted medicine** may be appropriate for members of a specific racial group, but not because of anything biologically *racial* about them (see Chapter 3). BiDil is race-targeted medicine.

Nevertheless, BiDil was welcomed by African Americans because of a broad perception that the standard pharmaceutical patient is a white male and nonwhites are underserved by the medical community (Lee 2005). Troy Duster, a sociologist at New York University (who is the grandson of African American antilynching activist and suffragist Ida B. Wells (1862–1931)), said the following about BiDil's FDA approval in a 2005 *New York Times* interview:

> I've heard geneticists say: "We're not concerned whether or not a person is in a higher or lower class position, or if they are white or black. We want to know what basic processes are going on." But few of these basic processes happen outside a social context. I believe you can't be creating ethnically based medicines, which is what a lot of biomedical research is about, without also doing some sociology. …Much of the racial genetic research is focused on finding drugs for diseases. I go to national meetings and I'm constantly facing geneticists who say to me: "Oh you sociologists, all you do is criticize. We're trying to save lives."
>
> I'm certainly for saving lives. But I wonder if this one-sided type of research will actually do that. When you're talking about genetic diseases, there's usually something in the environment that triggers their onset. Shouldn't we be talking about the trigger? Take the case of black men and prostate cancer. African-American males have twice the prostate cancer rate that whites do. Right now, the National Cancer Institute is searching for cancer genes among black men. They're not asking, How come black men in the Caribbean and in sub-Saharan Africa have much lower prostate cancer rates than all American men?
>
> A balanced approach might involve asking, Is there something in the American environment triggering these high rates? Is it diet, stress or what? The same thing goes for hypertension. All the studies on hypertension show that you reduce it when you take people out of stressful situations. American blacks have higher hypertension rates than whites. And it's undeniable that African-Americans face daily situations that are inherently stressful. They are routinely profiled when driving, shopping, applying for bank loans or

seeking relief from a natural disaster like Hurricane Katrina. A lot of money is currently being spent to try to find a drug for black hypertension. That's a lot cheaper than a war on poverty, which might alleviate the root cause of a lot of the hypertension.

When the reporter related that BiDil was being marketed as beneficial to black patients and asked Duster, "Would you take the drug?," he replied:

Actually, my brother is taking it. If I had a nitric oxide deficiency, which is what it is said to be effective for, I would, too. I'm opposed to the way it got to be marketed. BiDil came to market after a test where it was found to be ineffective for congestive heart failure in a large population. In the original test, there was the slight suggestion that it might help African-Americans. Rather than develop a clinical trial to show whites, Asians and blacks had different responses to the drug, the manufacturers went right to the F.D.A. and said, "Now let's try it on 1,050 black people." Good science is supposedly based on comparing things. (Dreifus 2005)

Duster's approach to BiDil is both practical and theoretical: Black people should take the drug if it helps them. (But so should people of any race.) Everyone should refuse a race-based approach to health that ignores social factors that ultimately cause differences in health according to race. Ignoring such social factors not only exaggerates myths and misunderstanding about race, but is an obstacle to research and public policy that would focus on real underlying causes and cures for many diseases.

Sickle Cell Anemia

In his 2005 *New York Times* interview, Troy Duster also observed the following:

There are genetic diseases in population groups. I don't believe they are race based. These diseases are a marker for the regions where certain populations originated. Sickle cell anemia, for instance, is thought of as a black disease. But it's also to be found among Greeks who hail from a swampy area north of Athens and among people from the Arabian Peninsula.

Conversely, cystic fibrosis is thought of as a white disease, though some African-Americans have it, too. I've been in a clinic where a black man with cystic fibrosis was told, "I believe you're in the wrong section of this hospital." So again, unless we're mindful of these variations, we're going to harm people. (Dreifus 2005)

Sickle cell anemia is a serious disease and the most common hereditary disease in the United States. In the early twenty-first century, average life expectancy for those who have it has been extended from 21 to 50 years, mainly through a vaccine that protects against pneumonia. About 1 in 13 African-American babies is born with sickle cell trait and 1 in 365 is born with sickle cell disease. One in 16,300 Hispanic-American babies is born with sickle cell disease, as are smaller numbers in the United States with ancestry from South America, the Caribbean, Central America, Saudi Arabia, India, and Mediterranean countries such as Turkey, Greece, and Italy (CDC 2017b). Approximately 100,000 people have sickle cell disease, and 2 million have sickle cell trait (North Alabama Sickle Cell Foundation 2017).

Two genes are relevant for the trait and the disease. Those who inherit one sickle cell gene and one normal gene have sickle cell trait (SCT) and they do not usually have symptoms of sickle cell disease (SCD), although their children can inherit either their normal gene or SCT gene. SCD is one or more of four red blood cell disorders. Red blood cells carry oxygen throughout the body. Normal red blood cells are round but an SCD red blood cell tends to have the shape of a C-shaped farm "sickle." In someone who has SCD, the red blood cells become hard and sticky and die early, resulting in a shortage of red blood cells and oxygen. Sickle cells also get stuck in small arteries and clog the flow of blood, which can cause stroke, as well as pain and infection. The only definitive cures are bone marrow or stem cell transplants (CDC 2017b).

For many years, it was popularly assumed that because African Americans suffered from sickle cell anemia, it was a race-based disease. In time, researchers identified it in individuals with Middle Eastern and southern European ancestry, as well as African Americans, which expanded their idea of the racial base for the disease. However, the scientific community also realized that there was no reliable means for determining race, so in the early 1990s, routine screening at birth came to include sickle cell testing (American Academy of Pediatrics 2002). Of course, such screening merely identifies SCD and does not disclose its origins.

In the 1940s, doctors in Africa noticed that patients with sickle cell anemia were more likely to survive malaria, which killed over a million people a year. A sickle cell mutation was identified in the hemoglobin gene (changing Hb to HbS), in either one or two copies of that gene, with one copy resulting in sickle cell trait, as described. In high malaria areas, up to 40% of the population had SCT. Those with HbS had resistance to malaria because when their sickle cells were destroyed in the spleen, the malaria parasite was destroyed along with them (Serjeant 2001; PBS 2001). Malaria itself is believed to have coevolved with humans as a result of stressed environmental and changed agricultural conditions, such as deforestation resulting in standing pools of water where mosquitos bearing malaria breed. While most severe in sub-Saharan Africa, due to ecological destruction under colonialism, HbS has occurred in other situations of great poverty and upheaval (Packard 2007). It is also interesting, in confirmation of the evolutionary account, that African Americans who have been in non-malarial environments for generations, have lower rates of SCT than their counterparts still living in the same sub-Saharan areas as their ancestors. In a non-malarial environment, HbS does not confer any special advantage (Relethford 1997, pp. 93–4).

The Pima Indians of Arizona and Mexico

In 1965, The National Institute of Diabetes and Digestive and Kidney Diseases began a longitudinal study of type 2 diabetes and obesity among the Pima Indians on the Gila River Reservation near Phoenix, Arizona. In 1991, the study was extended to genetically similar Pima Indians in Maycoba, Mexico. Both Pima groups descended from Hohokam who lived in the Sonoran desert and Sierra Madre regions before 300 BC, but the groups separated in 1853. The Pima in Arizona used irrigation canals to grow corn, beans, squash, and cotton until about 1900, when white settlers diverted their water supply and they could no longer farm. Their lifestyle changed from active to sedentary and from a low-fat to a high-fat diet, with periods of famine. Diabetes was documented at normal rates in 1937 but increased ten-fold by the 1950s, and by 1965, the Pima in Arizona had the highest rate of diabetes in any population ever recorded. A longitudinal study showed that they had nineteen times the rate of diabetes of a sample white population in Rochester, Minnesota. By 1970, 40% of Pimas age 35 and older had type 2 diabetes and by 1990 the rate was 50%. Pimas also had higher rates of obesity and a genetic cause was sought for both conditions. It was proposed that given the famine in their history, surviving Pimas had inherited a "thrifty gene" that had enabled them to efficiently store calories in times of famine. They also had variable resting metabolic rates that researchers believed contributed to "thrifty metabolism." Without famine, type 2 diabetes and obesity resulted.

The Pimas in Maycoba, Mexico had a subsistence, labor-intensive farming lifestyle when health investigators arrived in 1991. Nineteen men and 16 women were measured for weight, height, body fat, plasma glucose, cholesterol, and other factors, for comparison with the Pimas in Arizona. Only two women and one man had type 2 diabetes. A larger study began in 1994 and it was determined that the two Pima groups had the same gene pool. Results concluded that type 2 diabetes among the Mexican Pimas was less than one-fifth of the Arizona Pimas. Obesity was similarly lower, and the Mexican Pima had activity levels 2.5 times greater among men and 7 times greater among women. There were dietary differences in less fat and more fiber in the Mexican group. Researchers concluded that these lifestyle differences accounted for differences in diabetes 2 and obesity between the two Pima groups, despite a common gene pool (Schulz and Chaudharim 2015).

The history of the change in lifestyle imposed on the Pima Indians in Arizona and the comparative evidence that their health issues are life-style related together cry out for education and dietary and exercise habit changes. According to a 2014 "Needs and Assets Report," 30% of this population live in poverty, which is higher than state and national percentages. (Frances Mc Clelland Institute for Children, Youth, and Families 2014).

Social science researchers frequently refer to positive correlations between wealth/income, education, and health: The more money people have, the higher their education. Wealth/income and education combined, or separately, are positively correlated with health. With qualifications, this is referred to as the **education-health gradient** and **the wealth-health gradient** (Conti 2010). In some ways, this relates health to issues of social class, although it is not social class in the old sense of fixed groups, but social class in ways that get expressed and recognized through taste and consumption (cultural capital). And in addition the health-wealth gradient is affected by geography. For instance, there is a 20-year gap in US life expectancy between white men in the healthiest counties and black men in the unhealthiest counties (Murray et al. 1998).

Conclusion

Although race is a social construction, it is strongly bonded to family gene-alogy, so as to continually create intergenerational groups and identities for individuals. Beneficial social indicators, such as marriage rates, vary with race, although more due to external social and economic factors than eth-nic or racial culture or the preferences or values of individuals. Social class persists in a classless society but in many indirect ways that sociologists now claim includes the cultural capital of tastes and preferences. This means that as African Americans and other minorities apply or gain entry to institutions in which whites have the most power, their full upward mobility may stall, as reflected in persistently higher rates of unemployment compared to whites among recent young college graduates. Racial and ethnic health disparities can no longer be viewed as the effects of group cultures or biology, but need to be understood as the results of environmental restrictions on opportunities and/or causes of stress. Thus, BiDil, the so-called Black Heart Drug counteracts nitrous oxide deficiency that is not limited to blacks; sickle cell anemia provided resistance to malaria in sub-Saharan African groups; and Arizona Pima Indians had higher rates of diabetes and obesity than their genetic counterparts in Mexico. Overall, statistical views of well-being vary according to race and ethnicity, because health, education, and wealth/income are positively correlated, along with cultural capital, which vary among groups.

Glossary

authority—the recognition of power.
cultural capital—class status of individuals based on their preferences and practices in consumer society.
health-wealth gradient—gradual increase in health as wealth and income increase.
matriarchy—family and social structure in which women have the most power and resources, as well as resources and wealth.
patriarchy—family and social structure in which men have the most power and resources, as well as resources and wealth.
power—the ability to do something, influence others, or make things happen.
social status—a person's position or rank in any given pecking order or hierarchy that has to do with how others view them.
race-based medicine—medicine developed and applied because of hereditary or physiological differences among racial groups.
race-targeted medicine—medicine developed for and applied to a specific racial group, based on disease rates within that group.
racial climate—the degree and extent of hearts-and-minds racism on individual-to-individual levels, in specific contexts.
stratification—sociological analysis of "how where we start in life affects where we end up."

Discussion Questions

1. Do the low marriage rates for African American women indicate a "preference" for remaining unmarried? Explain the external factors.
2. If immigrant Mexican American women marry at younger ages, why is "ethnic culture" not a good explanation?
3. What does increasing interracial marriage indicate about white attitudes toward nonwhites, in your opinion? Explain how this is different from past ideas about miscegenation during segregation.
4. Why do older, Marxist notions of social class no longer apply?
5. If our ideas of social class are expanded to include cultural capital, how does that effect prospects for upward socioeconomic mobility among minorities?
6. Explain the difference between race-based and race-targeted medicine in reference to how BiDil was developed.
7. It what sense is sickle cell anemia related to racial identity and in what ways is it independent of even social ideas of race?
8. What does the difference in health among Pima Indians in Arizona and Mexico indicate about lifestyles and disease, more broadly?
9. How are education, wealth/income, and health related? Apart from the statistics can you imagine a concrete example, in narrative form?
10. If race in life plays out in comparatively disadvantaged ways for U.S. nonwhites, what can individuals do about this? Give specific examples.

References

American Academy of Pediatrics. "Health Supervision for Children with Sickle Cell Disease Pediatrics." Mar. 2002, vol. 109, no. 3. http://pediatrics.aappublications.org/content/109/3/526.

Aughinbaugh, Alison, Omar Robles, and Hugette Sun. "Marriage and Divorce: Patterns by Gender, Race, and Educational Attainment." *Monthly Labor Review.* U.S. Bureau of Labor Statistics, Oct. 2013. https://doi.org/10.21916/mlr.2013.32.

Blacker, Sarah. "Epistemic Trafficking: On the Concept of Race-Specific Medicine." *English Studies in Canada*, vol. 36, no. 1, pp. 127–48, 2010.

Bialik, Kirsten. "Key Facts About Race and Marriage, 50 Years After *Loving v. Virginia.*" Fact Tank—Our Lives in Numbers, Pew Research Center, June 12, 2017. http://www.pewresearch.org/fact-tank/2017/06/12/key-facts-about-race-and-marriage-50-years-after-loving-v-virginia/.

BiDil.com. 2017. https://www.bidil.com/.

Black Demographics.com. "Marriage in Black America," July 6, 2017. http://black-demographics.com/households/marriage-in-black-america/.

Blackpast.org. Patrick Moynihan. "The Negro Family: The Case for National Action," 2017.

Bottero, Wendy. "Class Identities and the Identity of Class." *Sociology*, vol. 38, no. 5, 2004, pp. 985–1003.

Bottero, Wendy. *Stratification: Social Division and Inequality*. New York, NY: Routledge, 2005.

Brody, Howard, and Linda M. Hunt. "BiDil: Assessing a Race-Based Pharmaceutical." *Annals of Family Medicine*, vol. 4, no. 6, 2006, pp. 556–60. PMC. Web July 8, 2017.

Cherlin, Andrew J., David C. Ribar, and Suzumi Yasutake. "Nonmarital First Births, Marriage, and Income Inequality." *American Sociological Review*, vol. 81, no. 4, July 9, 2016, pp. 749–70.

CDC. "Unmarried Childbearing." National Center for Health Statistics, Center for Disease Control and Prevention, July 8, 2017a. https://www.cdc.gov/nchs/fastats/unmarried-childbearing.htm and https://www.cdc.gov/nchs/data/statab/t001x17.pdf.

CDC. Sickle Cell Disease (SCD), July 8, 2017b. https://www.cdc.gov/ncbddd/sicklecell/data.html.

Conti, Gabriella, James Heckman, and Sergio Urzua. "The Education-Health Gradient." *American Economic Review*, vol. 100, no. 2, May 2010, pp. 234–8. https://www.ncbi.nlm.nih.gov/pmc/articles/PMC3985402/.

Dreifus, Claudia. "A Sociologist Confronts 'the Messy Stuff.'" *Science, The New York Times*, Oct. 18, 2005. http://www.nytimes.com/2005/10/18/science/a-sociologist-confronts-the-messy-stuff.html.

Fiscella, Kevin, Peter Franks, Mark P. Doescher, and Barry G. Saver. "Disparities in health care by race, ethnicity, and language among the insured: findings from a national sample." *Medical Care*, vol. 40, no. 1, Jan. 2002, pp. 52–9.

Frances McClelland Institute for Children, Youth and Families Norton School of Family and Consumer Sciences. "Needs and Assets Report," College of Agricultural and Life Sciences, The University of Arizona, 2014. https://www.firstthingsfirst.org/regions/Publications/Regional%20Needs%20and%20Assets%20Report%20-%202014%20-%20Salt%20River%20Pima%20Maricopa%20Indian%20Community.pdf.

Frieden, Thomas R. "Morbidity and Mortality Weekly Report (MMWR)." *Forward, Supplements, Center for Disease Control and Prevention*, vol. 62, no. 3, Nov. 22, 2013, pp. 1–2.

Godfrey, Phoebe. "Bayonets, Brainwashing, and Bathrooms: The Discourse of Race, Gender, and Sexuality in the Desegregation of Little Rock's Central High." *The Arkansas Historical Quarterly*, vol. 62, no. 1, 2003, pp. 42–67. JSTOR, www.jstor.org/stable/40023302.

Hacking, Ian. "Why Race Still Matters." *Daedalus*, vol. 134, no. 1, Jan. 2005 and 2006, pp. 102–16.

Holt, Douglas B. "Does Cultural Capital Structure American Consumption?" *Journal of Consumer Research*, vol. 25, 1998, pp. 1–25.

Hout, Michael, and Cumberworth. *The Labor Force and the Great Recession*. Stanford, CA: Stanford Center on Poverty and Inequality, Oct. 2012. https://web.stanford.edu/group/recessiontrends/cgi-bin/web/sites/all/themes/barron/pdf/LaborMarkets_fact_sheet.pdf.

Kahn, Jonathan. *Race in a Bottle*: *The Story of BiDil and Racialized Medicine in a Post-Genomic Age*. New York, NY: Columbia University Press, 2014.

Kroeger, Teresa, Tanyell Cooke, and Elise Gould. "The Class of 2016: The Labor Market Is Still Far from Ideal for Young Graduates." Economic Policy Institute, Apr. 21, 2016. http://www.epi.org/publication/class-of-2016/.

Lee, Kendra. "New Drug May Get to the Heart of the Problem." *Crisis*, Jan.–Feb. 2005, p. 12. https://books.google.com/.

Mazumder, Bhashkar. "Black–White Differences in Intergenerational Economic Mobility in the United States." *Economic Perspectives*, vol. XXXVIII, no. 1, Apr. 8, 2014. Available at SSRN: https://ssrn.com/abstract=2434178.

Minino, Arialdo."QuickStats: Life Expectancy at Birth, by Sex and Race/Ethnicity—United States, 2011." Centers for Disease Control and Prevention (CDC), Weekly Sept. 5, 2014, vol. 63, no. 35, p. 776. https://www.cdc.gov/mmwr/preview/mmwrhtml/mm6335a8.htm.

Mouzon, Dawne, M. "Blacks Don't Value Marriage as Much as Other Groups." *Getting Real About Race: Hoodies, Mascots, Model Minorities, and Other Conversations*, edited by Stephanie M. McClure and Cherise A. Harris. Los Angeles, CA, Sage, 2014, pp. 145–55.

Moynihan, Patrick. *The Negro Family: The Case for National Action*, United States. Dept. of Labor. Office of Policy Planning and Research. Jan. 1, 1965, chap. V.; Blackpast.org. http://www.blackpast.org/primary/moynihan-report-1965.

Murray, C.J.L. et al. "U.S. Patterns of Mortality by County and Race, 1965–94." Cambridge, MA: Harvard Center for Population and Development Studies, 1998.

NOLO. "Marriage Rights and Benefits," 2017. http://www.nolo.com/legal-encyclopedia/marriage-rights-benefits-30190.html.

North Alabama Sickle Cell Foundation. "Facts About Sickle Cell Trait and Disease," July 8, 2017. http://sicklecellna.org/facts-about-sickle-cell-trait-and-disease.html.

Packard Randall M. *The Making of a Tropical Disease*: *A Short History of Malaria*. Baltimore, MD: Johns Hopkins University Press, 2007.

PBS. "A Mutation Story." PBS Evolution Library, (c) WGBH Education Foundation and Clear Sky Productions, 2001. http://www.pbs.org/wgbh/evolution/library/01/2/l_012_02.html.

Psychology Today. "Marriage," 2017. https://www.psychologytoday.com/basics/marriage.

Raley, R. Kelly, T. Elizabeth Durden, and Elizabeth Wildsmith. "Understanding Mexican-American Marriage Patterns Using a Life-Course Approach." *Social Science Quarterly*, vol. 85, no. 4, 2004, pp. 872–90.

Relethford, John. *The Human Species: An Introduction to Biological Anthropology*. Mountain View, CA: Mayfield, 1997.

Rodrigue, Edward, and Richard V. Reeves. "Five Bleak Facts on Black Opportunity." Social Mobility Memos, Brookings Institute, Jan. 15, 2015. https://www.brookings.edu/blog/social-mobility-memos/2015/01/15/five-bleak-facts-on-black-opportunity/.

Russell, Lesley. "Fact Sheet: Health Disparities by Race and Ethnicity: Many Groups Suffer from Lack of Health Coverage and Preventable Chronic Illnesses." Center for American Progress, Dec. 16, 2010. https://www.americanprogress.org/issues/healthcare/news/2010/12/16/8762/fact-sheet-health-disparities-by-race-and-ethnicity/.

Saul, Stephanie. "U.S. to Review Heart Drug Intended for One Race." *New York Times*, June 13, 2005a.

Saul, Stephanie. "F.D.A. Approves a Heart Drug for African-Americans." *New York Times*, June 13, 2005b.

Serjeant, G.R. "The Emerging Understanding of Sickle Cell Disease." *British Journal of Haematology*, vol. 112, 2001, pp. 3–18.

Shin, Laura. "The Racial Wealth Gap: Why a Typical White Household Has 16 Times the Wealth of a Black One." *Forbes*, Mar. 26, 2015. https://www.forbes.com/sites/laurashin/2015/03/26/the-racial-wealth-gap-why-a-typical-white-household-has-16-times-the-wealth-of-a-black-one/#5714b9851f45.

Schulz, L.O., and L.S. Chaudhari. "High-Risk Populations: The Pimas of Arizona and Mexico." *Current Obesity Reports*, 2015, vol. 4, no. 1, pp. 92–8. https://doi.org/10.1007/s13679-014-0132-9.

Thernstrom, Abigail, and Stephan Thernstrom. *America in Black and White: One Nation Indivisible*. New York, NY: Simon and Schuster, 1997.

Wattenberg, Ben. "Daniel Patrick Moynihan Interview." PBS.org, 2004. http://www.pbs.org/fmc/interviews/moynihan.htm; Wattenberg, Ben. "Daniel Patrick Moynihan—In His Own Words, Moynihan Looks Back." Think Tank Transcript, TTBW 1220 PBS Feed Date 7/8/2004, http://www.pbs.org/think-tank/transcript1108.html#TOP.

Wilson, William Julius. *The Declining Significance of Race*. Chicago, IL: University of Chicago Press, 1978.

Wood, Robert G., Brian Goesling, and Sarah Avellar. "The Effects of Marriage on Health: A Synthesis of Recent Research Evidence." *ASPE Research Brief*, Department of Health and Human Services, June 2007. https://aspe.hhs.gov/system/files/pdf/180036/rb.pdf.

9

Political Philosophy, Law, and Public Policy

Introduction

Altogether, political philosophy, law, and public policy make up the official positions and practices regarding racial difference in society. However, it is useful to distinguish these different fields of research and practice. Standard political philosophy does not have a separate subfield addressing racial difference, although the tradition has resulted in principles of liberty and individual autonomy, as well as universal human rights, which many philosophers have applied to their concerns about race, for example, ideal theory and nonideal theory as developed by John Rawls in his 1971 *A Theory of Justice*.

Law consists of what is written, the rules for implementing it, and practices of interpretation and application, for example, the Fair Housing Act of 1965 that prohibited discrimination in public housing. Public policy consists of practices by government officials and other employees that create programs and institutions and their accompanying bureaucracies, which have different effects on racial groups, for example, Affirmative Action in higher education or the use of school busing to achieve integration in K-12. Also, there may be undesired effects of unspoken public policy on local levels, such as police killings of black people that have been preceded by racial profiling. While it is tempting to imagine that there is a path from political philosophy, to law, to public policy, with decreasing degrees of abstraction, in reality these levels of analysis are often all mixed up, for example, in litigation about public policy that seeks to

© The Author(s) 2018
N. Zack, *Philosophy of Race*, Palgrave Philosophy Today,
https://doi.org/10.1007/978-3-319-78729-9_9

change how laws are interpreted, and which is motivated by principles of political philosophy. This chapter is oriented toward contemporary examples of public policy and their associated laws, judicial interpretations, and underlying political principles. But first, a note on the democratic political tradition is in order.

In Chapter 2, several official oppositions to racist ideas and practices were discussed: key elements of the 13th, 14th, and 15th Reconstruction Amendments to the US Constitution, civil rights legislation, and the 1948 United Nations Declaration of Universal Human Rights. These egalitarian pronouncements have now become part of a contemporary living tradition that is invoked in reaction to racial injustice. The core ideas, for which legal support can be found in both US and international law, are that all human beings have the same legal and societal rights, regardless of race, and that law offers remedies when those rights are violated. Scholars draw on this tradition to argue that certain practices are just or unjust and lawyers and judges reason from elements of it in court cases.

It is comforting to think that the egalitarian legal tradition protects nonwhites, but as we know, there is often a slippage between what is written and promulgated in official and lofty language and how people are treated in concrete reality. Moreover, the egalitarian legal foundations provided from the Reconstruction Amendments onward, were additions to more foundational philosophical and legal doctrines of liberty and individual autonomy. And those foundations, for example, the US Constitution, although now revised by progressives as more inclusive today than they were in their time, were not intended to ground justice for everyone. The US Constitution originally allowed for slavery, and beyond that explicitly oppressive measure, in the late eighteenth century, women and poor white men who did not own property were not permitted to vote.

As we have seen in Chapter 1, historically, the philosophical tradition has not been racially egalitarian and anti-nonwhite racism was explicitly expressed by writers such as Hume, Kant, Hegel, and even John Stuart Mill. Nevertheless, there is a consensus about racial equality among contemporary political philosophers. Differences exist in their views of how racial equality should be interpreted and applied, but those differences do not preclude the shared commitment to racial equality or as it is sometimes called, **social justice**. The first part of this chapter takes up several contemporary philosophical/theoretical approaches to justice and injustice; the second part addresses issues of public policy in Affirmative Action and racial profiling by police officers.

Contemporary Philosophical/Theoretical Approaches to Justice and Injustice

John Rawls (1921–2002) provided a new paradigm for considering justice as a political ideal and is considered by many philosophers to have revitalized political philosophy from the 1970s on, with his idea of justice as fairness. Nonetheless, criticism of Rawls's project has been robust (Douglass 2012). The economist Amartya Sen (1933–) believed that Rawls's contribution was too abstract and he introduced the *capabilities approach*. Furthermore, if we begin with ideas of justice, as theorists, we may miss what most people care about, which is injustice. And beginning from injustice calls for new theoretical work.

John Rawls and Justice as Fairness

John Rawls's famous core idea is that justice is a universal social concept among all human societies, but that in specific application, it requires a *conception*. Rawls's conception of justice is that justice is fairness. He proposed a way to arrive at fairness through a thought experiment in which all stakeholders in society, who share background core democratic principles, deliberate behind a *veil of ignorance*, which means that they do not know their own interests in real life or their identities—rich, poor, male, female, black, white, able-bodied, disabled, and so forth. The task of the deliberators is to agree on the design of the basic institutions of their society. It is important to remember that Rawls is providing an ideal theory for liberal societies that are already **well-ordered**: citizens know what the laws are, accept them as just, and know that others regard them in the same way. In *Justice as Fairness* (1985), Rawls posits two fundamental principles to govern the basic institutions:

> First, each person has the same absolute claim to equal basic liberties, which is compatible with the same liberties for all.
>
> Second, Social and economic inequalities must meet two conditions: They must be attached to offices and positions open to all under conditions of *fair equality of opportunity*; They must be to the greatest benefit of the least-advantaged members of society (the *difference principle*). (Rawls 1999a, 42–3)

The difference principle has received great attention from Rawls's scholars because it addresses distributive justice, or how real goods ought to be distributed in society, given preexisting inequalities that may be unearned, such as inborn talents. According to Leif Wenar, writing for the *Stanford Encyclopedia of Philosophy*:

> The difference principle is partly based on the negative thesis that the distribution of natural assets is undeserved. A citizen does not merit more of the social product simply because she was lucky enough to be born with the potential to develop skills that are currently in high demand. Yet this does not mean that everyone must get the same shares. The fact that citizens have different talents and abilities can be used to make everyone better off. In a society governed by the difference principle, citizens regard the distribution of natural endowments as a common asset that can benefit all. Those better endowed are welcome to use their gifts to make themselves better off, so long as their doing so also contributes to the good of those less well endowed. (Wenar 2017, 4.3)

The difference principle thus takes into account natural inequalities and in *A Theory of Justice*, Rawls introduces the idea of moral equality which contains within it an awareness of justice in those individuals who are morally equal:

> Moral persons are distinguished by two features: first they are capable of having (and are assumed to have) a conception of their good (as expressed by a rational plan of life); and second they are capable of having (and are assumed to acquire) a sense of justice, a normally effective desire to apply and to act upon the principles of justice, at least to a certain minimum degree. … One should observe that moral personality is here defined as a potentiality that is ordinarily realized in due course.

This definition of moral equality is politically important because it entitles moral persons to just treatment. Thus, Rawls added, "We see, then, that the capacity for moral personality is a sufficient condition for being entitled to equal justice" (Rawls 1999a, p. 442).

There are problems with the egalitarian nature of Rawls's definition of moral personhood. First, universal human subjectivity is impossible to confirm and can only be imagined. Some human beings may not have Rawls's features for moral personhood, for example, the cognitively disabled, those who are unjust themselves, and those who have been so severely oppressed as to lose or not develop a sense of justice. In addition to the lack of universality of Rawls's features of moral equality, it does not tell us what it is that human beings all share that makes moral equality, or the moral equality of some of them, self-evident or factually grounded. Obvious candidates for universal human equality are not convincing, because they have been known to those who have acted unjustly: biological similarities; shared species identity; common basic needs; distinctive human subjectivity; being an actual or potential object of sympathy or compassion; the intrinsic goodness of human happiness, pleasure, and flourishing and the intrinsic badness of human suffering, pain, and destruction; a common creator of all humankind. Also, some of these candidates for human equality refer to what is distinct about human beings as though they could not be changed by distinctly human inventions and constructions, for instance, biological and species similarities could change due to genetic engineering. Furthermore, moral equality based on species identity may imply that humans do not have to behave morally to other forms of life.

As a result of the inability to define human equality in any factual sense that moral equality could be based on, there are problems with any political philosophy based on external ideas of human equality, because the fact of equality would not be sufficient to stop some people from acting as though other human beings were not equal to them. If, as in the past, the idea of equality comes from religion, there are no objective directives for which religion is the right one to follow and impose on others (Zack 2014, pp. 262–4).

Influential as he has been, Rawls's positive conception of justice was aspirational. He intended it to be a goal aimed for by well-ordered societies and his project was thus ***ideal theory***. He recognized that others in seeking to address real-life problems would engage in ***nonideal theory***, although it is generally understood that nonideal theory cannot have any effect on ideal theory (Simmons 2010). Regardless, in *Law of Peoples*, Rawls assumed that ideal theory was necessary before engaging in nonideal theory that would have the long-term goal of bringing society to the condition of being just according to ideal theory: "Nonideal theory asks how this long-term goal might be achieved, or worked toward, usually in gradual steps. It looks for courses of action that are morally permissible and politically possible as well as likely to be effective" (Rawls 1999b, p. 89; Simmons 2010, p. 7).

Amartya Sen and the Capabilities Approach

In 1998, Amartya Sen, who was born in India but lives and teaches in the United States and the United Kingdom, was awarded the Nobel prize for his contributions to welfare economics. **Welfare economics** is the study of how people benefit from different economic structures and systems. Sen's contributions have included original insights, backed up with statistical evidence and mathematical formulae, about the material conditions of some of the poorest people in the world who are non-European and nonwhite. Sen's research supported conclusions that: decline in aggregate food availability is less a cause of famine than is government inflation of currency and speculative hoarding; in India, specifically, illiteracy, government bureaucracy, and poor health care affect distribution among the poor. Sen's **capabilities approach** is a focus on the ability of individuals to transform goods available to them into instruments for their own well-being. Freedom of choice and security support capabilities and specific capability indexes have been developed for different countries (Shailesh 2016).

The importance of Sen's work lies in his specific and practical study of poverty, which is more nuanced and detailed than Rawls's abstract thought experiment, including his difference principle. Sen's conception of justice is meant to represent common sense ideals and expectations. Like Rawls, Sen assumes that the correct description of a just social structure is important for progress toward justice. However, unlike Rawls, Sen describes his point of departure as starting with perceptions of injustice:

> The requirements of a theory of justice include bringing reason into play in the diagnosis of justice and injustice. Over hundreds of years, writers on justice in different parts of the world have attempted to provide the intellectual basis for moving from a general sense of injustice to particular reasoned diagnoses of injustice, and from there to the analyses of ways of advancing justice. (Sen 2009, p. 5)

That is, Sen is concerned with peoples' real lives in a given society, rather than with the justice or fairness of formal institutional structures, or what he calls Rawlsian "transcendental institutionalism" (Sen 2009, pp. 4–12 and 24–7). Against transcendental institutionalism, Sen has argued that there may not be a uniquely just institutional arrangement, so in order to make social institutional choices under less than ideal conditions, we do not need to know what a perfect or fully just arrangement might be. His famous example is that in choosing between paintings by Dali and Picasso, it does not matter if we know that the Mona Lisa is the most perfect painting in the world (Sen 2009, 15–6).

Sen sums up the difference between his approach and Rawls's, with the distinction between *niti* and *nyaya* from Sanskrit literature on ethics and jurisprudence: *Niti* refers to "organizational propriety and behavioural correctness"; *Nyaya* refers to "the world that actually emerges." Sen writes, "A realization-focused perspective also makes it easier to understand the importance of the prevention of manifest injustice in the world, rather than seeking the perfectly just" (Sen 2005, pp. 20–22). We should note, however, that the distinction between *niti* and *nyaya* is like the expression, "The best laid plans of mice and men often go awry." Our focus may need to be not so much on the world that emerges in contrast to our ideals and plans, but more simply and directly, on the world that is.

Injustice Theory

An approach to racism and other social ills from the experience of injustice is more pragmatic and concrete than both ideal and nonideal theory. This approach is "justified" by the fact that ordinary people (i.e., neither academics nor specialists) are not concerned with abstract theories of justice but with the injustice they experience or observe in the experience of others.

Applicative justice is the process of extending justice already applied to some people to new groups or individuals, for example, granting women suffrage, freeing slaves, and enforcing civil rights for minorities. There can be applicative justice only when some are already treated justly. That is, the idea and process of applicative justice are relevant to situations where some are treated justly in specific ways, while others in the same society are not treated justly, and the principles of justice that some already enjoy are stated as though they apply to everyone. Often, there already is legal language implying universality, but practice or application is not universal. For example, the fourth amendment to the US constitution, granting voting rights to all, required the Voting Rights Act of 1965 for it to be extended to African Americans. Applicative justice is only as just as the justice already practiced, but, like Rawls's conception of justice, it aims to be fair.

However, applicative justice does not always work to correct injustice. For instance, just laws that presume equality of opportunity do not result in just outcomes for both the majority with access to opportunities and minorities who do not have access to those opportunities. Although the idea of rewarding merit is just, not everyone may have the opportunity to acquire the merit that gets rewarded, for example, poor children who cannot concentrate in school due to food insecurity at home, or students in communities without adequate resources for schools may not be able to develop the skills necessary for college preparation. Sometimes, the justice enjoyed by the majority is a norm to which those who do not conform, would not wish applied. Examples include Native Americans who may prefer their traditional ways of life over becoming part of majority consumer culture (Churchill 1983; Worland 2016), or deaf people who value their deaf culture as such and do not want cochlear implants for their children (Sparrow 2005). It cannot be assumed that even if conformity to a norm brings beneficial treatment, all who do not conform would be willing to pay the price of conforming, for a further example, Muslim women who resist giving up religiously modest clothing (Rubinaug 2016).

A broad view of people whose existential situations are unjust could require a broad view of injustice. This theory is difficult to construct because it breaks with philosophical tradition and may not seem abstract enough. What is injustice? We could say that injustice exists where there is great material inequality, although an absence of recognition and respect or of commitment not to repeat the same unjust acts and omissions in the future, are also factors. Injustice may also be viewed as dangerous, leading to social disruption. For instance, it has already been noted in Chapter 1 that in his *Letter Concerning Toleration*, John Locke referred to the dangers of what we could call racial discrimination, as an example to support religious toleration. In a similar way, the Preamble to the 1948 United Nations Universal Declaration of Human Rights (UDHR), warns that all human beings have inherent dignity and equal rights: "Whereas recognition of the inherent dignity and of the equal and inalienable rights of all members of the human family is the foundation of freedom, justice, and peace in the world." And then:

> Whereas disregard and contempt for human rights have resulted in barbarous acts which have outraged the conscience of mankind, and the advent of a world in which human beings shall enjoy freedom of speech and belief and freedom from fear and want has been proclaimed as the highest aspiration of the common people. (United Nations 1948)

That is, like Locke, the writers of the Declaration thought that the common people could only be pushed so far.

The beginning of injustice theory should define injustice, although that would be only the beginning. We've seen that this is more than simple unfairness, because not everyone who experiences injustice wants to be treated fairly or is able to be treated fairly. Some philosophers have thought it important to be able to distinguish between someone who is suffering from injustice and someone whose unwanted condition is her responsibility or who has suffered bad luck. They may believe that those who are disadvantaged because of their own acts or omissions have brought misfortune on themselves, so that others are, therefore, not morally required to help them and neither is it the job of the government to help them. For cases of bad luck, where no one is to blame and there is no real injustice, help may occur domestically as philanthropy and charity, or internationally as "humanitarian response" to disaster victims, civilian war refugees, and victims of disease and famine. Help in this sense is voluntary and optional, although it may be a cultural norm. But bad luck may turn into injustice if there have been opportunities to help and no one has stepped forth. (For example, natural disasters are not in themselves unjust but ongoing situations in which victims could be helped and are not helped may be unjust.) This would mean that injustice theory does not require proving that wrongs have been deliberately inflicted (Zack 2017). Justice theory, by contrast, is often an attempt to put deliberate wrongs right or prevent future wrongs.

Public Policy—Affirmative Action and Police Racial Profiling

Public policy is a set of directives for practices that establish routines and norms of behavior in society. In the United States, public policy is often the result of implementation of laws, which is designed by administrative agencies within the executive branch of the federal government, but it is not limited to that. Public policy also pertains to practices that are neither mandated by law nor prohibited by law. These policies often have controversial outcomes that become the basis for litigation on behalf of those who believe they have been treated unjustly. US Supreme Court rulings based on interpretations of the US Constitution, and legal precedents, do tend to settle these matters, although only until the Court agrees to consider fresh litigation. We will consider some of these legal mechanisms in terms of Affirmative Action and racial profiling, practices that in spirit seem to be in opposition: affirmative action seeks to support and assist racial minorities in employment and higher education; racial profiling by police seems to target racial minorities as criminal suspects.

Affirmative Action

Affirmative action has been practiced among government contractors, the military, and large business corporations, but it has received the most attention pertaining to higher education (Knowles 2014; Parloff 2015). Twentieth-century affirmative action began among federal contractors in 1961, when President John F. Kennedy issued Executive Order 10925 that instructed federal contractors to take "affirmative action to ensure that applicants are treated equally without regard to race, color, religion, sex, or national origin"; Kennedy also created the Committee on Equal

Employment Opportunity. After President Lyndon B. Johnson signed the Civil Rights Act of 1964, employment discrimination was prohibited by all employers with over 15 employees and the Equal Employment Opportunity Commission was created; in 1965, Johnson established the Office of Federal Contract Compliance in the Department of Labor, which required that government contractors and subcontractors expand job opportunities for minorities (in 1967, affirmative action for women was included). Johnson's initiatives continued under the Nixon administration with the Minority Business Enterprise Contracting Program in 1971–1973, but **quotas** (specified numbers of minorities) were by then prohibited (Martinez 2014).

Part of the rationale for affirmative action was that discrimination against minorities, which was believed to be widespread, was difficult to prove. Despite the 1964 antidiscrimination civil rights legislation, there was little change in the numbers of minorities in employment and higher education admissions outcomes—desirable employment and colleges and universities remained disproportionately white. While affirmative action was strongly supported by minorities and white progressives as a way to "level the playing field," from the beginning, it met opposition as "reverse discrimination." The reasoning was that whites would lose places as minorities gained them and it was widely believed that minorities were not as qualified as whites (Pious 1996). In *California v. Bakke* (438, US 912), in 1978 the US Supreme Court ruled that the University of California Medical School practice of setting aside 18 out of 100 admissions for minority students was unlawful. However, in *Bakke*, the Court also ruled that race could be considered as one factor in choosing among qualified applicants, stating in its opinion: "The goal of achieving a diverse student body is sufficiently compelling to justify consideration of race in admissions decisions under some circumstances" (*California v. Bakke* 1978, Syllabus).

After *Bakke*, the Court's qualified acceptance of affirmative action has continued. In *United Steel Workers of America, AFL-CIO v. Weber*, 444 U.S. 889, in 1979, the Court upheld temporary race-conscious affirmative action, provided that the rights of white employees were not violated. In 1989, in *City of Richmond v. J.A. Croson Co.* (488 U.S. 469), the Court banned a minority contracting program as unconstitutional and required that such programs fulfill a "compelling interest" and be "narrowly tailored" to do only that. This case was an example of the Court's application of the doctrine of *strict scrutiny* to practices involving race. The Court interpreted the Constitution as having zero tolerance for any degree of racial preference or racial discrimination, so that only a compelling government interest, such as ending discrimination, could override this principle of racial neutrality (Winkler 2006).

Some states have independently curtailed affirmative action. The effectiveness of affirmative action for nonwhite admission in higher education was demonstrated after Proposition 209 was passed in California, banning all affirmative action programs, beginning in 1998. Also In 1998, voters in Washington state passed Initiative 200 that prohibited affirmative action in higher education, public contracting, and hiring. In 2000, the Florida legislature passed the "One Florida" Plan, banning affirmative action (Martinez 2014). As a result of Prop. 209, UC Berkeley had a 61% drop in admissions of African American, Latino/a and Native American students, and UCLA had a 36% decline. However, the broader question is whether affirmative action in higher education has results that are beneficial to society.

In their 1996 book, *The Shape of the River: Long-Term Consequences of Considering Race in College and University Admissions*, William G. Bowen and Derek Bok, former presidents of Princeton and Harvard universities present the results of a long-term study of "race-sensitive" admissions policies at elite schools, beginning in 1951. (They focussed on 28 elite schools because 60% of US colleges and universities admit close to 100% of all who apply.) Bowen and Bok examined the academic records of 80,000 students and conducted interviews and submitted questionnaires to black and white students who began college in 1976 and 1989. Among black enrollees in 1989, 79% graduated, compared to a national 32% rate of black college graduation. Highly qualified black students were three times as likely to be admitted as highly qualified white applicants. Among about 700 black graduates who would not have been admitted without affirmative action, there were 60 lawyers, 70 physicians, and 125 business executives. Bowen and Bok predicted that without affirmative action policies, black enrollments at elite schools would fall from about 7 to 2%, with law and medical school enrollment to less than 1% (Bowen and Bok 1998) Recent surveys have found that affirmative action bans in medical schools in California, Washington, Florida, Texas, Michigan, and Nebraska have been followed by a 17% decrease in minority enrollment in medical schools (Garces and Mickey-Pabello 2015). Between 1993 and 2008, minority enrollment in US law schools also decreased (Lewin 2010).

In its first major higher education case after *Bakke*, in 2003, the US Supreme Court ruled in two University of Michigan cases. In *Gratz v. Bollinger* (539 U.S.) the Court rejected the undergraduate admissions program that granted automatic points for nonwhite race and ethnicity, without reviewing whole files (*Gratz v. Bollinger et al.* 2003). But in *Grutter v. Bollinger* (539 U.S.), the Court upheld the constitutionality of the Law School's use of race in considering candidates for admission, holistically, so that race is one factor among many. Nevertheless, the Court did not whole-heartedly approve even this restricted consideration of race and Chief Justice Sandra Day O'Connor speculated that it would be unnecessary by 2028, writing: "The Court expects that 25 years from now, the use of racial preferences will no longer be necessary to further the interest approved today" (*Grutter v. Bollinger et al.*, 539 U.S. 306, 2003, Opinion III, B.).

The two cases of *Fisher v. University of Texas at Austin* upheld the Court's perspective in *Bakke* and *Grutter*. The University of Texas has two ways in which minority students have opportunities for admission. Under UT's Top Ten Percent Program, the top ten percent of all high school graduates in the state are automatically admitted. Because this plan covers schools primarily attended by minorities as well as whites, it has been successful in increasing black and Hispanic enrollment. The second part of the UT program holistically considers applicants, with race as a factor among qualifications. In 2013, the Court first considered the case of Abigail Fisher, a white applicant who was denied admission under the second part of the program, but its ruling about whether she had unconstitutionally been denied admission on the grounds of race was inconclusive. However, in its second 2015 hearing of *Fisher v. University of Texas at Austin*, the Court once more upheld holistic affirmative action, after applying strict scrutiny and deferring to the institutional value of a diverse student body (*Fisher v. University of Texas at Austin*, 2013; Liptak 2016).

The value of diversity in higher education is not only a benefit to members of underrepresented groups who are admitted, but includes their distinct contribution to a whole cohort of students and professors, as a result of their different backgrounds and perspectives—Bowen and Bok's study has been received as confirmation of such claims about the wider benefits of affirmative action in higher education (Hacker 1998). It is commonly acknowledged that the US leadership class throughout societal sectors is trained in college. Having contact with racially and ethnically different people during formative years would seem to be an important component of future leadership skills. Part of the US Supreme Court's deference to institutional diversity, in this sense, is future-oriented. However, in accepting the overriding principle that any degree of racial preference is suspect, the Court has consistently refused to consider the effects of past discrimination on nonwhite college applicants who may not be as competitive as white applicants. The Court thereby considers racial difference without regard to status or inherited disadvantage. It may approve of limited affirmative action to correct past discrimination within an institution, but it has shown no acceptance of affirmative action as a remedy for inherited harms due to slavery and Jim Crow (Thomson 1973). Furthermore, the idea that affirmative action is "reverse discrimination" has not died out since it was first aired in the 1960s (Pojman 1998).

About two-thirds of Americans do not have college degrees (Ryan and Bauman 2016). But no one doubts the importance of a college degree for success in adult life in complex society. And no one doubts that minorities disproportionately lack college degrees. Therefore, part of what is at stake with the permissibility of affirmative action in higher education is upward socioeconomic mobility, from parents to children. In the early twenty-first century, only 35% of blacks, compared to 50% of whites, exceeded their parents' economic status by more than 20 percentiles (Upward mobility is highest for White men, followed by White women, Black men, and Black women.) (Mazumder 2008).

Upward socioeconomic mobility requires higher education. Grades on standardized tests administered in middle school are a stronger predictor of upward socioeconomic mobility from the status of parents, than any other indicator, including race and gender. According to a study by Columbia and Harvard University economists, which tracked 2.5 million elementary and middle school students over 20 years, good preparation for standardized tests affects college admission: Students whose teachers helped them raise standardized test scores had fewer teenage pregnancies, higher rates of college enrollment, and higher earnings at age 28 (Chetty et al. 2011). Returning to Amartya Sen's insights about capabilities, it may be that affirmative action is one way to support human capabilities and that teacher attention to college preparation is another.

Affirmative action can be judged on its intent and its result. If the intent of affirmative action is to unfairly give some people unearned advantages, it is not difficult to see why some call it "reverse discrimination." However, holistic consideration of minority candidates presupposes that these candidates are otherwise qualified. What remains is a small degree of preference based on race, again, "given all things equal," and that may or may not disrupt cherished principles of reward based on merit, and fairness. In considering those principles against the reality of college attendance, it should be kept in mind that there are other groups who are given boosts for admission that are not strictly related to their academic qualifications. The children of alumni have an easier time of getting admitted to most colleges and universities, as do athletes, in comparison to those who do not have such advantages (Massey and Mooney 2007).

Racial Profiling

Racial profiling is the use of nonwhite race or ethnicity by police officials to select likely criminal suspects. General US legal principles support **probable cause** or independent evidence of criminal behavior, before police are justified in interfering in the lives of civilians. But racial profiling may lead to police intervention in the absence of probable cause, for several reasons: anti-nonwhite racial bias on the part of individual law enforcement officers; high crime rate areas that are mainly populated by nonwhites; police suspicion of the presence of nonwhites in largely white areas; known high criminal conviction and incarceration rates for nonwhites. Racial residential segregation—minorities are more likely to live in segregated neighborhoods, regardless of their income—works together with high conviction and incarceration rates among minorities. For instance, 1 in every 15 African American men and 1 in every 36 Hispanic men are incarcerated in comparison to 1 in every 106 white men (Kerby 2013). The result is that minorities are more likely to live in high crime neighborhoods with other minorities (Andrews 2015), so that minority identity alone may be associated with crime in the minds of law enforcement officers.

Hearts-and-minds racism is difficult to predict or prove as existing in particular individuals. However, after the 2012 death of Trayvon Martin (CNN 2017), there has been heightened public concern about killings of unarmed young black men by law enforcement officials, followed by legal impunity for police perpetrators (Yancy and Jones 2013; Funke and Susman 2016). Reports indicate that young black men are nine times as likely as other demographic groups to be killed by police officers in the United States (Swaine and McCarthy 2017). Ongoing outrage and protests have been visible in mass and social media, perhaps most notably in the Black Lives Matter movement (Black Lives Matter 2017), which began after the killing of Michael Brown in 2014 (BBC News 2014). Such demonstration has been opposed by organizations in defense of police officers, pointing out the dangers of their jobs and objecting that "blue lives matter" and "all lives matter" (Blue Lives Matter 2017; All Lives Matter 2017). As of 2016, according to the Pew Research Center, about four in ten Americans support Black Lives Matter, while less than one in five strongly oppose it, although there is some confusion about what the slogan actually means (Horowitz and Livingston 2016). On the one hand, extra-juridical killings of black people by police officers send a message that the lives of black people do not matter; on the other hand, to emphasize that black lives matter suggests to some who are not black that *their* lives do not matter.

Many who support the Black Lives Matter Movement, and others, believe that police killings of unarmed young black men, in the absence of probable cause, and followed by legal impunity, are unjust. However, it is necessary to distinguish between what is just and what is legal, because final outcomes are not determined by strong intuitions of what is morally wrong, but by written law as interpreted by courts. US constitutional rights such as Fourth Amendment rights against searches and seizures without legal cause and Fourteenth Amendment rights to equal protection by government officials also seem to be at stake. But strictly speaking, racial profiling is not against the present law and neither is the fact that police homicide occurs with no legal penalties—even though both are unjust. In reality, the actions of police officers are no longer bound by "probable cause," and police discretion plus legal definitions of manslaughter and murder block indictments and convictions for police homicide. Several US Supreme Court Decisions have allowed for expanded police discretion and destroyed the doctrine of "probable cause" that would have required that police have an objective reason for stops and frisks or attempted stops and frisks: *Graham v. Connor, Plumhoff et al. v. Rickard*, and before then, *Terry v. Ohio*.

In *Graham v. Connor*, 1989, the Court introduced the "reasonable officer standard" for the use of deadly force: whether officers' actions are "objectively reasonable" in light of the facts and circumstances confronting them, *without regard to their underlying intent or motivation*. This case is of particular importance because it renders it legally irrelevant whether or not an officer is racially biased, to begin with. The "reasonableness" of a particular use of force must be judged from the perspective of a reasonable officer on the scene, and "its calculus must embody an allowance for the fact that police officers are often forced to make split-second decisions about the amount of force necessary in a particular situation" (*Graham v. Connor*, 490 U.S. 386 (1989)).

This reasonable officer standard inevitably refers to what is considered reasonable within police culture and it does not preclude the legality of using deadly force when the officer has instigated a confrontation that he then believes endangers his life. In *Plumhoff et al. v. Rickard*, the US Supreme Court ruled in 2013 that individuals' Fourth Amendment rights violations—that is the right against unreasonable stops and seizures, where death counts as a "seizure"—must be balanced against an official's *qualified immunity*, unless it can be shown that the official violated a statutory or constitutional right that was "clearly established" at the time of the challenged conduct.

In other words, police homicide in the recent high profile cases is protected until the laws or Supreme Court rulings change. We also need to recognize that the first attack on probable cause, and the background to both *Graham* and *Plumhoff* came with Justice Earl Warren's 1968 Opinion in *Terry v. Ohio*:

> It does not follow that because an officer may lawfully arrest a person only when he is apprised of facts sufficient to warrant a belief that the person has committed or is committing a crime, the officer is equally unjustified, absent that kind of evidence, in making any intrusions short of an arrest. (*Terry v. Ohio*. 392 I/S/1(1968))

That is, police officers may intrude based on evidence that falls short of the evidence needed to make an arrest. And if such intrusions escalate into the use of deadly force, police immunity applies, particularly if events have escalated to the point where an officer's life is in danger, or the officer so believes or is willing to claim.

Despite legal backing for police discretion culminating in what many view as unjust violence, public policy remains relevant for how these issues will ultimately play out. Changes in "Broken Windows Policy" are a case in point. The Broken Windows Theory was introduced by James Q. Wilson and George Kelling, in 1982 (Wilson and Kelling 1982). They proposed enforcing public order on a neighborhood basis, through police **stop-and-frisk** actions, to prevent more serious crime. Wilson and Kelling believed that minor offenses, such as drinking in public, loitering, and disorderly conduct, undermined civic pride and involvement. An important part of the new policy would involve community outreach programs with members of communities served. However, community outreach programs have not always been implemented when Broken Windows crime detection programs have been put into effect, especially in New York City. Also, it has not been confirmed that Broken Windows procedures put into practice in New York City, Chicago, and Los Angeles by the early 2000s, were effective in reducing more serious crime. A 2001 study by George Kelling and William Sousa about crime data from 1989 to 1998 in New York City suggests that there is no direct correlation between public disorder and serious crime (Harcourt and Ludwig 2005). Serious crime, especially violent crime, decreased by 48% from 1993–2011, a trend that began before widespread stop-and-frisk policies were adopted (Weisser 2014). Broken Windows type interventions have been curtailed in a number of municipalities, in favor of building better police-community relationships and interactions (Childress 2016).

Let's return now to the statistics on race and crime. As noted above: 1 in every 15 African American men and 1 in every 36 Hispanic men are incarcerated in comparison to 1 in every 106 white men (Kerby 2013). What is overlooked in this picture is that the figures entail that most African

American and Hispanic men, like most white men, *do not* commit the kinds of crimes for which police seek suspects. The problem with both racial profiling by police and the reasoning of those who defend it is a focus on the racial makeup of the criminal population. In *Floyd v. The City of New York*, Judge Schleindin ruled that NYPD's practice of stop-and-frisk in which half of 4.4 million suspects stopped from 2002–2012 were black, was unconstitutional because it did not represent actual crime statistics in the communities policed. What NYPD's policy did mirror was the proportion of blacks in the US prison population and it was not surprising that of all their stops and frisks in the period resulted in over 90% of suspects let go without further police action. Schleindin was removed from the case due to mayoral politics, but the subsequent administration has begun to implement the reforms she ordered, which included curtailment of stop-and-frisk based on racial profiling (Paybarah et al. 2016).

Further changes in policy in response to public outcry may be grounds for optimism. Among these is mandatory use of body cameras by police officers and growing awareness within local police departments of the need for positive relationships with members of minority communities in order to conduct their core work of fighting crime. But, body cameras are not a panacea and may raise privacy concerns (Pearce 2014). Still, new policies can be developed within police departments, requiring calls for backup, and again, white police officers can be trained in communication with minority suspects (Johnson 2017). In the meantime, disturbing violent incidents and reactions to them are likely to occur and recur (Zack 2015, pp. 93–100).

Conclusion

In democratic political life, political philosophy, law, and public policy are often interrelated. However, high theory, such as John Rawls's abstract thought experiment to develop basic institutions for already well-ordered and law-abiding societies, may not be directly relevant to the correction of practical injustice. Amartya Sen's idea of addressing human capabilities and practices of applicative justice, as well as injustice theory more generally, may be more effective for addressing practical concerns. As a policy, affirmative action has been a controversial method for achieving racial integration in employment and higher education. The US Supreme Court has upheld affirmative action by protecting the consideration of race in admissions only when it is part of a full range of individual qualifications. Police racial profiling has led to high profile homicides against young black men, although the police discretion involved has been upheld by the US Supreme Court. Policy changes in police methods are likely to change what is perceived to be unjust and racist about such extra-juridical killings, but there are no simple solutions to this problem or answers to the questions raised by it.

Glossary

Affirmative action—practice of positively considering nonwhite race and female gender for hiring and college admissions.

applicative justice—process of extending justice already applied to some people, to new groups or individuals.

autonomy—self rule.

capabilities approach—an economic focus on the ability of individuals to transform goods available to them into instruments for their own well-being.

difference principle—restriction on inequality in society, according to John Rawls, so that the least well off benefit from changes in distribution.

ideal theory—principles of justice for well-ordered liberal societies.

injustice theory —a method of starting from actual injustice instead of constructing ideals of justice.

nonideal theory—theories of justice for nonideal societies that seek to bring them closer to ideal societies.

probable cause—evidence of criminal behavior that justifies police intervention.

public policy—official practice that establishes routines of behavior in society.

racial profiling—the use of nonwhite race as a cause for police intervention.

quotas—unpopular practice of specifying numbers of minorities to be included.

strict scrutiny—judicial practice of closely examining the purpose of using race for employment and college admissions and determining that such usage does not exceed its purpose.

welfare economics—economic study of how people benefit from different economic structures and policies.

well-ordered society—people know what the laws are and know that others do also and that their society is just.

Discussion Questions

1. Explain how the relationship between political principles, law, and public policy may be complicated.

2. Describe how the consensus of racial equality among contemporary political philosophers is not grounded on foundational principles of democracy in a historical sense.
3. What are the major problems with moral equality as Rawls posits it? What are the problems with a factual basis for human equality? How is ideal theory related to nonideal theory, according to Rawls?
4. Explain why applicative justice does not always correct experiences of injustice.
5. Why does Amartya Sen call Rawls's ideal theory "transcendental institutionalism"? How does his capabilities approach avoid the pitfalls of ideal theory?
6. If legacies, or the descendants of alumni, and athletes receive preference in college admission, how is that different from race-based preference?
7. How is racial profiling related to residential racial segregation? Is it unjust?
8. In what ways are high profile cases of police homicide legally protected, based on Supreme Court rulings?
9. Discuss the relationships between "Black Lives Matter," "Blue Lives Matter," and "All Lives Matter."
10. Explain how public opinion is relevant to police behavior. What does this imply about the democratic nature of the US society?

References

All Lives Matter. "#All Lives Matter." *Wikipedia*, 2017. https://en.wikipedia.org/wiki/All_Lives_Matter.

Andrews, Edmund L. "Stanford Study Finds Blacks and Hispanics Typically Need Higher Incomes Than Whites to Live in Affluent Neighborhoods." *Stanford News*, June 25, 2015. http://news.stanford.edu/2015/06/25/segregation-neighborhood-income-062515/.

BBC News. "Ferguson Protests: What We Know About Michael Brown's Last Minutes." *Section US & Canada*, Nov. 25, 2014. http://www.bbc.com/news/world-us-canada-28841715.

Black Lives Matter. http://blacklivesmatter.com/. Consulted Aug. 7, 2017.

Blue Lives Matter. https://www.facebook.com/bluematters/. Consulted Aug. 7, 2017.

Bowen, William G., and Derek Bok in Collaboration with James L. Shulman, Thomas I. Nygren, Stacy Berg Dale, and Lauren A. Meserve. *The Shape of the River: Long-Term Consequences of Considering Race in College and University Admissions*. Princeton, NJ: Princeton University Press, 1998.

California v. Bakke (438, US 912) (1978). Syllabus, Legal Information Institute, Cornell Law School. https://www.law.cornell.edu/supremecourt/text/438/265. Accessed Aug. 7, 2017.

Chetty, Raj, John N. Friedman, and Jonah E. Rockoff. "The Long-Term Impacts of Teachers: Teacher Value-Added and Student Outcomes in Adulthood." *Columbia University and NBER*, Dec. 2011. http://www.nber.org/papers/w17699. Both Consulted Aug. 5, 2017.

Childress, Sarah. "The Problem with 'Broken Windows' Policing." *Frontline, PBS*, June 28, 2016. http://www.pbs.org/wgbh/frontline/article/the-problem-with-broken-windows-policing/. Consulted Aug. 7, 2017.

Churchill, Ward. *Marxism and Native Americans*. Brooklyn, NY: South End Press, 1983.

CNN. "Trayvon Martin Killing Fast Facts." *CNN Library*. http://www.cnn.com/2013/06/05/us/trayvon-martin-shooting-fast-facts/index.html. Consulted Aug. 7, 2017.

Douglass, R. Bruce. "John Rawls and the Revival of Political Philosophy: Where Does He Leave Us?" *Theoria: A Journal of Social and Political Theory*, vol. 59, no. 133, 2012, pp. 81–97. JSTOR, www.jstor.org/stable/41802535.

Fisher v. University of Texas at Austin. SCOTUSblog, June 23, 2013. http://www.scotusblog.com/case-files/cases/fisher-v-university-of-texas-at-austin-2/.

Floyd v City of New York Case 1:08-cv-01034-SAS-HBP (2013). Floyd, David, Lalit Clarkson, Deon Dennis, and David Ourlicht, Individually and on Behalf of all Others Similarly Situated, Plaintiffs, -Against- The City of New York, Defendant. United States District Court Southern District of New York Case 1:08-cv-01034-SAS-HBP Document 373, Filed 08/12/13. http://www.nysd.uscourts.gov/cases/show.php?db=special&id=317.

Funke, Daniel, and Tina Susman. "From Ferguson to Baton Rouge: Deaths of Black Men and Women at the Hands of Police." *Los Angeles Times*, July 12, 2016. http://www.latimes.com/nation/la-na-police-deaths-20160707-snap-html-story.html.

Garces, Liliana M., and David Mickey-Pabello. "Racial Diversity in the Medical Profession: The Impact of Affirmative Action Bans on Underrepresented Student of Color Matriculation in Medical Schools." *The Journal of Higher Education*, vol. 86, no. 2, 2015, pp. 264–94. *PMC*. Web. 7 Aug. 2017.

Graham v. Connor, 490 U.S. 386 (1989). Justia, US Supreme Court. https://supreme.justia.com/cases/federal/us/490/386/case.html.

Gratz v. Bollinger et al., (02-512) (2003). *Find Law*. http://caselaw.lp.findlaw.com/scripts/getcase.pl?court=US&vol=000&invol=02-516.

Grutter v. Bollinger et al., 539 U.S. 306 (2003). Find Law Justia LI. http://caselaw.findlaw.com/us-supreme-court/539/306.html.

Hacker, A. "The Bowen-Bok Study on Race-Sensitive College Admissions." *The Journal of Blacks in Higher Education*, no. 21, Autumn 1998, pp. 129–31. JSTOR, www.jstor.org/stable/2999027.

Harcourt, Bernard E., and Jens Ludwig. "Broken Windows: New Evidence from New York City and a Five-City Social Experiment." Public Law and Legal Theory Working Paper, 93. *University of Chicago Law Review*, 73. June, 2005. http://www.law.uchicago.edu/files/files/93-beh-jl-windows.pdf.

Horowitz, Juliana Menasce, and Gretchen Livingston. "How Americans View the Black Lives Matter Movement." Fact Tank—Our Lives in Numbers, *Pew Research Center*, July 8, 2016. http://www.pewresearch.org/fact-tank/2016/07/08/how-americans-view-the-black-lives-matter-movement/.

Johnson, Richard R. "Improving Police-Minority Relations: The Out of Car Experience." *Research Brief, Dolan Consulting Group*, Jan. 2017. https://www.dolanconsultinggroup.com/wp-content/uploads/2017/01/RB_OutOfCarExperiences_January-2017.pdf.

Kerby, Sophia. "The Top 10 Most Startling Facts About People of Color and Criminal Justice in the United States: A Look at the Racial Disparities Inherent in Our Nation's Criminal-Justice System." *Center for American Progress*, Mar. 13, 2013. http://www.americanprogress.org/issues/race/news/2012/03/13/11351/the-top-10-most-startling-facts-about-people-of-color-and-criminal-justice-in-the-united-states/.

Knowles, Robert. "The Intertwined Fates of Affirmative Action and the Military." *Loyola University Chicago Law Journal*, vol. 45, no. 4, 2014, pp. 1027–84. http://www.luc.edu/media/lucedu/law/students/publications/llj/pdfs/vol45/issue4/Knowles%20Cropped.pdf.

Lewin, Tamar. "Law School Admissions Lag Among Minorities." *New York Times*, Jan. 6, 2010. http://www.nytimes.com/2010/01/07/education/07law.html.

Liptak, Adam. "Supreme Court Upholds Affirmative Action Program at University of Texas." *New York Times*, June 24, 2016. https://www.nytimes.com/2016/06/24/us/politics/supreme-court-affirmative-action-university-of-texas.html.

Martinez, Kathleen. "More History of Affirmative Action Policies from the 1960s." *American Association for Access, Equity, and Diversity*, 2014. https://www.aaaed.org/aaaed/History_of_Affirmative_Action.asp.

Massey, Douglass, and Margarita Mooney. "The Effects of America's Three Affirmative Action Programs on Academic Performance." *Social Problems*, vol. 54, no. 1, 2007, pp. 99–117, http://www.margaritamooney.com/wp-content/uploads/2011/08/academicconsequencesofthreeaffirmativeaction.pdf.

Mazumder, Bhashkar. "Upward Intergenerational Economic Mobility in the United States." *Economic Mobility Project: Upward Mobility Project: An Initiative of The Pew Charitable Trusts*, 2008. http://www.economicmobility.org/assets/pdfs/EMP_ES_Upward_Mobility.pdf; http://www.pewtrusts.org/en/about/news-room/press-releases/2008/05/29/new-study-on-economic-opportunity-finds-that-americans-experience-upward-economic-mobility-but-for-many-the-magnitude-of-their-movement-is-minimal. Consulted Aug. 1, 2017.

Parloff, Roger. "Big Business Asks Supreme Court to Save Affirmative Action." *Fortune*, Dec. 8, 2015. http://fortune.com/2015/12/09/supreme-court-affirmative-action/.

Paybarah, Azi, Brendan Cheney, and Colby Hamilton. "De Blasio on Stop-and-Frisk: 'We Changed It Intensely.'" *Politico*, Dec. 8, 2016. http://www.politico.com/states/new-york/city-hall/story/2016/12/de-blasio-on-stop-and-frisk-we-changed-it-intensely-107886. Consulted Aug. 7, 2017.

Pearce, Matt. "Growing Use of Police Body Cameras Raises Privacy Concerns." *Los Angeles Times*, Sept. 27, 2014. http://www.latimes.com/nation/la-na-body-cameras-20140927-story.html.

Pious, S. "Ten Myths About Affirmative Action." *Journal of Social Issues*, vol. 52, 1996, pp. 25–31. https://doi.org/10.1111/j.1540-4560.1996.tb01846.x.

Plumhoff et al. v. Rickard, U.S. Supreme Court, October Term, 2013. http://www.supremecourt.gov/opinions/13pdf/12-1117_1bn5.pdf.

Pojman, Louis P. "The Case Against Affirmative Action." *International Journal of Applied Philosophy, Philosophy Documentation Center*, vol. 12, no. 1, 1998, pp. 97–115.

Rawls, John. *A Theory of Justice*, rev. ed. Cambridge, MA: Harvard University Press, 1999a.

Rawls, John. *The Law of Peoples*. Cambridge, MA: Harvard University Press, 1999b.

Rawls, John. *Justice as Fairness: A Restatement*, edited by E. Kelly. Cambridge, MA: Harvard University Press, 1985.

Rubinaug, Alissa J. "From Bikinis to Burkinis, Regulating What Women Wear." *New York Times*, Europe | Memo from France, Aug. 27, 2016. http://www.nytimes.com/2016/08/28/world/europe/france-burkini-bikini-ban.html.

Ryan, Camille L., and Kurt Bauman. "Educational Attainment in the United States: 2015 Population Characteristics." *Current Population Reports*, P20-578, Mar. 2016. https://www.census.gov/content/dam/Census/library/publications/2016/demo/p20-578.pdf.

Sen, Amartya. *The Idea of Justice*. Cambridge, MA: Harvard University Press, 2009.

Shailesh, Kirti. "7 Main Contributions of Amartya Sen to Economics." *Economics Discussion.net*, 2016. http://www.economicsdiscussion.net/economists/7-main-contributions-of-amartya-kumar-sen-to-economics/21123. Accessed Aug. 5, 2017.

Simmons, A.J. "Ideal and Nonideal Theory." *Philosophy & Public Affairs*, vol. 38, 2010, pp. 5–36. https://doi.org/10.1111/j.1088-4963.2009.01172.

Sparrow, Robert. "Defending Deaf Culture: The Case of Cochlear Implants." *Journal of Political Philosophy*, vol. 13, no. 2, 2005, pp. 135–52.

Swane, John, and Chiara McCarthy. The Counted: Young Black Men Again Faced Highest Rate of US Police killings in 2016." *The Guardian*, Jan. 8, 2017. https://www.theguardian.com/us-news/2017/jan/08/the-counted-police-killings-2016-young-black-men.

Terry v. Ohio. 392 I/S/1 (1968), No. 67. http://scholar.google.com/scholar_case?case=17773604035873288886&q=terry+v.+ohio,+us+supreme+court&hl=en&as_sdt=3,38.

Thomson, Judith Jarvis. "Preferential Hiring." *Philosophy & Public Affairs*, vol. 2, Summer, 1973, pp. 364–84.

United Nations, Universal Declaration of Human Rights, 1948. http://www.un.org/en/universal-declaration-human-rights/.

Weisser, Michael. "It's Clear Violent Crime Is Decreasing, but Less Clear Why." Posted 02/10/2014 1:12 pm, EST Updated 04/12/2014. Crime, *Huffington Post*, Posted 02/10/2014 1:12 pm, EST Updated 04/12/2014. http://www.huffingtonpost.com/mike-weisser/violent-crime-cities_b_4760996.html.

Wenar, Leif. "John Rawls." *The Stanford Encyclopedia of Philosophy*, edited by Edward N. Zalta, Spring 2017 Edition. https://plato.stanford.edu/archives/spr2017/entries/rawls/.

Wilson, James Q., and George L. Kelling. "Broken Windows: The Police and Neighborhood Safety." *Atlantic Monthly*, Mar. 1982. http://www.manhattan-institute.org/pdf/_atlantic_monthly-broken_windows.pdf.

Winkler, Adam. "Fatal in Theory and Strict in Fact: An Empirical Analysis of Strict Scrutiny in the Federal Courts." UCLA School of Law Research Paper No. 06–14, *Vanderbilt Law Review*, vol. 59, pp. 793–873, Apr. 18, 2006. https://papers.ssrn.com/sol3/papers.cfm?abstract_id=897360.

Worland, Justin. "What to Know About the Dakota Access Pipeline Protests." *Time*, Oct. 28, 2016. http://time.com/4548566/dakota-access-pipeline-standing-rock-sioux/.

Yancy, George, and Janine Jones, editors. *Pursuing Trayvon Martin: Historical Contexts and Contemporary Manifestations of Racial Dynamics*. Lanham, MD: Lexington Books, 2013.

Zack, Naomi. "Philosophical Theories of Justice, Inequality, and Racial Inequality." *Graduate Faculty Philosophy Journal*, Philosophy and Race, vol. 35, no. 1/2, 2014, pp. 353–68. https://doi.org/10.5840/gfpj2014351/216.

Zack, Naomi. *White Privilege and Black Rights: The Injustice of US Police Racial Profiling and Homicide*. Lanham, MD: Rowman & Littlefield, 2015.

Zack, Naomi. "Starting from Injustice: Justice, Applicative Justice, and Injustice Theory." *Harvard Review of Philosophy*, First Published on June 10, 2017. https://doi.org/10.5840/harvardreview2017679.

10

Feminism, Gender, and Race

The concerns of contemporary philosophical feminism have extended from the oppression of white middle-class women to **gender**, which includes heterosexual males and those of **LGBTQ** sexualities. However, all of these subjects do not peacefully coexist under the same umbrella of feminism, partly for historical reasons and partly due to ongoing tensions between feminists who are presently divided by their racial identities and experience.

Feminist philosophy, like philosophy of race, is a new addition to philosophy, with subjects of analyses that include the history of philosophy, neglected and reclaimed authors, contemporary social injustice, oppression, and identity. By the mid-nineteenth century, suffragists and abolitionists seemed to be natural allies. But following the Civil War, some educated suffragists resented freed black men for having attained the vote before they did. Black women were excluded from white women's political projects, as well as their club networks. (Social and activist clubs were an important institution at that time.) But black women organized on their own—they protested lynching and sought educational opportunities for black women; they vigorously corrected racist stereotypes of sexual immorality and sexual assaults on black women by white men; they created their own social organizations (Sterling 1997).

However, in spite of the eloquence and leadership from scholars and activists such as Ida B. Wells, Mary McLlyod Bethune, Sojourner Truth, Julia A. Cooper, Ella Baker, and Fannie Lou Hammer (Hine 2005), black women's issues were never center stage in general progressive action pertaining to race or gender. Even during the twentieth century Civil Rights

© The Author(s) 2018
N. Zack, *Philosophy of Race*, Palgrave Philosophy Today,
https://doi.org/10.1007/978-3-319-78729-9_10

Movement, black women did not share leadership with black men in activist and political organizations (Brown 1992; Barnett 1993; Collier-Thomas and Franklin 2001). Indeed, as black women began to find their political and activist voices after the civil rights movement, the prominence of men in that movement has increasingly been contrasted with the subordinate roles of women (Blumberg 1990). Black women may thus face a double oppression: racism from white women and men and sexism from black men.

Issues of the exclusion and oppression of women of color are an important part of contemporary philosophy of race. Philosophy of race has until the early twenty-first century had male leaders and male public intellectuals. White feminist philosophers have been more welcoming of philosophy of race and supported a focus on the work of female scholars of color, but this is not an easy alliance, either. In 1988, Elizabeth Spelman's *Inessential Woman* contributed to growing awareness within feminism of its assumptions that white middle-class women were its major subject, thus leaving out the problems faced by women of color and poor women of all races (Spelman 1998). This led to a strengthening of identity politics. More recently, the concept of *intersectionality* has been extensively used to explain differences in gendered experience, but it has not served to unite those who live with those differences (Zack 2017, pp. 598–600). In short, there are significant tensions among feminism, gender, and race and this concluding chapter will aim to examine several of the more pressing issues in contemporary life and scholarship: identity politics and intersectionality; black feminism and black feminist philosophy; black male philosophy; Representation and Theoretical Problems with Race and Gender.

Identity Politics and Intersectionality

In order to understand intersectionality, it is necessary to understand identity politics. The core idea behind **identity politics** and activism based on identities is that there are groups of people with broadly known characteristics that disadvantage them and progress should be sought by members of those groups, under the name or banner of their identities: women, black women, LGBTQ people, poor white people, and so forth. For instance, imagine a single mother who has difficulty keeping a job because her workplace commute takes two hours on three busses from where she lives. Not having a car, she has to rely on public transport, which is not reliable. A woman in that situation might struggle with issues of self-discipline, such as getting up at 5 a.m., or dependence on neighbors to take her children to school, as though these were her own individual problems. But in reality, the broader problems are a lack of adequate public transport or affordable housing close to her workplace (Puentes and Roberto 2008). For another example, a woman of color might suffer from overhearing racist jokes in her workplace and try not to be "too sensitive," when her problem is not her own emotionality but an implicitly racist culture or lack of training in her work environment. In both cases, organizing or banding together based on identities of low income or nonwhite race could result in solutions such as car-pooling, shared child care, or employee complaints and demands for change in workplace attitudes toward minorities. More broadly, people of color may become stuck in low-wage jobs due to both hearts-and-minds and institutional racism. They may be prevented from voting, voting may be made more difficult for them, or their votes may be discarded, because they are members of a racial group identified as unlikely to support candidates of a party dominant in their districts. (Minorities throughout the United States did not have full protection of the Voting Rights Act during the 2016 presidential election (Berman 2016)). Addressing problems tied to identities requires political solutions based on those identities, e.g., the Voting Rights Act of 1965 (Fryer et al. 2013). However, as Mary Bernstein points out, one of the biggest problems with identity politics is that the identities forged for the sake of resistance are the same identities that are the targets of oppression (Bernstein 2005).

The leading insight behind **intersectionality** as a method of analysis and way for describing social reality is that real human beings cannot be categorized in just one way. For instance, almost all individuals can be categorized by race, sex, social class, age, and ability. Intersectionality also takes into account the awkwardness of considering race and gender side by side as classificatory schemes: Anyone who has a race is likely to have a gender, but within the category of gender (males, females, nonbinary), there are different racial identities and within any one racial identity (among the census categories, at least) there are different genders.

Intersectionality in US feminism was begun by Kimberlé Crenshaw through her 1989 article, "Demarginalizing the Intersection of Race and Sex: A Black Feminist Critique of Antidiscrimination Doctrine, Feminist Theory and Antiracist Politics." Her aim was to show how black women are marginalized when feminists and others think about them in a "single-axis framework," as just one type of person. Crenshaw introduced the example of lack of legal remedies for workplace discrimination against black women who were the first to be fired: as women, there was no evidence of discrimination against them if there was no evidence of discrimination against women—because white women were not discriminated against; as black people, there was no evidence of discrimination against them if there was no evidence of discrimination against black people—because black men were not discriminated against. In legal terms, black women thus fell through the cracks as the combination of their race and gender resulted in discrimination unique to them (Crenshaw 1989).

In her 1991 *Stanford Law Review* article, "Mapping the Margins: Intersectionality, Identity Politics, and Violence Against Women of Color," Crenshaw observed that identity politics allowed for understanding and action that was group-based and to some extent external to individual struggles and suffering; she recognized that the problems often encountered by women as individuals are the result of wider practices in society. Crenshaw was specifically aware of the importance of identity politics for addressing problems shared by women of color. But she thought there were *homogenizing* problems with fitting people into the categories that identity politics requires—everyone in a recognized identity group was considered to have the same problems. Her example of immigrant women who are the victims of domestic violence shows how poverty, cultural barriers, lack of access to bureaucratic protections, and fears of deportation compound their plight. Crenshaw's point is that it is not just one thing about these women that oppresses them. More generally within communities of color, a desire to protect the community may stifle efforts to alleviate the plight of battered women (Crenshaw 1991).

In the abstract of a 2013 paper cowritten by Crenshaw there is a call for the development of *intersectionality studies*:

Intersectional insights and frameworks are put into practice in a multitude of highly contested, complex, and unpredictable ways. We group such engagements with intersectionality into three loosely defined sets of practices: applications of an intersectional framework or investigations of intersectional dynamics; debates about the scope and content of intersectionality as a theoretical and methodological paradigm; and political interventions employing an intersectional lens. We propose a template for fusing these three levels of engagement with intersectionality into a field of intersectional studies that emphasizes collaboration and literacy rather than unity. Our objective here is not to offer pat resolutions to all questions about intersectional approaches but to spark further inquiry into the dynamics of intersectionality both as an academic frame and as a practical intervention in a world characterized by extreme inequalities. At the same time, we wish to zero in on some issues that we believe have occupied a privileged place in the field from the very start, as well as on key questions that will define the field in the future. To that end, we foreground the social dynamics and relations that constitute subjects, displacing what often seems like an undue emphasis on the subjects (and categories) themselves as the starting point of inquiry. We also situate the development and contestation of these focal points of intersectional studies within the politics of academic and social movements—which, we argue, are themselves deeply intersectional in nature and therefore must continually be interrogated as part of the intersectional project. (Cho et al. 2013, p. 785)

In other words, intersectionality is theoretically self-reflective, with a core commitment to focusing on wider social factors that make up individual subjects and oppress them.

Intersectionality has not been without its critics. One problem is that there is no limit to possible intersections, so that there is an **ad hoc** quality to any newly discovered intersection. A second issue is that "intersection" is a metaphor, so it is not clear to what extent different identities add up to, or result in, new identities. A third issue is that intersectionality depends on the same kind of identities that motivate identity politics, as in Crenshaw's initial example of black women in the workplace, who would be both black and women (Zack 2005, pp. 1–22). Jennifer Nash has noted that the primary subject of intersectionality seems to have been black women, to the exclusion of other "intersections" (Nash 2008). If Nash is correct, intersectionality may be viewed as a subfield of identity politics. One could speculate further and claim that when any given project of intersectionality is successful, the result is new identities with political motivations, e.g., black working-class women who seek to further their rights in the workplace. In this sense, intersectionality faces the same strategic problem as identity politics: the intersections around which people organize to resist oppression are also the targets of oppression. However, the important contribution of intersectionality studies is that the oppression of women of color is situational and complex, so that understanding and analyzing that oppression requires extensive understanding of its contexts.

Black Feminism and Black Feminist Philosophy

Black feminism is not new in reality. African-American women's rights activist and abolitionist Sojourner Truth (1797–1883) delivered her famous "Ain't I a Woman?" speech to the Women's Convention in Acron, Ohio, in 1851:

That man over there says that women need to be helped into carriages, and lifted over ditches, and to have the best place everywhere. Nobody ever helps me into carriages, or over mud-puddles, or gives me any best place! And ain't I a woman? Look at me! Look at my arm! I have ploughed and planted, and gathered into barns, and no man could head me! And ain't I a woman? I could work as much and eat as much as a man - when I could get it - and bear the lash as well! And ain't I a woman? I have borne thirteen children, and seen most all sold off to slavery, and when I cried out with my mother's grief, none but Jesus heard me! And ain't I a woman? (Truth 1851)

Intersectional theory would show that as a black woman, Truth experienced both the oppression of slavery and unrecognized oppression against her gender—"thirteen children, and seen most all sold off to slavery." When Truth spoke out against the general idea that women needed to be protected by speaking of her own strengths, she was implicitly drawing a distinction between herself and white women—they were protected, while she wasn't—but nonetheless asserting her female identity.

Twentieth-century feminist scholars of female gender identity have emphasized how women's roles as compliant, decorous, fragile, and nurturing were socially constructed for the benefit of men, but described as determined by nature. This literature often leaves out how such traditional roles were assigned to white women, while different theories of gender were used for describing the gender of women of color, particularly black women, during and after slavery.

An emphasis on the nuclear family structure resulted from the industrial revolution when workplaces were relocated outside of the home and white middle-class men, although not white middle-class women, left their homes for the workday. Cultures of domestic economy, community service, child rearing, and women's proper comportment, including sexual fidelity and/or chastity, structured female gender norms, which were assumed to be racially white. Widely circulated manuals on interior decoration and home management, such as *The American Woman's Home, Or Principles of Domestic Science: Being a Guide to the Formation and Maintenance of Economical, Beautiful and Christian Homes*, first published in 1869 by Harriet Beecher Stowe and her sister Catherine E. Beecher, simply assumed a white readership. The same can be said about the 1939 *Delineator Cookbook*, later known as the *American Woman's Cookbook* (Stowe and Beecher 1869; Berholtzheimer 1939). During and after slavery, black women worked agriculturally and domestically in the homes of white women and their gender identity did not have the same status or protection as that of white women. Their work roles were limited to laborers, nurturers, and servants, and their sexuality was not viewed as a value to be protected, but rather as a free resource to be exploited: it was not unusual for white male slave owners to "breed" their female slaves or during Jim Crow, for white men to assume that they had an unrestrained right to black women's bodies. Anti-miscegenation laws, prohibiting interracial marriage and sex were primarily enforced against black men (Zack 1997; Robinson 2003).

Differences in aesthetic evaluations have also been related to race. In his *Notes on the State of Virginia*, written between 1781 and 1787, Thomas Jefferson insisted on a fundamental difference in beauty, based on skin color. He wrote:

> The first difference which strikes us is that of colour. Whether the black of the negro resides in the reticular membrane between the skin and scarf-skin, or in the scarf-skin itself; whether it proceeds from the colour of the blood, the colour of the bile, or from that of some other secretion, the difference is fixed in nature, and is as real as if its seat and cause were better known to us. And is this difference of no importance? Is it not the foundation of a greater or less share of beauty in the two races? Are not the fine mixtures of red and white, the expressions of every passion by greater or less suffusions of colour in the one, preferable to that eternal monotony, which reigns in the countenances, that immoveable veil of black which covers all the emotions of the other race? Add to these, flowing hair, a more elegant symmetry of form, their own judgment in favour of the whites, declared by their preference of them, as uniformly as is the preference of the Oranootan for the black women over those of his own species. The circumstance of superior beauty, is thought worthy attention in the propagation of our horses, dogs, and other domestic animals; why not in that of man? (Jefferson 1785, p. 145)

Jefferson here not only claims the aesthetic superiority of whites over blacks, from a white perspective, but also attributes to blacks an aesthetic preference for whites.

Black women, in particular, have been oppressed by, and themselves internalized, beauty ideals for white women. In the late nineteenth and early twentieth century, Sarah Breedlove (1867–1919), known as "Madame Walker," made a fortune and became a philanthropist for African American causes, through her line of hair products with grooming instructions for black women. Breedlove's products were more gentle to the skin and scalp than those containing lye, which were in wide use at the time. However, the subtext of "beauty culturists" who sold the "Walker System" door-to-door was not only relief from damaging products, but closer approximation to white beauty ideals. Walker invented the first hair-straightening formula and her advertisements typically featured light-skinned African American women with flowing hair (Walker 2007). (In Toni Morrison's *The Bluest Eye*, Pecola shares her last name (see Chapter 6).)

Many African American women continue to be sensitive to the tyranny of white beauty ideals, perhaps because in US history, aesthetic disparagement of black people has been deeply linked to issues of self-regard and racial progress. Tommy Curry has traced the connection of racial aesthetics to nineteenth-century theories of gender which held that "inferior races," particularly Africans, did not have gender distinctions. Self-help racial uplift practices for African Americans included "feminizing" personal beauty and hygiene routines, as well as housekeeping standards, which disproportionately became the obligations of black women (Curry 2017a).

The influence of Thomas Jefferson's racist aesthetics has been taken up by T. Denean Sharpley-Whiting in relation to the misogyny of gangsta rap music. Sharpley-Whiting argues that such devaluation and stereotyping is reproduced in white entertainment; at the same time, white women appropriate selected aspects of black women's physical appearances, such as hairstyles and skin tones (Sharpley-Whiting 2017).

In general, black feminist scholarship has sought to center black women by focusing on their agency, political power, and knowledge production. Patricia Hill Collins has questioned official constructions of knowledge that exclude the experience of black women. Her theoretical standpoint in sociological theory of knowledge, has been inspiring to black feminist philosophers (Collins 1986, 1989, 1990, 1998). However, the concerns of black feminism across disciplines do not in themselves constitute black feminist philosophy. Although philosophers have been inspired by voices from related disciplines, many believe it is important to self-consciously develop black feminist philosophy as a subfield in the academic discipline of philosophy. Thus, V. Denise James writes:

> Although some might say the idiosyncratic quotes that eccentric philosophy professors choose to post on their doors mean little in the greater scheme of things, I thought long and hard before deciding to greet students, colleagues, and other visitors with words from a black feminist statement and not a quote from one of the canonical philosophical thinkers. The quote makes a declaration.
>
> I am a black feminist philosopher.
>
> I want to work on projects that will contribute to understanding the lived experiences of black women and girls. I believe that philosophy done from

a black feminist standpoint can help to define, clarify, assess, and suggest changes in our social world that would greatly improve the lives of all people. I am happy to admit that commitment to this standpoint is a rejection of the supposed neutrality and universalist claims made by other philosophers.

I am a black feminist philosopher. (James 2014, p. 189)

That James wrote this for 2014 publication indicates that black feminist philosophy is a (very) new academic subfield. But even in its beginnings, there is room for diversity of opinion. Kristie Dotson, speaking as a black feminist philosopher in 2013, defines black feminist philosophy as "radical love for the lives and cultural artifacts of black women" (Dotson 2013, p. 38). The focus on history through black feminist philosophy leads to the reclamation of black feminist thinkers and activists, through analysis of their core ideas and principles, as well as their relevance to problems still faced by black women. For example, Joy James considers the political persona of Ida B. Wells in her opposition to lynching. James relates how Wells called for black self-defense against racial terrorization and insisted that white women did enter into voluntary sexual relationships with black men, contrary to received mythology that demonized black men as rapists. James relates Wells's insights to principles of the contemporary resistance movements, Black Lives Matter, and the Black Women's Blueprint (James 2017).

It is reasonable to expect that as the number of black feminist academic philosophers increase, they will both ply philosophical methodology to subjects of interest to and about black women and illuminate the distinctively philosophical aspects of thought developed in other disciplines. It is also to be expected that black feminist philosophy will continue to show concern about philosophical methodology more generally, as in the 2010 anthology *Convergences*, edited by Maria del Guadalupe Davidson, Kathryn T. Gines, and Donna-Dale L. Marcano. The editors' aim was to provide a forum to explore issues of agency, identity, alienation, and power shared by black feminist thought and continental philosophy. And in another direction of disciplinary unification, V. Denise James has written about connections between black feminist concerns and the pragmatist philosophy of John Dewey. Others are taking up issues of contemporary concern to black women, for instance Camisha Russell's *The Assisted Reproduction of Race: Thinking through Race as a Reproductive Technology*, philosophically examines how race is used in assisted reproduction and to determine kinship (Russell 2018).

Black Male Philosophy

There are two kinds of black male philosophy. The first is simply philosophy done by black men. Black men were the first to introduce African American thought to philosophy in the 1970s, as well as philosophy of race. Their assumption that scholarship about race was inclusive of all members of "the race" implicitly centered their own gender. To that extent, black male philosophy, as philosophy conducted by black men, has been antithetical to feminism as generally understood to be resistance to male dominance. However, as black women have entered the field of academic philosophy, there have been anecdotal accounts of their reaction against this professional dominance of black men. Quayshawn Spencer reports on the results of a 2014 demographic study of black graduate students and professors in philosophy that most respondents declared their AOS (Area of Specialization) as Africana Philosophy (including African American Philosophy) or Philosophy of Race. However, Africana Philosophy was male-dominated, whereas Philosophy of Race was gender-neutral (Botts et al. 2014.)

The second kind of black male philosophy is an explicit focus on the experience of black men, conducted by black male philosophers. Strictly speaking, black male philosophy as philosophy by and about black men should be broadly accepted as part of the same feminist philosophy that includes black feminism, because feminism, as now broadly understood, includes gender. However, it is not clear that is always the case, insofar as black feminist philosophers may not agree with some of the conclusions of black male philosophers. We can begin with this last source of tension through the main ideas in Tommy T. Curry's 2017 book, *The Man-Not: Race, Class, Genre, and the Dilemmas of Black Manhood*, which introduces Black Male Studies to philosophy.

Curry refers to demographic and sociological data and theory to develop a view that black males have been unjustly portrayed by academic progressives, as well as white racists in the outside public. He notes that counter to white trends, black men have not progressed in undergraduate and graduate enrollment compared to black women and receive only 40% of the degrees awarded to African Americans; black male compared to black female representation among professors in higher education is 48,000–70,000. Moreover, Curry charges that contemporary theorists portray black men as sexist, homophobic, and misogynistic, counter to evidence that they are more progressive about gender than white men, white women, and black women. He claims that black feminist theorists have portrayed black men as lacking agency and seeking to emulate the masculinity of white men, through the oppression and abuse of black women. According to Curry, such views ignore studies of social class within patriarchal capitalistic societies, which are structured to valorize dominant males while oppressing those from subordinate groups and viewing them as biological and cultural threats to the high-status group, in the US case, whites. Curry calls for **Black Male Studies** as a philosophical research program that will incorporate dominance theory into gender studies of patriarchy and include accounts of their own experience by black men (Curry 2017b).

Curry's views are novel in criticism of attitudes toward black men by black feminist theorists. However, the ways that black men have been deprived of respect and honorific rewards compared to white men have long been discussed and expressed in African American literature, film, and political aspirations. In philosophy, Leonard Harris in "Honor, Eunuchs, and the Postcolonial Subject," claims that no "eunuch, slave, serf, or peasant, can be recognized as having the traits of courage, temperance, or sagacity that would result in their being honored—the subject of exalted deference or regard—as a eunuch, slave, serf, or peasant. Instead, if a member of such a group is honored, it is in spite of that identity" (Harris 1997). About 20 years earlier, Harris had written about how William Fontaine was honored:

> In 1936, Fontaine was the first Black to receive a doctorate in philosophy from the University of Pennsylvania. His doctoral dissertation, *Fortune, Matter and Providence: A Study of Ancius Severinus Boethius and Giordano Bruno* evoked favorable reviews. In 1947, he joined the philosophy faculty at the University of Pennsylvania after teaching at Southern University, Baton Rouge, Louisiana, and Morgan State University, Baltimore, Maryland. In the course of his career, he published several critiques of C. I. Lewis, C. L. Stevenson, and Ruth Benedict in respectable philosophy journals. Fontaine was well known for his concern with racial issues. As the first Black professor of philosophy at Penn, he was frequently queried on race relation problems of his day. Fontaine's *Segregation, Desegregation, and the Power of Morals* (1967) is seen by former colleagues and students as his principal statement on racial issues. According to those same persons, Fontaine was an excellent teacher. A rare honor was posthumously accorded Fontaine in 1969; Penn established an ongoing graduate fellowship program in his name, the Fontaine Fellows. The university community recognized Fontaine as an accomplished philosopher, and this, in spite of being Black. (Harris 1978, p. 417)

Harris does not explicitly mention gender in his account of Fontaine, but this omission is contextual. Almost all academic philosophers were male at the time of Fontaine's career, so that the main demographic basis for comparing Fontaine with his colleagues would have been race, by default.

It, therefore, seems important not to view history anachronistically from a feminist perspective. Overall, the male dominance in specific historical periods and contexts cannot be read into contexts that were predominantly male, but needs to be understood as more general and external to such contexts. Within all-male contexts, where "no eunuch, slave, serf, or peasant" is honored, as such, gender is not a factor, although race and status are.

However, in his accounts of reclaiming the neglected philosophical contributions of Alain Locke—who was honored for his contributions to black culture during the Harlem Renaissance—Harris does focus on gender as part of the reason for Locke's decades-long oblivion:

> Not one paper on Locke, besides mine, was presented at any of the seven queer theory conferences I attended between 2000, at the graduate Center of the City of New York, to 2007 at UCLA: he had no story of being uncomfortable with his homosexuality and no drawer of pictures at the New York Public Library full of nude Black males with particular attention to their penises like Carl van Vechten. Besides a few stories of flirtation, his story was not a source of inspiration. Without a story like James Baldwin's, author of *Giovanni's Room*, (1953), who was alienated from his American homeland and lived openly abroad, Locke was boring. He was not an alienated wounded being that overcame or openly advocated; and nothing titillating. Locke critiqued what he termed 'proprietorship' as a source of heterosexual prejudice – ownership of mates – and an array of prejudices against difference. His normality, self-confidence, counseling of gays from Bruce Nugent to Countée Cullen, wonderful relationship with his mother and his steadfast effort to infuse a respect for difference simply made him unfit as a hero.
>
>   Locke has been buried beneath a mountain of books that needed a Negro type to talk about – bourgeois, uncle-tom, white lackey, gentile, closeted gay, professional, middle-class non-threatening or just 'niggeratti'. He is usually described as a gentile scholar that used verbose language. Yet, whether Harold Cruse's *Crisis of the Negro Intellectual* (1967), where he is pictured as the white man's lackey and delusional romantic, Anna Pochmara's *The Making of the New Negro* (2011), where he is pictured as a paternal patronizing gay homophobe or Barbara Foley's *Spectres of 1919* (2008), where he is pictured as a ruling class puppet, Locke is pictured as an agent for an agenda not of his making.
>
> Locke is never an agent. (Harris 2017, pp. 128–9)

There are interesting intersections implied by Harris's claim that Locke was ignored because he did not dramatize his homosexuality—Locke did not fit into stereotypes of black male homosexuals. This claim highlights the intersection of race with sexual preference, which itself intersects with an inability to be categorized (Harris 2017).

George Yancy gives a different contemporary account of both the lack of black male agency and the demonization of black males. In "The Violent Weight of Whiteness: The Existential and Psychic Price Paid by Black Male Bodies," he begins by describing an experience at a philosophy conference, when white philosophers congratulated another black philosopher who did not resemble him, for a plenary talk he (Yancy) had given on Franz Fanon. Yancy writes:

> When the other Black philosopher shared his experiences with me, I could feel the existential weight of being any Black male. Being thanked for a talk that he had not given was just one register of the burden. He had to endure the process of dis-identifying himself from me, of being mistaken. In absentia, I endured the burden of being where I wasn't, of being "the Black." Imagine the mantra, "A Black man did it!" And then watch as whites engage in hysterics and fanatic insularity, where all Black men begin to look alike ("criminals," "aggressors," "rapists") and thus needing to be stopped, and, indeed, in so many cases, stopped dead. Susan Smith, a white woman who in 1994 drowned her two children and blamed it on a Black man, and Charles Stuart, a white man who in 1998 shot and killed his pregnant wife and blamed it on a Black man, were not only guilty of murder, but guilty of invoking the white racist historical sedimentation of the white imago of the Black male body as inherently and unconscionably violent and cruel, which is a form of death by racist semiosis, one that can and does easily translate into an actual killing of Black men who "fit the description." ...
>
> I wanted to move lithe in that conference space, to move with effortless grace, but my individual embodiment's meaning had been confiscated and I was returned as racially static. ... Within another context, I would have been lynched because some white woman said that a Black man had accosted and raped her, though I was nowhere close to the alleged act. Lynching any Black male body that "fit the description" would have been sufficient; indeed, within the context of North American white supremacy, any Black body would have served the larger purpose of white nation building, of performing what it meant not to be Black. (Yancy 2017, 589–91)

This interchangeability of black bodies in the imaginations of white people becomes dangerous for black males when otherwise rational and benevolent white people experience fear at the sight of a black man. In the first chapter of his *Black Bodies/White Gazes: The Continuing Significance of Race*, Yancy relates a stressful ride in an elevator with a white woman, who he realizes, regardless that he is well-dressed, "sees" his black body, as a threat. She reacts to this perceived threat by almost imperceptibly cowering, trembling, receding, and clutching her purse. Her apparent fear is a threat to Yancy, because if she falsely accuses him of assaulting her when they both get out of the elevator, her word will be more readily accepted than his. Yancy also describes his experience in walking down a street with people sitting in their cars and hearing a series of "clicks" as they lock their car doors (Yancy 2008, pp. 4–8; xix–xx).

The alienation Yancy describes in the conference experience, riding the elevator with the white woman, and hearing the car doors click, occurs in relatively safe social contexts. But Yancy also relates an earlier experience in which the stereotype of black males as dangerous was life-threatening to him:

"Man, I almost blew you away!"

Those were the terrifying words of a white police officer — one of those who policed black bodies in low income areas in North Philadelphia in the late 1970s — who caught sight of me carrying the new telescope my mother had just purchased for me.

"I thought you had a weapon," he said.

The words made me tremble and pause; I felt the sort of bodily stress and deep existential anguish that no teenager should have to endure.

. …

This officer had already inherited those poisonous assumptions and bodily perceptual practices that make up what I call the "white gaze." He had already come to "see" the black male body as different, deviant, ersatz. He failed to conceive, or perhaps could not conceive, that a black teenage boy living in the Richard Allen Project Homes for very low income families would own a telescope and enjoyed looking at the moons of Jupiter and the rings of Saturn.

A black boy carrying a telescope wasn't conceivable — unless he had stolen it — given the white racist horizons within which my black body was policed as dangerous. To the officer, I was something (not someone) patently foolish, perhaps monstrous or even fictional. My telescope, for him, was a weapon.

In retrospect, I can see the headlines: "Black Boy Shot and Killed While Searching the Cosmos."

That was more than 30 years ago. Only last week, our actual headlines were full of reflections on the 1963 March on Washington, the Rev. Dr. Martin Luther King's "I Have a Dream" speech, and President Obama's own speech at the steps of the Lincoln Memorial to commemorate it 50 years on. As the many accounts from that long ago day will tell you, much has changed for the better. But some things — those perhaps more deeply embedded in the American psyche — haven't. In fact, we should recall a speech given by Malcolm X in 1964 in which he said, "For the 20 million of us in America who are of African descent, it is not an American dream; it's an American nightmare." (Yancy 2013)

These writings in black male philosophy by Curry, Harris, and Yancy, altogether leave us with a puzzling question: How can members of a group believed to lack agency, who would thereby be passive, nonetheless be viewed as dangerous? One could answer this question by claiming that stereotypes and myths need not be consistent, because they do not come from rational thought. Alternatively, we could return to the concept of a widely shared white imaginary or what a large number of white people all imagine to be true, and have sufficient dominance and power to make true in reality. In an enigmatic 1997 article, "Sex, Race, and Matrices of Desire in an Anti-Black World," Lewis Gordon analyzes gender in terms of race. In an anti-black world, the ultimate object of desire is white and the ultimate object of rejection is black. Desire is evaluative as well as erotic, so in an antiblack world, the phallus (symbol of male power) is actually white skin. The result, according to Gordon is that "the logic of gender in an antiblack world can be demonstrated to converge with the logic of race in ways that question the very meaning of sex" (Gordon 1997, pp. 129–30).

For Gordon, racism is racial desire. White women are "coded" with the helplessness of their femaleness, which is black, given the white-skin color phallus; and black women occupy the lowest position of helplessness and passivity, so that they are doubly black, that is, black because they are female and black because they are racially black. Black men, on the other hand, are simply female in being black. However, many theorists of race and gender would consider that Gordon's analysis takes race as a leading concept to an extreme (Zack 2017, p. 603). This underscores radical differences in perspectives within racial gender theory. And those kinds of differences can influence how ideas and proposals are received within a pluralistic audience in philosophy of race, as we will now see in our final section of this chapter and book.

Representation and Theoretical Problems with Race and Gender: The Tuvel Affair

In one sense, the 2017 "Tuvel Affair" was a tempest in a teapot, but it raised issues about feminist scholarship that swirled around the question, "How and by whom should the subjects of race and gender be researched?"

The "how" part of the question concerns the race or gender of the authors of sources used by the researcher; the "who" part concerns the race or gender of the researcher. The "facts" here were mainly of interest to academic philosophers, but the issues extend more broadly into representation in the sense of who can speak for whom, and the ethics of scholarship and race.

On March 29, 2017, *Hypatia: A Journal of Feminist Philosophy* published an article by Rebecca Tuvel, "In Defense of Transracialism." (The article had been subjected to Hypatia's review process, which many in philosophical feminism regard as extremely rigorous.) Tuvel suggested that it should be morally permissible for people to change their racial identities, analogously to why it is morally permissible for people to change their gender identities. Angry and accusatory reactions by self-called "marginalized" scholars immediately followed. Because of the public abuse of Tuvel on social media, few defended her according to the standards of professional philosophy that were upheld in her writing—her article was well-reasoned and scholarly. However, Kelly Oliver and Jesse Sengal did step up (Oliver 2017; Sengal 2017). The Associate Editors of Hypatia issued a statement and another was signed by more than 800 people, both stating that Tuvel's article should not have been published because it did not seriously refer to work by women of color and/or transgender people (Schuessler 2017). More recently, the Board of *Hypatia* and its editor, Sally Sholtz, disavowed the associate editors' statement and stood by Tuvel's article, because it had been peer-reviewed according to *Hypatia's* procedures. Sholtz and Shelley Wilcox, editor of *Hypatia Reviews Online* subsequently resigned. The Hypatia Board of Directors disbanded the associate editors and basically declared an emergency situation for Hypatia, the leading feminist journal of philosophy (Weinberg 2017; McKenzie et al. 2017).

Tuvel became well known and has been viewed as unprofessionally, if not unjustly, attacked. Tuvel is white and her self-proclaimed marginalized critics are feminist women of color. The controversy raises a number of questions: Is racial identity analogous to gender identity? Why are some people incensed at the idea that racial identities are chosen? Who has the right to decide which identities others may choose and what are the criteria for such decisions? Do white philosophers who write about race and gender have an obligation to refer to the work of philosophers who may be marginalized because they are people of color and/or LBGTQ? These questions raise issues in professional ethics, which are neither legal nor empirical, although they are important for collegiality, reputation, and the atmosphere of the discipline of academic philosophy. To answer them is not to advocate any particular public or institutional policy and neither do answers constitute magic wands for changing how people think and behave in reality. But considering such questions is an intellectual choice that many philosophers would think they have a right, if not an obligation, to make.

Tuvel based her suggestion that people may change their racial identities on an analogy to the reasoning behind the widespread progressive consensus that changing gender identities is morally permissible. It's not self-evident that such analogical reasoning is valid, because racial identities and gender identities are different kinds of social identities, even though both require choice. Usually, these choices are not evident because most people comply with both the racial and gender identities others assume are theirs or attribute to them. But racial identities have genealogical connections within families—people tend to be the same race as their family members. By contrast, gender identities, while also assigned and constructed within families and communities, are applied to individuals as separate units. This suggests that racial identities are overall more communal, whereas gender identities are more individualistic. Thus, individuals already have more social freedom in choosing their gender identities than their racial identities. Therefore, Tuvel's analogy may not be apt, apart from the facts and possibilities of choice, in both cases. Also, progressives might be skeptical of treating race and gender as analogues in moral reasoning. White males have left an uncomfortable history of lumping nonwhites, straight women, and LGBTQ people together in one nontraditional category, particularly within institutional structures, as in the expression, "women and minorities" or the term "diversity." That alone is reason to insist that these identity types be treated separately, out of respect for the autonomy of their members.

Some people have always been incensed at the idea that racial identities can be chosen. In the late nineteenth and early twentieth centuries, there was widespread white public hysteria about people with black ancestry passing for white. But now, there is agitation among blacks about whites passing for black. (This attitude surfaced when Rachel Dolezal, a white NAACP official who presented herself as black, was revealed to be white (La Ganga and Pearce 2015)). Part of such reaction may be due to perceived "unearned" advantages of having a racial identity other than one's birth race, part may be the result of people feeling that the racial identities they possess include a right to assess the claims of others to possess them. And this leads to the third question: Who does have the right to decide what racial identities others may have?

Racial identities are not now imposed by law in the United States, although they are recorded for legal and institutional purposes. The US Census is based on voluntary self-reporting of respondents' racial categories. Contemporary biological science provides no system, independent of social divisions, for racial categories. Race in society is attributed to people and claimed by them, based on known ancestry and appearance. There is nothing compelling or necessary about how individuals are racially categorized—custom is king. People do not easily change their birth race identities because members of the group they were born into, who they usually know, do not approve of such changes. For example, many mixed black and white people in the United States claim black identity and are claimed by black family members, especially if they "look" black (whatever this may mean). But many others identify as multiracial or claim stand-alone identities, based on their life circumstances and experiences, gender, religion, and social class (Davenporta 2016). The choices of such mixed black and white people, as well as others who are mixed, when they make their choices known, have been broadly recognized and respected. Indeed, as discussed in Chapter 6 in 1993, psychologist Maria P.P. Root published a "Bill of Rights for People of Mixed Heritage," which claimed a right to choose and change one's racial identity (Root 1993). Root was neither excoriated or vilified for that proclamation, which was embraced by scholars of mixed race. Apart from the fact that mixed race may be a better analogue for thinking about "transracialism" than is transgender, what else does the recognition of mixed-race choice tell us? Such choice arises at the boundary between custom and individualism; but it may be tolerated only because mixed race, although uncommon but not rare, is a small exception to the American racial system.

Many blacks, and to some degree whites, have tolerated the fact that some black Americans have "passed" into the white group. Are Americans ready for exceptions to custom in the form of white people passing as black? Apparently not, although there are no laws against it. However, to put it this way is only to *describe* a social situation. *Morally*, we should ask why such choices and those who advocate them are intolerable to some black people. This question of tolerance is important because it entails limiting the freedom of other people, for which there needs to be a good reason(s). It is not self-evident that if a white person advocates a choice to be black made by other white people, that her white identity disqualifies her advocacy. If that choice is a matter of communal moral consensus, it belongs to everyone in the racial community, which in this case includes both whites and blacks. But, black scholars who are intolerant of such choices also have their principled reasons, which can be buried in the aftermath of controversial cases, such as Tuvel's article. We can expect further discussion about such choices in the future of philosophy of race.

Here is the final question: Do white, heterosexual philosophers who write about race and gender have an obligation to refer to the work of philosophers who may be marginalized because they are people of color and/or LBGTQ? There cannot be a good argument for personal diversity in choice of research sources, because research is broadly presumed to stand on its own. But a very good argument can be made for seeking out the best work in any subfield that one engages. Some of the best work on race and gender has been done by philosophers who are nonwhite, nonmale, or LGBTQ. When those philosophers and their work are simply ignored by white philosophers interested in these subfields, it is very understandable, especially when it happens repeatedly, that those who have been marginalized in that way will be very hurt, very angry, and very frustrated. Nevertheless, the response as philosophers to inadequate, shallow, or even opportunistic philosophy should always be a civil, reasoned, unemotional response that is the result of the best intellectual work the person responding can put forth. Philosophy is, after all, a cold and dry intellectual discipline!

Conclusion

Gender as a subject has its roots in feminism. During the nineteenth century, black abolitionists and white suffragists were allies. But after freed black men received suffrage and educated white women did not, there was a rift that to this day has not fully healed. The wave of feminism that began in the middle of the twentieth century came to be criticized for its focus on the concerns of white middle-class women. At the same time, identity politics developed, as a means for people to identify and organize based on disadvantaged identities. Some feminist theorists became critical of identity politics for its tendency to homogenize all members of a group sharing the same identity. The result was intersectionality as a method of analysis and basis for political action, which was more contextualized than identity politics because, in effect, multiple identities were conceived as constituting subjects. In philosophy, first white feminism and then African American philosophy became established academically. Black feminist philosophers proceed by reclaiming historical figures for philosophical analysis and inspiration, forging connections between different traditions in philosophy, and philosophizing contemporary concerns of black women. Black male philosophy is in one sense the result of the fact that when African American philosophy first entered a field that was dominated by men—the first black academic philosophers in the twentieth century were men. However, given the history of feminism, black male philosophy can also be understood as a philosophical focus on the experience of black men. Accounts of that experience have protested injustice against black men and shared the social and physical vulnerability of being falsely stereotyped as dangerous.

Gender studies by and about people of color have become well enough established in philosophy to raise questions about who has the authority to write about whom and whether there is a general obligation to include work by minority scholars in sources. A recent controversy involving whether people should be permitted to change their race as they have changed their gender focused on this issue.

Glossary

ad hoc—added or done for a specific purpose, only, and not following from a general principle previously agreed upon; arbitrary, in terms of theory.
philosophy—inquiry and advocacy for the well-being of black women and justice for them, undertaken with the methodology of academic philosophy.
black male studies—proposed philosophical research into the experience of black men as members of a subordinate, out-group under white-dominated patriarchal society.
black male philosophy—philosophy by and explicitly about the experience of black men.
feminism—thought and action about injustice toward women, with advocacy of improvement in their circumstances, based on general and specific analysis; now broadly includes gender.
gender—umbrella term for social aspects of human sexuality, including male, female, nonbinary, heterosexual, LGBTQ.
identity politics—group organization or identification for the sake of dealing with common problems for people with specific identities.
intersectionality—theoretical method and description of people who experience multiple oppressions based on multiple identities.
LGBTQ—acronym for people who identify as: Lesbian, Gay, BiSexual, Transgender, or Queer.

Discussion Questions

1. Explain a double or triple oppression experienced by black women.
2. How is identity politics different from the methodology of intersectionality?
3. Explain the identity politics in which you or people you know directly participate.
4. Provide some examples of intersectionality from your own experience.

5. How is black feminist philosophy different from black feminism?
6. Who do you think benefits from the demonization of black men in the United States?
7. How is the "unmanning" of black men related to their demonization?
8. Do you agree that people should be allowed to choose their gender?
9. Do you think that people should be allowed to choose their race? Who gets to decide and why?
10. Do you agree that even in matters of race and gender, philosophy should remain "cold" and "dry" in presentation? Give reasons for or against.

References

Barnett, Bernice McNair. "Invisible Southern Black Women Leaders in the Civil Rights Movement: The Triple Constraints of Gender, Race, and Class." *Gender & Society*, vol. 7, no. 2, 1993, pp. 162–82.

Berholtzheimer, Ruth. *The American Woman's Cookbook*. Chicago, IL: Consolidated Book Publishers, 1939.

Berman, Ari. "The GOP's Attack on Voting Rights Was the Most Under-Covered Story of 2016." *The Nation*, Nov. 9, 2016. https://www.thenation.com/article/the-gops-attack-on-voting-rights-was-the-most-under-covered-story-of-2016/.

Bernstein, Mary. "Identity Politics." *Annual Review of Sociology*, vol. 31, 2005, pp. 47–74. JSTOR, www.jstor.org/stable/29737711.

Blumberg, R.L. Dialect Anthropol, vol. 15, 1990, p. 133. https://doi.org/10.1007/BF00264648.

Botts, T.F., L.K Bright, M. Cherry, G. Mallarangeng, and Q. Spencer. "What Is the State of Blacks in Philosophy?" *Critical Philosophy of Race*, vol. 2, no. 2, 2014, pp. 224–42.

Brown, Elaine. *A Taste of Power: A Black Woman's Story*. New York, NY: Doubleday, 1992, 185–9.

Cho, Sumi, Kimberlé Williams Crenshaw, and Leslie McCall. "Toward a Field of Intersectionality Studies: Theory, Applications, and Praxis." *Signs*, vol. 38, no. 4, 2013, pp. 785–810. https://doi.org/10.1086/669608.

Collier-Thomas, Betteye and V.P. Franklin, editors. *Sisters in the Struggle: African American Women in the Civil Rights-Black Power Movement*. New York: New York University Press, 2001.

Collins, Patricia Hill. "Learning from the Outsider Within: The Sociological Significance of Black Feminist Thought." *Social Problems*, vol. 33, 1986, pp. 14–32.

Collins, Patricia Hill. "The Social Construction of Black Feminist Thought." *Signs*, vol. 14, 1989, pp. 745–73.

Collins, Patricia Hill. *Black Feminist Thought: Knowledge, Consciousness, and the Politics of Empowerment*. Boston: Unwin Hyman, 1990.

Collins, Patricia Hill. *Fighting Words: Black Women and the Search for Justice*. Minneapolis: University of Minnesota Press, 1998.

Crenshaw Kimberlé. "Demarginalizing the Intersection of Race and Sex: A Black Feminist Critique of Antidiscrimination Doctrine, Feminist Theory and Antiracist Politics." *The University of Chicago Legal Forum*, 1989, vol. 140, pp. 139–67.

Crenshaw, Kimberlé. "Mapping the Margins: Intersectionality, Identity Politics, and Violence Against Women of Color." *Stanford Law Review*, vol. 43, no. 6, 1991, pp. 1241–99. http://multipleidentitieslgbtq.wiki.westga.edu/file/view/Crenshaw1991.pdf.

Curry, Tommy J. "Ethnological Theories of Race/Sex in Nineteenth-Century Black Thought: Implications for the Race/Gender Debate of the Twenty-First Century." *Oxford Handbook of Philosophy and Race*, edited by Naomi Zack. New York, NY: Oxford University Press, 2017a, pp. 565–75.

Curry, Tommy J. *The Man-Not: Race, Class, Genre, and the Dilemmas of Black Manhood*. Philadelphia, PA: Temple University Press, 2017b.

Davenporta, Lauren D. "The Role of Gender, Class, and Religion in Biracial Americans Racial Labeling Decisions." *American Sociological* Review, vol. 81, no. 1, pp. 57–84, Article First Published Online: Jan. 27, 2016; Issue Published: Feb. 1, 2016, https://doi.org/10.1177/0003122415623286.

Davidson, Maria del Guadalupe, Kathryn T. Gines, and Donna-Dale L. Marcano. *Convergences*. Albany, NY: SUNY University Press, 2010.

Dotson, Kristie. "Radical Love: Black Philosophy as Deliberate Acts of Inheritance." *The Black Scholar: The Role of Black Philosophy*, vol. 43, no. 4, 2013, pp. 38–45.

Fryer, R.G, D. Pager, and J. Spenkuch. "Racial Disparities in Job Finding and Offered Wages." *The Journal of Law & Economics*, vol. 56, no. 3, 2013, pp. 633–89. https://doi.org/10.1086/673323.

Gordon, Lewis R. "Sex, Race, and Matrices of Desire in an Anti-Black World." *Race/Sex: Their Sameness, Difference, and Interplay*, edited by Naomi Zack. New York, NY, 1997, pp. 73–85.

Harris, Leonard. "Philosophy in Black and White." *Proceedings and Addresses of the American Philosophical Association*, vol. 51, no. 3, American Philosophical Association, Feb. 1978, pp. 415–24.

Harris, Leonard. "Honor, Eunuchs, and the Postcolonial Subject." *Postcolonial African Philosophy*, edited by E.C. Eze. Malden, MA: Blackwell, 1997, pp. 252–59.

Harris, Leonard. "Looking for Alain Locke." *Oxford Handbook of Philosophy and Race*, edited by Naomi Zack. New York, NY: Oxford University Press, 2017, pp. 125–34.

Hine, Diane Clark, editor. *Black Women in America*. Malden, MA: Blackwell, 2005. 3 vols.

James, Joy. "The Quartet in the Political Persona of Ida B. Wells." *Oxford Handbook of Philosophy and Race*, edited by Naomi Zack. New York, NY: Oxford University Press, 2017, pp. 309–18.

James, V. Denise. "Theorizing Black Feminist Pragmatism: Forethoughts on the Practice and Purpose of Philosophy as Envisioned by Black Feminists and John Dewey." *The Journal of Speculative Philosophy*, vol. 23 no. 2, 2009, pp. 92–9. Project MUSE, muse.jhu.edu/article/316248.

James, V. Denise. "Musing: A Black Feminist Philosopher: Is That Possible?" *Hypatia*, vol. 29, no. 1, Special Issue: Interstices: Inheriting Women of Color Feminist Philosophy, Winter 2014, pp. 189–95.

Jefferson, Thomas. *Notes on the State of Virginia*, edited by Frank C. Shuffelton. New York, NY: Penguin Classics, 1785/1999, Query XIV, Laws.

La Ganga, Maria L., and Matt Pearce. "Rachel Dolezal's Story, a Study of Race and Identity, Gets 'Crazier and Crazier.'" *LA Times*, June 15, 2015. http://www.latimes.com/nation/la-na-spokane-naacp-rachel-dolezal-resigns-20150615-story.html.

McKenzie, Lindsay, Adam Harris, and Fernanda Zamudio-Suaréz. "A Journal Article Provoked a Schism in Philosophy. Now the Rifts Are Deepening." *The Chronicle of Higher Education*, May 6, 2017. http://www.chronicle.com/article/A-Journal-Article-Provoked-a/240021.

Nash, Jennifer C. "Re-thinking Intersectionality." *Feminist Review*, vol. 89, no. 1, June 2008, pp 1–15.

Oliver, Kelly. "If This Is Feminism … ." *The Philosophical Salon*, May 8, 2017. http://thephilosophicalsalon.com/if-this-is-feminism-its-been-hijacked-by-the-thought-police/.

Puentes, Robert, and Elizabeth Roberto. "Commuting to Opportunity: The Working Poor and Commuting in the United States." *Brookings*, Mar. 14, 2008. https://www.brookings.edu/research/commuting-to-opportunity-the-working-poor-and-commuting-in-the-united-states/.

Robinson, Charles F., II. *Dangerous Liaisons: Sex and Love in the Segregated South*. Fayetteville, AR: University of Arkansas Press, 2003.

Root, Maria P.P. "Bill of Rights for People of Mixed Heritage." 1993, http://www.drmariaroot.com/doc/BillOfRights.pdf. Consulted Aug. 8, 2017.

Russell, Camisha. *The Assisted Reproduction of Race: Thinking Through Race as a Reproductive Technology*. Bloomington: Indiana University Press, 2018.

Schuessler, Jennifer. "A Defense of Transracial Identity Roils Philosophy World." *New York Times*, May 19, 2017. https://www.nytimes.com/2017/05/19/arts/a-defense-of-transracial-identity-roils-philosophy-world.html?_r=0.

Sengal, Jesse. "This Is What a Modern-Day Witch Hunt Looks Like." *New York Magazine*, May, 2017. http://nymag.com/daily/intelligencer/2017/05/transracialism-article-controversy.html.

Sharpley-Whiting, T. Denean. "Jefferson's Paradox, or a Very Brief History of Black Women's Sexuality, Hip-Hop, and American Culture." *Oxford Handbook of Philosophy and Race*, edited by Naomi Zack. New York, NY: Oxford University Press, 2017, pp. 576–87.

Spelman, Elizabeth B. *Inessential Woman*. Boston, MA: Beacon Press, 1998.

Sterling, Dorothy, editor. *We Are Your Sisters: Black Women in the Nineteenth Century*. New York, NY: W. W. Norton, 1997.

Stowe, Harriet Beecher, and Catherine E. Beecher. *American Woman's Home, Or Principles of Domestic Science: Being a Guide to the Formation and Maintenance of Economical, Beautiful and Christian Homes*, 1869. https://wwnorton.com/college/history/america-essential-learning/docs/CEBeecher-Womans_Home-1869.pdf.

Truth, Soujourner. "Ain't I a Woman?" *Modern History Sourcebook*, Fordham University, Dec. 1851. https://sourcebooks.fordham.edu/mod/sojtruth-woman.asp.

Weinberg, Justin. "Statement from Hypatia Board Regarding Tuvel Controversy." *Daily Nous*, July 21, 2017. http://dailynous.com/2017/07/21/hypatias-editor-reviews-editor-resign-authority-associate-editors-temporarily-suspended/.

Walker, Susannah. *Style and Status: Selling Beauty to African American Women*, 1920–1975, University Press of Kentucky, 2007. JSTOR, www.jstor.org/stable/j.ctt2jcm09.

Yancy, George. *Black Bodies/White Gazes*. Lanham, MD: Rowman and Littlefield, 2008.

Yancy, George. "Walking While Black in the 'White Gaze'." The Stone, Opinionator, *New York Times*, Sept. 1, 2013. https://opinionator.blogs.nytimes.com/2013/09/01/walking-while-black-in-the-white-gaze/.

Yancy, George. "The Violent Weight of Whiteness: The Existential and Psychic Price Paid by Black Male Bodies." *Oxford Handbook of Philosophy and Race*, edited by Naomi Zack. New York, NY: Oxford University Press, 2017, pp. 587–597.

Zack, Naomi. "The American Sexualization of Race." *Race/Sex: Their Sameness, Difference and Interplay*, edited by Naomi Zack. New York, NY: Routledge, 1997, pp. 145–55.

Zack, Naomi. *Inclusive Feminism: A Third Wave Theory of Women's Commonality*. Lanham, MD: Rowman & Littlefield, 2005.

Zack, Naomi. "Gender Theory in Philosophy of Race." *Oxford Handbook of Philosophy and Race*, edited by Naomi Zack. New York, NY: Oxford University Press, 2017, pp. 598–607.

Index

Made in the USA
Middletown, DE
25 May 2019